Soviet-American
Academic Exchanges,
1958-1975

Soviet-American Academic Exchanges, 1958-1975

ROBERT F. BYRNES

Indiana University Press   *Bloomington and London*

Published in Canada by Fitzhenry & Whiteside, Limited, Don
Mills, Ontario

Manufactured in the United States of America

Library of Congress Cataloging in Publication Data

  Byrnes, Robert Francis.
    Soviet-American academic exchanges, 1958-1975.

    Bibliography
    Includes index.
    1. Educational exchanges--United States.
  2. Educational exchanges--Russia. 3. International Research and Exchanges Board. I. Title.
  LB2285.R9B93 1976   370.19'6   75-10718
  ISBN 0-253-35402-1   1 2 3 4 5 80 79 78 77 76

Contents

In Memory of and in Tribute to
PHILIP E. MOSELY
GEROID T. ROBINSON
ERNEST J. SIMMONS

PREFACE

I propose in this volume to analyze academic exchanges between the United States and the Soviet Union, as well as some of the states of Eastern Europe, from 1958 through 1975 in the framework of Soviet-American cultural relations and of the larger Soviet-American relationship. Academic exchanges with the Soviet Union, which began formally in 1958 and which continue under many of the principles then established, have increased our understanding of the Soviet Union and have created new relationships between our universities and our government. They have often provided the closest and most significant form of personal contact between American and Soviet citizens. They have also played an important political role, although they are called the "neglected aspect" of our foreign policy. They reveal the basic philosophies and policies that separate the two systems and the adversary character of Soviet-American relations.

Negotiations on the issues involved in these exchanges reflect the same Soviet policies and attitudes and create the same problems as do those over SALT. The right of an American scholar who is a guest in the Soviet Union under agreed-upon conditions to travel from Moscow to

Leningrad, and the endless actions that he and an
American organization must take to secure that
right, reflect as clearly the nature of the Soviet
system and the Soviet-American relationship as
does the prolonged wrangle over West Berlin's
relationship with the Federal Republic of Germany.
They reveal the benefits each state derives and
the costs it must pay for these new relations,
which create critical dilemmas for both parties.
Moreover, the skill with which American academic
administrators negotiate with the centralized
Soviet system affects the total relationship,
as does the effectiveness with which our businessmen complete commercial agreements with Soviet
state agencies.

I have written this book not only because
the subject is interesting and significant, but
also because I was deeply involved in the Inter-
University Committee from its first days in 1956
until it transferred its activities to the
International Research and Exchanges Board (IREX)
in May 1969. I helped found the Committee, a
league of American universities that established
and administered the principal American exchange
programs with the Soviet Union and Eastern Europe.
I served on the policy committees that defined
the principles under which these exchange programs
began. I participated in countless meetings of
scholars and academic administrators to discuss
principles, policies, and procedures, and to
prepare requests for funds to the Carnegie
Corporation, the Ford Foundation, and the Bureau
of Educational and Cultural Affairs of the
Department of State. I attended the alumni
meetings the Committee organized in the early
years and all of the Committee's annual conferences.
I profited throughout these years from discussions
on campuses in every part of the country with
alumni and with all those engaged in any way with
academic and other cultural exchanges.

I was a participant in the original travel
program to the Soviet Union, Poland, and Czechoslovakia in the summer of 1957. In 1963 I enjoyed
four months of research in the Institute of
History in the Soviet Academy of Sciences as a

participant in the program that the American
Council of Learned Societies (ACLS) and the
Soviet Academy of Sciences established in 1961.
I spent much of the summer of 1974 in Eastern
Europe on a grant from IREX to help make arrangements for one institution in each country to
provide Indiana University with a copy of every
important book and journal published, in return
for copies of American books in which they were
especially interested.

Above all, I served as chairman of the
Inter-University Committee from July 1960 through
May 1969, when the administrative offices were
at Indiana University. Throughout those years,
with many others, I represented American universities in discussions with the Department of
State and the Ford Foundation. I also dealt
frequently, in person and through correspondence,
with officials in the Soviet Embassy in Washington,
the Ministry of Higher and Specialized Education
in Moscow, Moscow State University, Leningrad
State University, and the Soviet Academy of
Sciences. I made eleven trips to the Soviet
Union for reviews and negotiations and to visit
universities from which the Committee accepted
scholars and in which we hoped the Soviet government would allow our scholars to study.

After 1962, when I was among a group of
Committee representatives who visited Czechoslovakia, Hungary, and Bulgaria to discuss
initiating exchange programs, I enjoyed the same
kinds of experience in Eastern Europe. Between
1956 and 1969 I also served on a number of
occasions on selection and advisory committees of
the Foreign Area Fellowship Program, ACLS, and
the National Academy of Sciences. In the 1960s
I served on committees the Ford Foundation sent
to Eastern Europe, in particular to Yugoslavia,
Hungary, and Czechoslovakia, to help choose
scholars from those countries for research
opportunities in the United States. I spent
the summer of 1967 reviewing the work of the
Ford Foundation's International Affairs Division,
both here and abroad. From 1957 through 1974
I made fourteen different trips to Eastern

Europe for periods from two to seven weeks in
duration.

Over the years I talked informally with a
good number of American participants in the
various academic exchange programs, and with
perhaps forty Soviet participants, and I became
well acquainted with a number of Soviet officials
and scholars. In addition, I have enjoyed long
conversations with Jesse Clarkson, John Shelton
Curtiss, Merle Fainsod, Calvin Hoover, Philip E.
Mosely, Ernest J. Simmons, and Geroid T. Robinson
about their experiences as scholars in the Soviet
Union in the 1930s. I benefited from long talks
with Schuyler Wallace concerning his role in the
Foreign Area Fellowship Program and in establishing
the Committee. Frederick T. Merrill and Frank
Siscoe often described for me their experiences
in the Department of State in the early years of
academic exchanges, and our Embassy officials in
Moscow were equally helpful. Conversations with
Richard Speaight and George West of the British
Council concerning their experiences and practices,
and less-frequent ones with Wolfgang Kasack of
the Deutsche Forschungsgemeinschaft, provided
insight concerning the British and German
academic exchange programs. Gordon Skilling and
Donald V. Schwartz have been equally candid
concerning the University of Toronto's program.
Indeed, Skilling for a number of years attended
the Committee's annual meetings. Throughout the
1960s, in particular, Shepard Stone and Stanley
Gordon of the Ford Foundation, Frederick Burkhardt
and Gordon Turner of ACLS, and Lawrence Mitchell
of the National Academy of Sciences were generous
in sharing experiences and in responding to
queries, as Allan Kassof of IREX has been since
1969. In fact, all of those in organizations
that had exchange programs with these countries
have showered me with information and views.

In short, I have been active, with many
others, in the main element of the exchanges I
seek here to analyze. I have therefore written
with a particular sense of responsibility. I
have learned again from this effort how difficult
it is for a historian, perhaps especially one

writing about an activity in which he has been
engaged, to ascertain the facts, to understand
the points of view involved, and to appreciate
the hazards created by the climate or atmosphere
in which he lives and the assumptions under which
he works.

I have tried to be complete, candid, accurate,
objective, and resolutely fair. I have attempted
to describe what has happened, not what I wish
had happened. I have written nothing I would not
repeat in the Soviet Union or defend there. At
the same time, I have not provided any means for
identifying Soviet citizens who were notably
helpful or who were critical of their government
or its policies. I therefore cannot thank many
Soviet scholars, men and women of great professional
ability and of the finest human qualities.

I take especial pleasure in expressing warm
appreciation to those officials of the Department
of State involved in Soviet-American cultural
relations. The greater my knowledge of the
Soviet Union and of the difficulties our diplomats
face negotiating with Soviet representatives,
the deeper my admiration has grown for them. I
would like to commend in particular Boris Klosson
and the late Frank Siscoe, who were directors
of the Soviet and East European Exchanges Staff
during most of the period from 1958 until 1969,
and Guy Coriden of the Bureau of Educational and
Cultural Affairs. These men showed a profound
understanding of our national interests, of the
nature of Soviet-American relations, of the
character of American higher education, and of
the need to preserve the independence of our
universities and scholars.

I refrain from thanking several scholars
and administrators well-informed on this subject
who have made helpful critical comments concerning
this volume, but they know how grateful I am.
John Gallman of the Indiana University Press
provided candid insight. Robin Byrnes served
as a dedicated and immensely conscientious copy
editor, and Emily Sharrow typed the final
manuscript.

My wife and children uncomplainingly tolerated
my trips to the Soviet Union and Eastern Europe
and my struggle with this volume when it competed
with other responsibilities. I could have
accomplished nothing without their full understanding and support.

                        Robert F. Byrnes
Indiana University

CHAPTER ONE

Introduction:
The Principal Themes

The relationships between the Soviet Union
and the United States, the two great giants of
today's world, dominate international politics
as few other such relationships have in the past.
In these complex and direct arrangements,
military power and resolution, economic strength,
political vitality, and diplomatic skill, in the
short run at least, are more significant than
ideas and those who deal with them. Nevertheless,
as all appreciate who understand the role that
political philosophy, music, and art alone have
played in twentieth-century politics and international affairs, culture and cultural relations
between states are of enormous importance, perhaps
more significant than ever before.

One of the central themes of this volume is
the role dedicated individuals have played, even
in this age of great powers and intercontinental
crises. Russian studies in the United States
were launched by a handful of outstanding scholars
who acquired extraordinary knowledge of Russian
history and culture and who devoted their lives
to increasing their learning and to training
others. The qualities of these men, especially
their high standards, objectivity, dedication to
teaching, and cooperative spirit, have helped

shape the entire field and have given it a different character than, say, Chinese studies have acquired.

The original impulse that led to academic exchanges and to the cultural exchanges agreement came from these individuals and from some of those whom they had taught. Their concern with providing opportunities for young scholars to study in the Soviet Union helped shape the peculiar pattern of the first agreement in 1958. Their initiatives were supported by private institutions, such as American universities and foundations, that helped organize other institutions, such as the Inter-University Committee, to continue work they had started.

Similarly, individuals such as Sol Hurok were mainly responsible for the beginning and rapid expansion of the flood of Soviet artistic performers to this country, as Gabriel Reiner launched the flow of tourists to the Soviet Union and Eugene Rabinowitch the Pugwash Conferences of scientists. In short, individuals took the lead: the universities, the public, and the government followed, a pattern common in American history. The role individuals have played throughout this brief history, and that they continue to perform, reflects our society and also helps explain the vigor and the outward thrust of American intellectual power. Likewise, the absence of such bursts of energy, the apathy, and the defensiveness of the Soviet Union reveal both the overwhelming power of the state in society and the cultural stagnation such state power has produced.

In Eastern Europe individual scholars and administrators played the same kind of role in very difficult circumstances by pressing their governments to end their isolation from the West and to accept the challenge and opportunity of academic exchanges with the United States. The work of these scholars in influencing national policy, in negotiating agreements, and in persuading their universities to arrange direct relations with American and other Western

universities helps illuminate the differences that
distinguish the countries of Eastern Europe from
the Soviet Union.

   A central theme that pervades this volume
is the relentless American interest in increasing
knowledge and understanding of Russia and Eastern
Europe, which remain even now quite deficient.
This manifests both the inquisitiveness concerning
the unknown that has distinguished the Western
mind since the Renaissance and the pioneering
spirit of this country as well. In addition,
this interest reflects the freedoms that grace
American life and the way in which universities
have accepted their responsibility to study every
part of the universe. The absence of a powerful
parallel Soviet interest in increasing learning
and insight concerning the United States, and the
restrictions placed upon all Soviet citizens,
serve to highlight the differences between the two
societies and this second theme.

   Even before the United States burst out
of its isolation from the rest of the world
and long before the cold war, a growing number
of men and women, working closely with colleagues
in Germany, France, and Great Britain, began
to devote their time and energy to research,
teaching, and increasing public knowledge of
Russia and Eastern Europe. The quality of
American learning and public knowledge has
therefore risen sharply. Even so, the fields
of study that were neglected two decades ago,
such as the arts, education, religion, and
sociology, remain feeble, and our knowledge
of Marxism-Leninism and its effect on the
Soviet mind is slight. Moreover, few of our
specialists today possess the language facility
and the well-grounded knowledge of Russian
history and culture that all of the smaller
band of founders commanded before World War II.
Indeed, a careful analysis reveals that only
about seven percent of our more than two
thousand specialists on Russia and Eastern
Europe have fluent command of at least one
language and also have resided there for more

than a year.[1] This awareness of our deficiencies
and our determination to overcome them again
underline this second theme.

It is unfortunate that the conditions under
which American scholars have continued their
studies in the Soviet Union since 1958 have not
been so free, pleasant, or productive as the
founders of Russian studies enjoyed. The actions
of various Soviet government agencies toward
American participants have clearly increased their
insight into the Soviet Union, but they represent
a colossal Soviet political blunder because the
critical view these personal experiences have
produced deeply affects American scholarship on
every aspect of Soviet life. In fact, these
perceptions and resentments add a special sharpness to views that Stalinism, the concentration
camps, the repression of the Hungarian revolt,
and the invasion of Czechoslovakia had already
influenced. Surely the search for insight that
this theme summarizes has deepened public awareness
of the character of the Soviet system and will
long influence national policy.

The changing nature of relations between the
government and universities constitutes the third
central theme of this study. The transformation
of higher education in the 1950s and 1960s and
its general contours, in particular the rapid
expansion of the number of students and faculty
and the growth in quality of graduate education
in every part of the country, have helped destroy
the mythical ivory tower. The universities'
acceptance of modernization and of new responsibilities has brought with it additional problems.
All of these changes have carried educational
institutions and educators directly into public
service, politics, and international affairs.
The academic exchange programs as a minor part
of this process have placed the scholar in the
front line. They have above all engaged the
university and the government in relationships
new to both.

[1]Richard D. Lambert, Language and Area Studies Review
(Philadelphia, 1973), 368-70.

Americans have traditionally emphasized the
individual and private organizations. We have had
a heritage of suspicion of government and a
determination to limit its authority, especially
over the mind. However, social and economic
changes, the need to organize knowledge for
public use, and the world crises of this century
have turned our government toward the universities
and colleges for advice, research, and training.
At the same time, our educational institutions
have had to turn more to the government for
funding. The new relationship has therefore
become a critical theme, one that threatens the
independence and freedom of the universities.
It has led them to establish cooperative enterprises to coordinate their activities and defend
their interests. It has also produced a remarkably
successful effort by men and women in both
universities and government to ensure the independence of the university and of the scholar,
even in delicate affairs involving central
principles for the university and relations with
a rival state. Whether the various private
organizations engaged in cultural exchanges can
retain their independence over the long run
remains a serious question, in particular because
the growing emphasis on science, technology,
industry, and agriculture in the exchanges
involves both governments ever more deeply.

The fourth theme, one that permeates the
entire volume, is the contrast between the two
societies and governments which these programs
illumine. These diversities contribute to
the difficulties the two peoples have in understanding each other. They also contribute to
the complications that arise in all their
relations.

Soviet-American relations constitute the
fifth theme, perhaps the major one. In fact
academic exchanges serve as a minor paradigm of
these relations, as would also a study of
Soviet-American trade in recent years. However,
because these exchanges involve the presence of
a number of highly trained scholars for several
months or an academic year in some of the leading

educational institutions of the rival state, they
provide a particularly clear illumination of
the character of the two societies and of the
special problems that their relationships raise.
One society is of course authoritarian, unfree,
centralized, closed, and incredibly inefficient.
The other is open, plural, relaxed, free.
Academic exchanges underscore these characteristics
as well as others central to our difficulties:
the conflict in ideology, purpose, and national
interest; the asymmetry in level and goal; the
wrangles that seem petty but which reflect
principles vital to both; and the styles or
methods of operation of the two governments and
societies. Their role, and the growing part
played by contacts of all kinds between the two
societies, indicate that cultural affairs broadly
defined should no longer remain a neglected
aspect of international politics.

The changes that have occurred during the
past two decades within the United States and
the Soviet Union and in their relationships
are also part of this theme. In this country
authority has drifted away from the scholar and
the university, and that of the government has
grown. As the American programs have become
well established, those involved in administrating
them have relaxed somewhat their standards and
emphases upon maturity and stability. In fact,
we have all begun to accept some of the indecencies
and indignities of the Soviet system as we have
become more accustomed to them.

On the other hand, the Soviet government
has become more civil and somewhat more relaxed
and efficient. The substantive controls remain,
but some of the major causes of friction have
been softened. The exchanges therefore outline
the stage of Soviet-American relations called
detente, to which they may have contributed and
from which they benefit. However, the survival
of an arrangement that the American scholars,
universities, and government accepted most
reluctantly in 1958 and which all hoped would
be temporary demonstrates the relentless character
of Soviet control over the movement of men and

ideas. Indeed, the Soviet government has shown
the same persistence in maintaining and re-
inforcing this system as it did in the two years
of negotiating spent by 492 diplomats at Geneva
to produce the document on European security
and cooperation.

The final theme includes the paradoxes of
the academic exchange programs and the dilemmas
they raise for the American people and for both
of the governments, thus revealing in another
way the nature of international politics in the
final third of the twentieth century. The
programs have benefited the United States by
increasing our knowledge and understanding,
educating the Soviet government and some of the
Soviet intellectual elite about our society,
and contributing in some way to increasing ties
and reducing tension. At the same time, they
have enabled Soviet scholars to profit from
research opportunities and the opportunity to
travel. They have also allowed the Soviet Union
to obtain important scientific and technical
information from the United States, to use
patronage as an instrument of control over Soviet
intellectuals, to persuade some in the West that
peace is at hand, and to acquire respectability
and prestige for a despotic and unloved system.

Academic exchanges raise a dilemma for us
because formal exchange agreements undermine
free trade in ideas, increase the role of our
government over intellectual activity, and grant
legitimacy to governments that deny the freedoms
essential to civilized life. However, they raise
an even more acute dilemma for the Soviet
government, desperately eager to obtain advantages
from cultural exchanges and economic relations
but fearful of the infections these relationships
bring into their controlled society and into
Eastern Europe as well.

The dilemma, which will continue to grow for
the Soviet Union, raises the same questions as
our total relationship does. Can a society
import a skill or a product from another culture
without also introducing other alien elements

that produced that skill or product and that carry destructive potentialities? Because of the scientific and technical revolutions, in transportation and communications in particular, can any state isolate itself from the rest of the world? Would such a policy of isolation, if it could be implemented, condemn that state to ever more critical scientific-technical and economic-military backwardness? Does communism bear within itself the seeds of its own decay, ripened into flower by necessary contact with the outside world?

These relations raise questions and dilemmas for us as well. In particular, are Soviet changes in recent years substantial, genuine, and permanent, and are they creating a major shift in Soviet policy; or are they slight, tactical, and temporary? Which side benefits the most? Do these relations enable the Soviet Union both to borrow heavily from the West and to lull it into indifference? Do they contribute toward a new spirit and a "new structure of peace"? Can the Soviet Union tolerate peace?

In addition, can our government give respectability and prestige to the Soviet government, and to other repressive governments, by agreements that are inherently restrictive and counter to our essential traditions without undermining our own freedom? Can we allow our government to assume controls over our cultural and economic relationships with another part of the world without subverting that same freedom? On the other hand, do we have a choice? If we do continue, can our government retain the support of the American people, the confidence of our allies, the faith of those who seek freedom, and the respect of the Soviet leaders if it grants free access to Soviet scholars, scientists, and business leaders but does not insist upon equal rights of interpenetration? Can an open, flexible society maintain close relationships with a closed and secret society without being infected by totalitarian practices? Indeed, has this already happened?

In summary, the themes that run through
this study of a minor element in the major
confrontation of our times help illuminate the
nature of the two competing societies, the
fundamental issues at stake, and the changing
character of international politics in this
unstable era. They suggest, too, that the
phase of Soviet-American relations labeled detente
will probably remain brief, that the struggle
between the Soviet Union and the West will
be marked by direct disagreement over every
aspect of that relationship, and that academic
exchanges are a part of the discord concerning
free movement of men and ideas that will continue
to serve as a paradigm and a symbol of the
nature of the two societies and their conflicts.

CHAPTER TWO

The Origins: American Scholarly Interest in Russia and Soviet Policy Shifts after Stalin

Until the 1880s the American people were generally ignorant of and indifferent to developments in other parts of the world. We lived in a kind of splendid isolation, without even limited external interests, and we concentrated almost entirely upon Western Europe, from which had come most of our population, traditions, culture, and values. The first crack in this isolation came in Asia, where China and Japan attracted commercial and missionary activity. Classical Oriental studies of Sanskrit, the Near East, and China were well established more than a half century before a university offered the first course dealing with Russia.

American interest in Russia began in the mid-1880s, when English translations of the novels of Tolstoy and Dostoevsky led to something on the order of a "Russian craze." These works, as well as those of Chekhov, Turgenev, and other Russian novelists and playwrights, were incorporated into general literature courses before World War I and helped to establish Russian literature as an essential part of the intellectual background of educated Americans. The great writers also helped break the path for other representatives of Russian culture, such as

Tchaikovsky and Musorgsky, Diaghilev and Chaliapin, Repin and Stanislavsky, whose influence then made simple our universities' absorption of the distinguished "Huguenot" exiles from the Soviet Union who enriched our faculties after 1920. In the 1920s alone, outstanding historians such as Michael Karpovich at Harvard University, George Vernadsky and Michael Rostovtzeff at Yale University, and Alexander A. Vasiliev at the University of Wisconsin began to increase our knowledge and understanding of Russia and the Soviet Union.

An important new force began to influence the United States when massive numbers of Jews and Poles reached these shores, beginning in the 1890s. The critical view of the Russian political system that they brought supplemented those of Russian liberals and radicals who began to reach the United States at about the same time, somewhat later than they had affected Western Europe.

The study of Russia by Americans was launched not by universities or by the government but by gifted amateur scholars, diplomats, and journalists. The intellectual qualities of these men, their mastery of Russian and of other languages, their thorough knowledge of the culture and geography from long residence and travel, and the scholarly and literary qualities of their publications have had a profound formative influence on our scholar-ship and on our view of Russia. The first of these men was George Kennan, whose book Tent Life (1870), describing his travel from San Francisco to northern and eastern Siberia to investigate the problems involved in laying a telegraph line from Alaska to Europe, was published in more than one hundred printings. His two-volume Siberia and the Exile System (1891) and the articles he wrote at that time, brilliant exposés of the Russian political system and of its treatment of political prisoners, had a significant impact precisely at the time our interest was beginning to grow.

Jeremiah Curtin's contribution was of the

same high quality. An extraordinary polyglot,
Curtin was in the American ministry in St.
Petersburg from 1864 until 1870. This experience
and his travels, particularly into Central Asia,
enabled him to write fascinating and influential
books concerning Turkestan and the Mongols, to
translate some of the important novels of Gogol
and Zagoskin, and to become the first American
specialist on the folklore of Russia and parts of
Eastern Europe. His translations of some of the
novels of Sienkiewicz also helped to make that
great Polish author known throughout the English-
speaking world.

Curtin's contemporary, Eugene Schuyler, spent
almost ten years in the diplomatic and consular
service in Reval, Moscow, and St. Petersburg. He
was the first to translate Turgenev's Fathers and
Sons into English, and he also translated Tolstoy's
The Cossacks. However, Schuyler is most important
for his volumes on Central Asia and his biography
of Peter the Great. Like Curtin, Schuyler was
fascinated by Eastern Europe, especially the
Balkans, where he served for a number of years
and about which he wrote important books, in
particular on the Balkan wars.

The formal history of Russian studies in the
United States began in 1894 when Archibald Cary
Coolidge introduced the first course in Russian
history at Harvard University. This was approximately five decades later than in France
and Germany and three decades later than in
England. Coolidge was appointed assistant
professor in 1893 in a Department of History
whose sole instructional concerns were ancient,
West European, and American history. Fresh from
six-year's study abroad, including a year's
travel throughout Russia and a trip around the
world, he received permission in his second year
to introduce a course on northern Europe, that is,
Russia, Poland, and Scandinavia. The following
year he taught a new course on the Eastern
Question, or the Balkans and the Near East.
In December 1895, in Washington, he presented
the first paper on Russia given at an annual
meeting of the American Historical Association.

In it he urged that we cease neglect of "Northern Europe" and of Russia, "for everything connected with the development and conditions of such a mighty Empire is obviously worth our attention." Since Harvard was unwilling to increase its attention to Russia, Coolidge discovered and for several years paid the salaries of specialists, such as Leo Wiener, who in 1896 began instruction in Russian language and literature. Coolidge provided financial assistance for graduate students to travel to Russia for research, even if it was not central to their concerns. He attracted into Russian studies and helped train a number of other early leaders, such as Robert H. Lord, who taught at Harvard after 1910; Robert J. Kerner, who played a prominent role at the University of California in Berkeley from 1928 until 1956; Frank Golder, who helped begin the great Russian collection and who was the first director of the Hoover Institution on War, Revolution, and Peace; and Philip E. Mosely. In 1927 Coolidge brought to Harvard Michael Karpovich, who has trained more Americans in the field of Russian history than anyone else. His own books and articles, like those of the men he helped train, also served to increase knowledge and understanding of the Slavic world. Finally, through large gifts of Slavic materials to the Harvard Library and his service as Director of the Library from 1910 until his death in 1928, Coolidge helped make Widener Library one of the largest and best storehouses of materials on Russia, Eastern Europe, and other areas of the world.

Charles Crane demonstrated in a different way the significant role individuals played. A wealthy industrialist who sold his firm in 1914 to concentrate on travel and world affairs, Crane became interested in Russia from reading Tolstoy's novels. He made twenty-five trips to and through Russia between 1890 and 1937. He played the role of an aggressive private foundation. He persuaded President William Rainey Harper of the University of Chicago to travel with him to Russia in 1900. He then paid the salary of his son, Samuel, at Chicago from 1906 through 1909 and from 1914

through 1917 in an effort to begin instruction there
in Russian language and studies. Crane gave funds
to the library and financed publication of Russian-language textbooks. In addition, he stimulated and provided funds for lectures at the
university by distinguished statesmen. In the
1920s he provided travel fellowships for graduate
students at Harvard University and established the
Institute of Current World Affairs in New York,
which enabled Bruce Hopper in the 1920s and John
Hazard in the 1930s to enjoy prolonged periods of
study in the Soviet Union.

President Herbert Hoover's contribution was
of a still different character. He became interested in Russia from his numerous trips between 1909 and 1915 as an "industrial doctor" and
through his service in directing the American
Relief Administration after World War I. During
the early 1920s he began the collection that became the great library of the Hoover Institution
by employing men such as Golder to purchase
historical materials in Russia.

One should note that these men, and others
like them--such as Professors Samuel Cross,
George R. Noyes, Philip E. Mosely, Geroid T.
Robinson, and S. Harrison Thomson, and great journalists such as William Henry Chamberlin--were not
of Slavic origin and that the base of Russian and
East European studies was not influenced significantly by men and women of Slavic origin or by
those who came from Russia or Eastern Europe. Immigrants played a significant role later, but even
early immigrants such as Professors Wiener, Alexander Kaun, George Patrick, and Henry Lanz were
not among the most important founders. One
should note, too, that our government played no
role in launching Slavic studies. Perhaps the
best indication of its lack of interest in this
part of the world is that in 1901 the Library
of Congress had only 569 volumes in its collection on Russia and 97 on Poland. The Foreign
Service began training specialists on the
Soviet Union only in 1928, when Robert F.
Kelley established a program in which George
Kennan and Charles Bohlen received training

in Berlin and Paris, respectively, and then in Riga.

The next generation of founders had the same high qualities. They also enjoyed living freely and traveling widely in Russia and had close relations with Russians of all classes. For example, Geroid T. Robinson, the founder of the Russian Institute at Columbia University, received a Dunning Fellowship and spent thirty months between 1924 and 1927 in Moscow and on travels throughout European Russia. He returned to the Soviet Union in 1937 for more than four months. Hopper, a special protégé of Coolidge, spent 1926-27 in research and travel in Russia and returned in 1930 for an extensive stay. Ernest J. Simmons, on a Sheldon Fellowship from Harvard, lived fifteen months in a three-room Moscow basement apartment with several Russians in 1928 and 1929, while Philip E. Mosely enjoyed two years in similar circumstances from 1930 to 1932. Calvin Hoover, supported by the Social Science Research Council (SSRC), which made its first research grant to a scholar interested in Russia in 1924, lived from August 1928 until May 1930 in a small apartment with a Moscow family and made six later visits to the Soviet Union.

Russian studies have benefited enormously from the high intellectual quality of their founders, who were attracted by the vastness, the distinctive history, and the exciting culture of Russia. Their careers at a time when study of Russia was not significant or prestigious are themselves tributes to their capabilities, as are their published volumes, still honored and studied. None was, or considered himself, a specialist or expert on a self-contained area of the world. They had a genuine and deep knowledge of the societies in which they were interested that extended far beyond history and politics. Indeed, they possessed the kind of information and insight our universities now try, generally unsuccessfully, to instill through multidisciplinary area programs. These men were also interested in the states and peoples of Eastern Europe,

which they saw as part of Europe. Perhaps because
their knowledge emphasized economic development,
the zadruga, and Kossuth, while ours is based on
Katyn, the Berlin blockade, and the invasion of
Czechoslovakia in 1968, they approached Eastern
Europe from Western Europe. Today, we often
view it from Moscow and as part of a Soviet empire.

The founders of Russian studies started the
practice of living and working in Russia and
Eastern Europe at a time when knowledge of other
languages and cultures was rare among Americans.
They were not only outstanding and remarkably
objective and unpolitical scholars but dedicated
teachers, almost missionary in their activities to
expand knowledge and understanding. They sought
to educate and inform their fellow Americans by
a steady flow of articles in newspapers and
journals that were widely read, such as The Nation
and Foreign Affairs. Finally, they devoted
enormous energy and skill to creating the library
collections that are at the base of our studies
today. The selfless contributions of Kerner at
Berkeley, Mosely at Columbia, and Golder and
H. H. Fisher at the Hoover Institution resemble
those of Coolidge in their significance.

They also established professional friend-
ships with scholars in Germany, France, and
especially Britain. The works of Aylmer Maude,
Mackenzie Wallace, Maurice Baring, and Sir Bernard
Pares were widely used in the United States.
Coolidge, Harper, and Crane were members of the
Anglo-Russian Literary Society, founded in
January 1893, that had four hundred members,
largely scholars and social leaders, in the first
two decades of the twentieth century. Coolidge,
Kerner, and Lord were among the specialists on
Russia and Eastern Europe at Versailles in 1919.
Their close cooperation with British scholars,
such as Robert W. Seton-Watson and Harold W.
Temperley, and their general agreement on
boundaries and other problems helped strengthen
these connections. Harper taught at the
University of Liverpool from 1911 through 1913,
and he retained especially close English ties
throughout his life. When the Slavonic Review

was established in London in 1922, Harper, Kerner, and Noyes served as co-editors, making the journal in a sense Anglo-American.

In December 1924, Pares, Seton-Watson, and Temperley participated in a large session devoted entirely to Russian studies at the annual meeting of the American Historical Association in Richmond, Virginia. Seton-Watson spoke on "The Future of Slavonic Studies" at a luncheon attended by almost 150, and he later lectured at seven universities and five other organizations in the East and Midwest. Pares taught one summer at Berkeley and spent the last eight years of his life in the United States.

Late in the 1930s England served as a kind of staging area for a new flow to the United States of specialists on Russia and Eastern Europe from newly darkened Eastern and Central Europe. Thus, scholars such as Gleb Struve, Father Francis Dvornik, René Wellek, Fritz Epstein, Sergius Yakobson, and Otokar Odložilík earned important academic and library positions here after they had taught or worked in the School of Slavonic and East European Studies in London. The relationship with British scholars was so close that the December 1940 cable from Pares asking the Americans to delay founding their own journal and assume responsibility instead for the Slavonic Review brought quick and unanimous acceptance. In fact, relations between scholars in the Eastern part of the United States and British scholars were probably closer than with scholars from the Midwest and the Pacific Coast. These relations were important for many reasons, in particular because of the foundation they established for close cooperation after the war in research and instruction and in the administration of the exchange programs when they began in the late 1950s.

By the end of the 1930s, about twelve native Americans were engaged in the scholarly study of Russia. They were of high intellectual quality, were thoroughly dedicated to their craft, represented no special interests, remained aloof

from the political controversies concerning the
Soviet Union, and were unaffected by financial
considerations, since neither foundations nor the
government had begun to devote funds to this field.
All had lived and studied for prolonged periods in
the Soviet Union. All were devoted scholar-
teachers convinced that any prospective academician,
particularly those whom they trained, should also
live and work in the country of their special
interest. However, these were rare and isolated
apostles. In 1914 only three universities,
Harvard, Columbia, and California in Berkeley, had
professorships in Russian language and literature,
only five taught the Russian language, and only
two, Harvard and Berkeley, offered courses in
Russian history. After the war, in 1920, only
thirteen institutions offered Russian and even
fewer the other Slavic languages. Moreover,
efforts in the early 1920s to establish a journal,
a research center, and professional organizations
of scholars and language teachers all failed.

Even in 1936 only fifty-three institutions
offered a total of 320 courses dealing with Russia
or Eastern Europe. Thirty-three institutions
offered courses in Russian history and eighteen
in Russian language. Twenty-nine offered courses
on the Balkans and the Near East, and nine on
Slavic history and literature. Russian and East
European studies were still concentrated at
Harvard, Columbia, and Berkeley. Only one other
institution even had a Department of Slavic
Languages and Literatures in 1939. Berkeley,
which had the largest, most complete, and best-
organized program, produced only twenty Ph.D.'s
in all disciplines between 1920 and 1947.

The international crisis that began after
1933 and the threat of war in Europe persuaded
many Russian scholars who had earlier emigrated to
Eastern and Western Europe, and many East European
scholars, to come to the United States, thus
enormously enriching our national resources for
the study of these areas. At the same time, the
tightening of Soviet controls closed the Soviet
Union to opportunities for research there. After
1933, few and, after 1936, no American scholars

were able to study in the Soviet Union until 1956.
This denial of access heavily influenced the
system of instruction and research just when it
began to expand most rapidly. Thus, the ACLS in
1938 urged establishment of multidisciplinary
programs or area studies in part because the Soviet
Union denied scholars the opportunity to acquire
understanding of Russian history and culture
from living there.

In summary, Russian studies was not a thriving
or dynamic field before World War II. Scholars in
the field did not form an organization until 1938,
when Mortimer Graves of the ACLS helped establish
the Committee on Slavic Studies, which brought
together a number from different disciplines, but
almost all in language and literature. There was
very little student interest, even in the major
centers, despite the fact that the United States
recognized the Soviet Union in 1933. Yale
University, which had the largest library on
Russia in 1906, began Russian instruction in 1910
but abandoned it in the 1920s. The universities
were conservative and lacked funds to develop
such fields of study. The atmosphere was not con-
ducive to expansion because of ignorance and disinterest. Isolation reigned supreme.

In the twentieth century the role of Russia
as a European and then as a world power has no
doubt been the principal influence upon popular
interest in that country. This began with the
surprising Japanese triumph over Russia in 1904-05
and the Revolution of 1905. Russia's role in
World War I naturally increased our attention,
which surged with the revolutions in 1917, the
civil war, American intervention in that war, and
the Bolshevik triumph in full authority by 1921.
However, in spite of the extraordinary developments
in the Soviet Union in the 1920s and 1930s, interest
remained low until the crisis in the late 1930s
increased our concern with the affairs of other
countries. The unfavorable impression created by
the Soviet role from 1939 until the invasion in
1941 was quickly overcome by the savage resistance
that the Soviet population offered as soon as it
understood Nazi policies. This admiration

expanded enormously when we became allies, and our
bright hopes for the democratization of the Soviet
Union, continued cooperation after the war, and
establishment of a true United Nations that would
promise peace and some kind of stability concentrated popular interest upon the Soviet Union.

The war and our new relationship with the
Soviet Union drew hundreds into language and area
programs established by the armed services,
persuaded many colleges and universities to
establish courses for teaching languages of value
to the war effort, and helped the universities
understand more clearly the level of our ignorance
and the nature of their educational responsibilities.
In addition, some institutions established special
schools for the armed services, of which nineteen
were devoted to various Slavic countries.

In September 1941, when Thomas P. Whitney
reported to Geroid T. Robinson in the Ethno-
graphic Board of the Smithsonian Institution for
work that he learned involved research on the
Soviet Union, the government employed less than
twenty men and women (including secretaries) to
study the Soviet Union. By 1943 Robinson directed
a staff of forty specialists in the USSR Division
of the Office of Strategic Services. The needs
of government departments, in particular the
Department of State, the Lend-Lease Office, the
Office of Economic Warfare, and the military
services, grew so rapidly that the Navy Language
School in Boulder in 1944 employed fifty Russian-
language instructors, almost as many as had been
teaching Russian throughout the United States
five years earlier.

At the end of the war, popular interest in
things Russian and in Eastern Europe remained
vigorous, especially because Stalin demolished our
high hopes concerning transformation of the Soviet
system and cooperation in creating a peaceful
world, and instead intensified controls against all
contact with the West, expanded Soviet authority
over Eastern Europe, and was intransigent in all
relations. However, until after sputnik in 1957,
our government's role in expanding Russian studies

was limited largely to improving the resources of
the Library of Congress and to providing opportunities for employment.

Expansion of research and instruction on
Russia and Eastern Europe was by no means an
automatic development, nor was it caused entirely
by our new role in world politics or the cold war.
The main thrust came from a handful of committed
scholar-teachers, interested in expanding knowledge
and understanding and aided now by their universities, by learned societies, and by private
foundations. Study of other so-called non-Western
areas also increased, but not as rapidly, because
the leadership was not so dedicated or able.
Moreover, other countries as deeply affected by
the transformation of world politics did not
react as we did.

Many universities disbanded the faculties they
had collected during the war for the special
defense programs and returned to the traditional
curriculum. Others, especially the major
institutions that were to serve as the important
centers, decided to maintain and expand their
resources, creating the foundation on which
improvement of research and instruction has been
built. In addition, the ACLS and the SSRC, the two
organizations that link professional groups of
scholars by discipline in the humanities and
social sciences, helped to provide national
long-term planning, served as an intellectual bank
for those interested in all foreign areas, and
brought scholars together from competing institutions for a common effort. The ACLS and SSRC
Joint Committee on Slavic Studies was enormously
influential as a coordinating agency and as a
source of ideas and information. The SSRC's
Committee on World Area Research established
principles for the study of foreign areas that had
enormous national influence. In 1948 it also
created an Area Research Fellows Program that in
five years distributed $700,000 from the Carnegie
Corporation for research and travel and enabled
214 established young scholars to "reconvert"
by acquiring knowledge of another part of the
world.

The third element in this massive increase was provided by three large philanthropic foundations, the Rockefeller Foundation, the Carnegie Corporation, and the Ford Foundation, which contributed the funds necessary for enlarging faculties, expanding and improving libraries, and providing graduate students with fellowships.

The fourth factor, by far the most important, was the small group of dedicated and far-sighted scholar-teachers. They recognized the need to produce a number of specialists on the Soviet Union for education, government, business, and journalism and to raise the general level of public information. They decided to sacrifice their careers as scholars to meet this new need. This group, which included the three men to whom this book is dedicated, and others, including Clyde Kluckhohn at Harvard and Kerner at Berkeley, provided the crucial leadership, imagination, and energy.

The personal and professional qualities of those who founded Russian and East European studies and who later directed the postwar explosion were as important as the dedicated training they provided, and they helped to make the cooperative university effort of the exchange program both possible and effective. These men worked well within their institutions and cooperated closely in interuniversity ventures and in programs sponsored by the ACLS and the foundations. Because of their good sense, these programs avoided the feuds between traditionalists and modernists, the generational conflicts, and the bitter wrangling and suicidal conflicts that afflicted Chinese studies. Instead, scholars and universities cooperated at every level, so that the Inter-University Committee was a natural and logical development. Another impressive demonstration of university cooperation in this field was the $287,000 contribution that thirty-seven institutions made between 1964 and 1970 to support the Current Digest of the Soviet Press and the Slavic Review, and the agreement of a larger number of institutions to cooperate in maintaining these national tools or instruments after 1970, when all universities faced financial difficulties.

These joint efforts helped transform the
character of American higher education with regard
to the rest of the world; spread the multidisciplinary approach throughout the university world;
trained the scholar-teachers who have increased
our knowledge and understanding through teaching
and writing; and, of course, created a core of men
and women who were eager to live and work within
the Soviet Union, but who were denied that opportunity until 1958.

The most significant step was the opening of
the Russian Institute at Columbia University in
1946. This Institute, the Russian Research Center
at Harvard, and the simultaneous expansion of
Russian studies at Berkeley and other institutions
were planned during a period of close cooperation
between the Soviet and American governments and
preceded the cold war. All five members of the
Institute's faculty were prominent research
scholars, native Americans who had lived extensively in the Soviet Union in the 1920s and '30s.
Two, Robinson and Abram Bergson, had worked in the
Office of Strategic Services during the war; the
third, Mosely, had been a high official in the
Department of State; the fourth, Hazard, had
served in the Office of Economic Warfare and in
Lend-Lease; and the fifth member, Simmons, had
created the first Russian area program in 1943
at Cornell University.

The government played no role in this explosion of interest. In fact, Robinson's work
as head of the USSR Division of OSS persuaded him
that the United States needed bases for independent
study of the Soviet Union outside government. He
wrote to Dean Schuyler Wallace at Columbia University on October 11, 1943, urging him to consider
establishing a coordinated multidisciplinary
program to train scholar-teachers on Russia at
the graduate level. His views were shared by
Wallace, who was influenced by his work within
the university in administering interdisciplinary
training programs for the government, in particular
the Naval School of Military Government and Administration. Even before the war ended, Wallace
began discussions with officials of the Rockefeller
Foundation, some of whom had reached similar

conclusions from their broad review of international
affairs and of likely developments within the
academic world. In April 1945 Columbia University
established a School of International Affairs, and
in 1946, the Russian Institute, with a grant of
$250,000 from the Rockefeller Foundation.

This Institute was of central importance
because university administrators, scholars, and
foundation officers throughout the country adopted
the principles on which it was built. Its example
not only affected procedures within universities,
but it also established principles concerning
relations between the universities and the
government that significantly influenced the
academic exchange programs. Thus, when the
cultural exchange agreement with the Soviet Union
was signed in 1958 and when federal funds began to
pour into Russian and other foreign area programs
through the National Defense Education Act later
that year, the crucial principles that Robinson
had identified were already well established
throughout the country.

First, Robinson was persuaded by his experience
at Columbia since 1924, as well as by his work in
government, that Russian studies constituted a
university responsibility, should be incorporated
into the academic structure, and should be utterly
free from government influence. His knowledge of
organized Russian studies in other countries
strengthened this conviction. Therefore, even
though he was widely admired in Washington and
could have readily acquired funds there, he turned
his back to government relationships. The
university provided all funds for the faculty
appointments, the administration, and the library;
the Rockefeller Foundation made available the
money necessary for fellowships and later for
faculty research, travel, and publishing.
Robinson also devoted the Institute program almost
entirely to Russia, and to just five disciplines,
on the ground that resources were scarce and that
providing effective instruction on that vast
country would itself be a considerable achievement.

Robinson had been a member of the SSRC

Committee on World Area Research since its
establishment in 1941. This experience and his
service during the war convinced him of "the
great value of the regional approach" and of "the
need for some form of organization which will
break down the isolation between disciplines, that
will foster some kind of cross-fertilization, and
that will not so blatantly violate the unity of
knowledge as does most of our present structure."
In the words of Robert B. Hall, chairman of that
committee, Robinson saw that "the vertical pillars
of knowledge," the traditional disciplines, leave
twilight zones and vales between them. An
integrated curriculum would overcome this fragmen-
tation and specialization. In short, Robinson saw
that study of another society was like that of a
human ailment: a number of disciplines were
involved, and they should be closely related in
the scholar's mind and approach because of the
nature of the body.

The Institute's pattern was especially
important because it brought together into a
coherent group a number of individuals who would
have otherwise been scattered, isolated, and
powerless in their departments. It provided
consistent and effective intellectual and
administrative leadership. It created a power
base within the university and a compelling magnet
for funds from outside the institution. It was
so successful in meeting a recognized need that
its graduates everywhere served as disciples.
Fifteen years later, when the Hayter Commission
in the United Kingdom reviewed research and
instructional programs on all the so-called
non-Western areas, it identified Robinson's
emphasis upon a center that provided "unity,
driving force, and direction" as a principal
reason for America's remarkable advance in
Russian studies.

The role of philanthropic foundations in the
expansion of Russian studies has been most important. Indeed, the original grants to Columbia
and Harvard by the Rockefeller Foundation and the
Carnegie Corporation in 1946 and 1947 were crucial,
as were the Carnegie grant to the SSRC in 1948 and

other smaller Rockefeller awards then to other
institutions. Above all, the foundations provided
the fellowships that supported graduate students
during the required extra years of study of
language and of courses outside the major discipline. Finally, the foundations, interested in
but not directly involved in education and free to
direct funds to new ideas, provided support for
venturesome and innovative arrangements that
university administrators could not recognize or
assist.

The Ford Foundation, the largest and wealthiest
of all foundations, played the most important role
after 1951, when it established the Board of
Overseas Training and Research to help support
American graduate students and young scholars
studying other parts of the world. Between 1951
and 1969, the Foundation devoted $294,000,000 to
expanding international studies in the United
States and abroad. Of this, American universities
received $155,000,000. The International Training
and Research Program (later Division) under this
Board from 1952 through 1962 played an absolutely
decisive role in the expansion of foreign studies,
in particular that of the Soviet Union and Eastern
Europe. Above all, it provided graduate fellowships, in some cases for several years, to 430
young men and women interested in Russia and
Eastern Europe.

The Russian Institute's opening announcement
in 1946 indicated that study in the Soviet Union
would be a major part of the work, that Soviet
scholars would be invited to lecture, and that the
faculty "planned to continue their pre-war
practice" of research there at frequent intervals.
However, since the Soviet Union and Eastern Europe
were closed to Western scholars until 1958,
American training was restricted to work in
libraries and classrooms here and in Western
Europe. This offered some advantages. It
prevented a flood of young men and women to the
Soviet Union before they were able to make
effective use of the opportunity: fewer than
one-half of those entering the Harvard and
Columbia graduate programs in 1948 had studied

Russian, and only one-quarter had had courses of any kind on Russia. Moreover, it forced our scholars to develop special skills in the search for and analysis of published information.

The principal achievement of this postwar expansion was the establishment of a number of graduate centers with significant library collections and research and instructional programs of high quality. The responsibilities accepted originally only by Harvard, Columbia, and Berkeley were thus distributed among a large number of institutions throughout the nation, a tribute to the original centers as well as to the administrators and scholars in the "newer" institutions. While in 1939-40, for example, 18 and in 1942 only 20 colleges and universities taught Russian, 128 taught the language in 1946, 211 in 1953, and 600 in 1965. The first Russian area program was established in 1946; by 1951 the United States had five and by 1971, fifty-eight.[1]

Between 1946 and 1956, more than 500 received M.A.'s in Russian studies, 235 from Columbia alone and about 100 from Harvard. During the same period, about 50 who had received multidisciplinary area training also achieved doctorates, and about 30 received Ph.D.'s without the benefit of full area training. In all fields of Russian studies between 1950 and 1959, sixty-eight universities awarded approximately 600 doctorates, 275 of them in history. In the next five years, 400 more young men and women obtained doctorates, 130 of them in history. In the 1960s, 610 received Ph.D.'s in Russian and East European history, three-quarters as many as had been produced in all fields on Russia before 1960.

The expansion of East European studies has been just as impressive, with 375 M.A. degrees awarded (276 of these at Columbia) between 1945 and 1965. During the same years, 184 received Ph.D.'s,

[1]The most complete survey of the growth of foreign area studies in the United States is Richard D. Lambert, Language and Area Studies Review (Philadelphia, 1973), pp. 490.

seventy-five percent of these at Columbia. Seventy-six percent of these young men and women entered teaching.

Membership in the American Association for the Advancement of Slavic Studies (AAASS), founded in 1948, reflects this growth, which was much more rapid than that of groups in other foreign areas or in professional disciplines. In 1960 the AAASS had 633 members; in 1968, 2,200 members, an increase of 310 percent; in 1971, 2,844 members. The organization for language teachers, the American Association of the Teachers of Slavic and East European Languages, founded in Indianapolis in 1941, had 350 members in late 1953 and 1,500 in 1966.

In the first decade after 1946, slightly more than one-third of the graduates of the Russian area programs entered government service, while about one-third, including almost all who obtained doctorates, became scholars and teachers. After that period, approximately three-quarters entered the academic profession, and only a few went into government service. Even a suspicious Soviet scholar in 1966 noted that only nineteen percent of our historians in the Russian field had had any military, diplomatic, or other government service.[2]

The handful of scholars who studied in Russia before and after World War I reflected accurately the low level of American interest in the Soviet Union and in any kind of commercial or intellectual contacts. The new Soviet state began to attract American visitors only in the late 1920s, especially when the first five-year plan began in 1927-28. Soviet success in persuading the Ford Motor Company, General Electric, and Calder, McKee, and Company to

---

[2]B. P. Kanevskii, "K kharakteristike amerikanskogo 'sovetovedeniia'" [Concerning the Character of American "Sovietology"], Voprosy istorii, 5 (May 1966), 185. A 1971 study concluded that between seventy-five and one hundred university-trained specialists on Russia and Eastern Europe worked in American government agencies (John M. H. Lindbeck, Understanding China. An Assessment of American Scholarly Resources [New York, 1971], 47, 62, 74).

assist in industrializing the Soviet Union brought
as many as a thousand engineers in 1930. In 1932,
six hundred American engineers were working in
Soviet automobile and tractor plants alone. In
the late 1930s social workers, such as Jane Addams,
labor leaders, such as Sidney Hillman and Walter
Reuther, progressives, such as Senator Robert M.
LaFollette and Rexford Tugwell, and leaders of
ethnic minorities, such as W. E. B. DuBois,
visited Moscow and Leningrad. From 1929 through
1937, Intourist assisted two thousand and sometimes
ten thousand tourists each year, and tourists
wrote seventeen of the twenty-one books published
about Russia in the United States in 1928 and 1929.

The Rockefeller Foundation in 1927 and again
in 1937 sought to aid medical research and
instruction in the Soviet Union, as in Bulgaria,
China, and other countries, but it encountered
such fear and anxiety that it provided only a few
fellowships and minor laboratory equipment.
W. Horsley Gantt spent five years in the 1920s in
the laboratory of Academician I. P. Pavlov, and a
few scientists attended national and international
conferences in Moscow, but these contacts did not
create important relationships. George R. Havens
and Norman L. Torrey each used the Diderot and
Voltaire archives in Leningrad for two summers with
full satisfaction, but their studies of eighteenth-
century French literature from materials Catherine
the Great had purchased had little effect on
Russian studies or on Soviet-American relations.
Stephen P. Duggan, director of the International
Institute of Education (IIE), also had little
impact when he investigated educational exchanges
in 1925, although Duggan through Lunacharsky and
Trotsky was later able to arrange some student
tours, with Mosely, Maurice Hindus, Henry Shapiro,
and Louis Fischer serving as tour leaders.

In 1933, VOKS, the All-Union Society for
Cultural Relations with Foreign Countries that
was established in 1925 to assist prominent foreign
visitors, and Intourist together attracted only
twenty-five American teachers and students to the
Anglo-American Summer Institute at Moscow State
University. Duggan, because of his earlier

interest and because of the successful IIE
seminars he and Edward R. Murrow had arranged in
Western Europe, was suddenly invited in the winter
of 1934 to help attract American professors,
teachers, and students to another such institute.
The following summer, more than two hundred
Americans from about sixty colleges and universities, plus about thirty Englishmen, therefore
enjoyed two weeks of travel and six weeks of
courses given by Soviet professors in English on
education, literature, art, sociology, and
psychology. However, when two hundred American
and English students arrived in June 1935, they
learned that the summer school had been canceled.
Duggan's inquiries to the Soviet embassies in
Washington and London and to VOKS brought no
response, and IIE was later denounced as "the
center of international propaganda for American
reaction."[3]

Over the Christmas holiday in 1935 Pares
sought to persuade Foreign Minister Maxim Litvinov
to accept an exchange of students between Great
Britain and the Soviet Union and to allow Soviet
scholars to lecture at the School of Slavonic
Studies. This effort failed, as did another in
1937 to establish a dormitory for British and
American students. In short, Western efforts for
study opportunities and exchange programs before
World War II led nowhere.

However, American admiration for the Soviet
war effort, desire to help overcome Soviet sus-
picions, and enthusiasm for working together led to
a flood of proposals for close intellectual and
scholarly cooperation during the last years of the
war and the immediate postwar period. After the
Moscow Conference in October 1943, Ambassador
Averell Harriman requested Soviet approval from
Foreign Minister Viacheslav Molotov for distribution
of two bimonthly magazines on the American war
effort and American life, direct contact between
Soviet and American news editors to exchange

[3]Senator Joseph McCarthy later attacked Edward R. Murrow
for his role in the 1934 summer school (Alexander Kendrick,
Prime Time. The Life of Edward R. Murrow [Boston, 1969], 67).

information, publication by the Embassy of a
daily news bulletin for diplomatic missions,
distribution of films to the American-Soviet Film
Committee, and permission to discuss cultural
exchanges with VOKS. Molotov's reply on December
13, 1943, was extremely cold, and it only per-
mitted distribution of the daily issue of the
Department of State's Radio Bulletin to a limited
number of Soviet institutions and distribution of
Amerika in Russian. In 1944, when the Rockefeller
Foundation offered a number of fellowships in
agriculture, forestry, public health, and library
service, the Soviet government did not even reply.
In January 1945, John Parker, a member of the
House of Commons, thought Stalin and Moscow State
University administrators and faculty had welcomed
his proposal for a program like the Rhodes fellowship. But again, the Soviet government took no
action.

American interest in expanding cultural
relations with all parts of the world exploded
after World War II. In the academic field, private
institutions and the splendid legislative achievement of the Fulbright program brought thousands of
foreign students here and enabled similar numbers
of Americans to study and teach abroad. As part of
this changed interest, a flood of invitations from
the United States reached the Soviet Union. The
Department of State in October 1945 invited the
Red Army Chorus to tour, and the Department urged
the exchange of ballet dancers, theater groups,
orchestras, and exhibits of art and handicrafts.
Ambassador Harriman on November 13, 1945, told
Deputy Foreign Minister Andrei Vyshinsky that the
United States wanted to exchange students,
beginning in 1946-47. There was no response, as
there was none to invitations from groups such as
the Boston Symphony Orchestra and the National
Federation of Women's Clubs. Princeton and other
universities offered fellowship and research
opportunities for Soviet scholars and students, and
Cornell sought Soviet teachers of Russian--to no
avail. The Soviet Ministry of Health did not even
respond to an August 1946 offer of a complete
penicillin plant. Those veterans who sought to use
the G.I. Bill for study in the Soviet Union were

unable to obtain entry. Scholars in fields as
diverse as geology, clinical pathology, Russian art,
and diabetes were denied visas. Admittedly, Soviet
universities were crowded, and living conditions
were Spartan. However, in the academic year
1946-47, more than five hundred students from
Eastern Europe, including fifty from tiny Albania,
were studying in Moscow, Leningrad, and Kharkov.

However, these initiatives failed miserably
because they occurred just as the Soviet government
was establishing firm control over Eastern Europe
and assisting the Greek communists in the Greek
Civil War. Above all, they collided with the
Zhdanovshchina, the Soviet drive launched early in
1946 as a "gigantic ideological reconversion
operation" to restore cultural purity and eliminate
Western influences produced by cooperation with the
United States and Great Britain during the war.
Thus, Dr. Vasili V. Parin of the Soviet Ministry of
Health and the Academy of Medical Sciences, who had
been most cooperative with Western colleagues,
in December 1946 was dismissed from the Ministry
and sentenced to a forced labor camp for six years
when he returned from an official trip to this
country that had been arranged by the Public
Health Service.[4] Attacks on "servility before the
rotten West," "rootless cosmopolitanism," "kow-
towing to bourgeois culture," and "survivals of
capitalism in the consciousness of the people"
helped isolate the Soviet peoples and were
accompanied by efforts to glorify Soviet achievements, particularly scientific discoveries. A
February 15, 1947, law forbade the marriage of
Soviet citizens to foreigners. The State Secrets
Act of June 1947, which established severe
penalties for divulging information to foreign
citizens, was amended in December 1947 to provide
that no individual or organization could have
relations with foreigners except through the
Ministry of Foreign Affairs or the Ministry of
Foreign Trade. In April 1949, massive jamming of
foreign radio broadcasts began. In that same

[4]Prominent Personalities in the USSR. A Biographic
Dictionary... Compiled by the Institute for the Study of
the USSR (Metuchen, New Jersey, 1968), 468-69.

year, Metropolitan Nikolai called Pope Pius XII an "agent of American imperialism."

Consequently, the efforts of the Department of State in 1947 to establish cultural exchanges were doomed. Ambassador Walter B. Smith's message to Molotov in February 1947, summarizing the proposals for cultural exchanges that various organizations had made, received no reply. In April 1947, when Smith informed Vyshinsky that the United States would welcome some fifty Soviet scholars "to confer with American scholars in the same fields on matters of mutual professional interest" and would appreciate similar invitations, the Soviet response was negative.

The final American endeavor was also a failure. However, both the principles on which this was made and the proposals themselves foreshadow later initiatives that launched the academic exchange programs. First, these proposals were the product of a cooperative effort among a group of dedicated individuals who had long experience in Russian studies; a university that had special interest; agreement of a group of universities to have one institution and one man speak for all; aid from the ACLS in collecting and culling proposals; financial support for travel from the Rockefeller Foundation; and the assistance of the American Embassy, when requested, in trying to open doors in Moscow.

After careful preparation, Columbia's Russian Institute confidently sent Ernest J. Simmons to present its proposals for academic exchanges. Simmons spent the period from July 15 through August 14, 1947, in Moscow. He was unable even to talk with most of the administrators and scholars whom he wished to invite to the United States, and his reception from those he did meet was cold. The Lenin Library responded that Soviet librarians were too heavily engaged to work on a combined bibliography and that it did not wish to accept the entire Yudin collection of eighty thousand volumes, but only the volumes that Lenin had used. With this failure and a subsequent vicious attack on Simmons in the Soviet press, American initiatives

to surmount or bypass the Iron Curtain ended until
after the death of Stalin, when the thaw began in
the Soviet Union.[5]

Arrangements under which our scholars ultimately were able to study in the Soviet Union came
slowly and gradually. The Soviet government after
Stalin's death continued its policy of maintaining
positions of strength in dealing with foreign cultures, but its tactics became more subtle, flexible,
and skillful as smiles and bouquets for Western
leaders replaced the wintry blasts of the Stalin
period. Some observers likened the process to
opening "the massive groaning gate of a medieval
castle." Others noted that the thaw affected only
the visible surface and that the deep permafrost
of the system remained solid and unbroken.

The new turn no doubt reflected a number of
pressures and ambitions, beginning with the desire of
the new rulers to win the favor of the Soviet public,
especially the intellectuals. They also wanted increased access to the latest scientific and technical discoveries of the West. They recognized, too,
the new situation created by the failure of communist
forces in Greece, the Soviet disasters in Berlin and
Yugoslavia, the defeat and stalemate in Korea, and
the extraordinary recovery of Europe, spurred by the
Marshall Plan, NATO, and the move toward West European unity. The policy of the new collective leadership toward slightly increased freedoms within the
Soviet Union, for less-tense dealings with the West
and for controlled cultural relations, was reflected
in the Austrian State Treaty in May 1955, the "visit
to Canossa" by Khrushchev and Bulganin when they
went to Yugoslavia that June, and the establishment
of diplomatic relations with the Federal Republic
of Germany in September.

The beginnings of a more relaxed policy in
cultural relations appeared as early as 1953, when
Western music began to appear occasionally on
Soviet programs and Western art in Soviet exhibits.

[5]After this trip Izvestiia denounced Simmons as a spy.
At the same time, the New York World Telegram accused him
of being a Soviet agent.

Allowing Soviet women who had married foreigners
during World War II to leave the country represented
another step. In late 1953 delegations of high
party officials began to travel abroad, followed
soon by delegations that included scientists.
Then the Soviet government encouraged groups of
tourists, particularly from countries that
communists ruled. In April 1954 the Comédie
française played for three weeks to large and
enthusiastic audiences in Moscow and Leningrad, as
well as on television. That same month, the Soviet
Union joined UNESCO. In February 1955, it joined
the Inter-Parliamentary Union. In July of that
year it resumed its membership in the World
Health Organization.

The Soviet government in September 1954
allowed two Soviet specialists to attend the
Second World Congress of Cardiologists in Washington, D.C.,and to tour the United States.[6] This led
to invitations to American cardiologists and other
doctors, notably Paul Dudley White, to visit the
Soviet Union, and in January and February 1955
to reciprocal visits by groups of medical doctors.
In fact, following an epidemic of polio in Moscow
in 1955, the assistance from the Salk vaccine that
the Soviet Union obtained from the exchange of
specialists demonstrated most vividly to Soviet
leaders the value of increased contacts.

The number of Western news correspondents in
Moscow rose in 1955 to twelve, of whom nine were
American, two British, and one French. Approximately two thousand Soviet citizens were
allowed to travel to Poland or to Finland on
holidays, a great step forward from the years in
which no Soviet citizen was allowed to visit even
another state that communists ruled. In December
1955 the Soviet government allowed the American
producers of Porgy and Bess to present this opera
in Moscow and in Leningrad, stunning Soviet
audiences. It also allowed its most distinguished

[6]One of the two was Dr. Boris V. Petrovsky, who became
Soviet Minister of Health in 1965, played an important part
in expanding medical exchanges, and signed the Agreement on
Health Cooperation in Moscow in May 1972.

pianist, Emil Gilels, to perform with Eugene
Ormandy and the Philadelphia Orchestra, the
first time an important Soviet artist had played
in the United States since the Prokofiev tour in
1938. Here the initiative of Sol Hurok, the
celebrated American impresario, was of particular
importance because he persuaded the Soviet
leaders that Gilels, David Oistrakh, and other
artists would have a significant impact on world
opinion. Hurok thus released a flood of Soviet
entertainers.

This slow but visible change led Americans
to renew direct and vigorous efforts to expand
relations. At the official level, the Department
of State supported invitations to Soviet individuals and groups and encouraged travel to
the Soviet Union. President Dwight Eisenhower's
speech at the General Assembly of the United
Nations in December 1953 on the peaceful uses
of atomic energy led to the conference on that
subject in Geneva in August 1955, which produced
scientific cooperation on a most sensitive
subject. At the Geneva Conference of the four
Great Powers in July 1955, the United States
pressed for "lowering the barriers," and the
Soviet leaders warmly agreed. At the Foreign
Ministers' conference in October, our government
made seventeen specific proposals for increasing
contacts. However, the Soviet Union vetoed
our suggestions that all curbs on the press be
removed, that jamming of radio broadcasts end,
and that information offices be established.

The turning point in Soviet policy apparently
came at the twentieth congress of the Soviet
Communist Party in February 1956. This congress
launched the attack on Stalin, agreed that
peaceful means could be used to achieve socialism
and that there were several roads to socialism,
and justified increased contacts with the West.
Khrushchev himself supported study of "the best
of the West," and the program of the Sixth
Five-Year Plan urged "maximum use of the
achievements of Soviet and foreign science and
technology by design and planning organizations."
The National Security Council on June 29, 1956,

concluded that a "vast possibility for peaceful change" existed within the Soviet Union and urged a vigorous policy toward increasing contacts.

While the federal government was acting with imagination and vigor, but not in such a way as to alarm Soviet leaders, growing numbers of individual Americans demonstrated interest in visiting Russia and establishing personal contacts. Only forty-three had visited the Soviet Union in 1953, but the dribble grew to a trickle in 1955 when numbers of churchmen, businessmen, journalists, farmers, congressmen, veterans, and tourists began to visit, creating contacts and discussing their experiences back home.

Gabriel Reiner of the Cosmos Travel Agency in New York in 1955 again demonstrated the role enterprising individuals played by accompanying a chess team to Moscow. There he met the Soviet leaders at the American ambassador's July 4 reception and obtained improved opportunities for tourists. Two thousand American tourists then visited the Soviet Union in 1956, accompanied by Intourist guides and traveling in tightly restricted areas.

Hopes were raised so absurdly high that the New York Times Moscow correspondent in 1955 suggested that we invite one hundred thousand Soviet young men and women to live in our homes and study in our schools. Chester Bowles in August 1957 suggested a more modest exchange of five hundred students. His friend William Benton proposed that ten thousand Soviet college graduates be invited to live with American families and travel freely around the country, with our government providing the $30,000,000 he thought necessary and with the program reciprocal if Khrushchev agreed. President Eisenhower talked of exchanging ten thousand Soviet and American students. C. Wright Mills urged that the American government adopt a target of fifty thousand students as a suitable goal.

The new "crack in the Kremlin wall" naturally attracted close attention among those engaged in

Russian studies. Harvard University as early as
1955 invited the Soviet Academy of Sciences to
send a Soviet medievalist to lecture. After the
Soviet national bibliography, the Knizhnaia
Letopis', had again become available in the West,
American universities persuaded leading Soviet
libraries to resume book exchanges. The few
scholars who had visited the Soviet Union in the
1930s wished to test what they might see against
the knowledge they had acquired from reading and
from talks with refugees. However, fearful
because of their experience with abrupt shifts in
Soviet policy that any new opportunity might be
a brief one, and deeply committed to improving
the training of their graduate students, they
preferred that our young scholars benefit first.
One hundred twenty-six young Americans had
received fellowships for study of the Soviet Union
or Eastern Europe from the Ford Foundation alone
between 1953 and 1955; these men and women and
their colleagues who had continued their studies
under other auspices naturally were eager to
visit the country on which their professional
concerns concentrated. Individual scholars began
to suggest as early as the spring of 1955, before
the Geneva summit conference, that the Ford
Foundation "give serious thought to the quick
establishment of a fund for travel to the Soviet
Union for qualified American scholars and teachers."
A group that became the nucleus of the Inter-
University Committee on Travel Grants then made
a formal application early in October that year
for such a fund.

As the apparent "thaw" developed within the
Soviet Union and as our scholar-teachers reviewed
prospects for travel and the financial and other
questions such ventures would raise, they
recognized the need for cooperation. Their
traditional multidisciplinary instruments that
also served to mute university rivalries, the
ACLS and the SSRC, both declined to administer
a program that provided for thirty-day trips,
because they considered it a "crash" affair and
one devoted to increasing understanding, not
research, which was their principal function. In
consequence, some other organization was considered

essential. Twelve scholars representing ten
universities--those most interested then in
Russian and East European studies--at a meeting
in New York on February 22, 1956, therefore established the Inter-University Committee. They
agreed that it should be a temporary organization
and that its functions should be transferred
whenever the specialists could safely surrender
their responsibilities to another qualified
organization.

Those who created the Committee came largely
from the East. Of the twelve, one, Charles
Jelavich, then at the University of California in
Berkeley, was from the Far West, and one, Chauncy
Harris of the University of Chicago, from the
Midwest. The others were all from the East:
Frederick C. Barghoorn of Yale; Abram Bergson
and Marshall Shulman of Harvard; Cyril E. Black
of Princeton; M. Gardner Clark of Cornell; Evsey
Domar of Johns Hopkins; William B. Edgerton of
Pennsylvania State; Henry L. Roberts and Schuyler
C. Wallace of Columbia; and Oscar Halecki of
Fordham. Of the twelve, five had received their
Ph.D. degrees from Harvard University and three
from Columbia.

Columbia University, which then had the
largest and most important center for Russian
studies, contributed those most responsible for
creating the Committee. Wallace, the first
chairman, was the first Dean of the School of
International Affairs at Columbia. The deputy
chairman was David Munford, a graduate of the
Russian Institute, one of the first SSRC Fellows
for study of foreign areas, and after 1953 an
executive associate in the Ford Foundation. His
work there had acquainted him with the interests
of scholars throughout the country and had
provided him a national view that few members
of the academic community possessed. Thus, in
1953 and 1954 alone, Munford and his colleagues
visited almost one hundred campuses.

The second meeting of the Inter-University
Committee in March 1956 added seven others to the
policy committee. Of these, five were from the

East, one from the Midwest, and one from the
Northwest. All spoke as individuals but had
university support. Informal meetings in the
summer and early fall of 1955 and the more formal
meetings in 1956 proved extraordinarily important
for the history and development of Russian and
East European studies and of academic exchanges.
One should note that the scholars participating
in these meetings were interested solely in
opportunities for Americans to study for a short
time in the Soviet Union. They also established
a program for Eastern Europe and encouraged those
especially interested in the Soviet Union to visit
Eastern Europe as well. Above all, they had no
interest in an exchange program. This became
necessary later, when the Soviet government would
allow Americans to study in the Soviet Union for
prolonged periods only if the two governments
concluded an agreement that ensured Soviet scholars
opportunities to study in the United States.

The numbers involved in the original program
were relatively small. Forty-one scholars
traveled to the USSR in 1956, fifty-eight in
1957, and thirty-eight in 1958, at a total cost
of somewhat more than $300,000. When the
cultural exchanges agreement signed in January 1958
provided opportunities for study throughout the
academic year, those grants became less significant.
Even so, especially after the Soviet government
announced in 1959 that one could travel for up
to seventy-five days for only $16.00 per day, the
Committee renewed the faculty grants program and
made additional awards for 1959 and 1960. Between
1956 and 1960, the Committee thus enabled somewhat
more than two hundred scholars from fifteen
disciplines and seventy-five academic institutions
to visit the Soviet Union as tourists, generally
for thirty days. The program was thus far more
successful than anyone had dreamed. In fact, in
its first year the Committee had expected perhaps
25 or 30 qualified applications; it received 109.

These awards had a significant influence upon
the participants, of whom I was one, and upon
Russian and East European studies. Without
exception, the trips enormously stimulated the

interest and ambition of the participants. They
also led to increased emphasis upon improving
Russian language instruction and upon greater use
of Russian sources in both teaching and research.
Above all, however, these visits persuaded everyone
involved to seek extended opportunities for study.

The changes in Soviet leadership and policy
that occurred after the death of Stalin in March
1953 launched the process which led more than four
years later to the Soviet decision to negotiate
the 1958 cultural exchanges agreement with the
United States. Presumably, the artists, medical
doctors, and others who met American colleagues
on their return provided information and insights
to Soviet leaders who were reviewing long-term
policies. In 1956 the Soviet government concluded
cultural exchange agreements with Belgium and
Norway, although neither treaty was implemented
until 1960. In October 1957, it signed a similar
agreement with France. Finally, in the same month,
the Soviet Union launched the first sputnik, so
that it entered negotiations in a strong position.

The negotiations in Washington began on
October 29, 1957, and ended on January 28, 1958.
They were conducted by Ambassador William S. B.
Lacy, President Eisenhower's special assistant for
East-West exchanges, and by the Soviet Ambassador
in Washington, Georgi Zarubin. Ambassador Lacy
indicated that our government disliked the concept
of a cultural exchange agreement and had never
signed one. He described our goals as "removing
barriers currently obstructing the free flow of
information and ideas" and enabling both peoples
to obtain the benefit of "free discussion, criticism,
and debate on the vital issues of the day." He
advocated establishment of normal intellectual
relations and urged the Soviet Union to end
censorship, jamming radio broadcasts, and all
controls over access to information and travel.
As far as education was concerned, he hoped that
individuals and universities themselves would be
able to arrange regular periods of study, with
their wives and families accompanying the scholars.

Ambassador Zarubin described the purpose of

the agreement as "the normalization of Soviet-
American relations and the relaxation of
international tensions." He then proposed the
exchange of fifty-six delegations, each for
short tours, in fields such as metallurgy, mining,
automobile manufacture, chemicals, electronics,
machine tools, plastics, various forms of energy,
cattle-breeding, and horticulture.

The ultimate agreement had fourteen sections,
only one of which dealt with higher education.
Perhaps the most important section from the
Department of State's point of view then was the
first, which provided for an exchange of radio and
television broadcasts. Other sections provided
for carefully regulated, reciprocal visits of
artists, dancers, athletes, scientists, doctors,
youth groups, and agricultural specialists.
Another section provided for the exchange of large
national traveling exhibits. An agreement "in
principle" provided for direct air flight between
the two countries; this was signed eight years
later, in the fall of 1966. Both sides agreed to
encourage tourism. In short, neither government
achieved its purposes through this agreement, or
its later versions. Both compromised in order to
obtain a compact and to open prospects for closer
contacts and for other larger long-term goals. In
the words of then Senator Lyndon B. Johnson, the
agreement was "the beginning of a beginning."

As far as higher education was concerned, the
first paragraph dealt with exchanges in the fields
of natural science and engineering, which were not
completed. The second provided for exchanges of
professors and instructors between Columbia
University and Moscow State University and between
Harvard University and Leningrad State University.
The third section, the most important, provided
for the exchange of twenty graduate students and
young scholars between the two countries in the
academic year 1958-59 and of thirty in 1959-60.
The Soviet government sought an exchange of senior
scientists between the Soviet Academy of Sciences
and the National Academy of Sciences, but the
Department of State, pressed by Russian specialists
through the Committee, preferred instead

an exchange of junior scholars, with all of the
American participants in the first year to be
Russian specialists. The organized concern of the
American scholars in the Committee with providing
their younger colleagues their first opportunity
to visit the Soviet Union explains the exchange
program for these juniors, rather than one for
senior scientists with the Soviet Academy of
Sciences. This had a powerful effect upon the
history of academic exchanges with the Soviet
Union, determined the Committee's basic policies,
and froze it into a relationship with the Soviet
Ministry of Higher Education that proved unsatisfactory, but which the Committee could not revise
or escape. In short, if the Inter-University
Committee had reached the same decision as the
Committee on Scholarly Communications with the
People's Republic of China, which in 1973 decided
to choose only those who already had a Ph.D., this
history would have been greatly different.

After this basic decision had been made, the
Soviet government proposed an exchange of ten
graduate students each year between Moscow and
Leningrad, on one hand, and Columbia and Harvard,
on the other. The Department of State succeeded
in raising the figures and in obtaining agreement
that half of the participants would come from and
go to the four universities named, but that the
other ten Soviet scholars the first year would be
placed in five other universities and that scholars
from other American institutions could participate.

As soon as the agreement was signed, the
Department of State asked the Committee to become
the administrative agent for the exchange of
"graduate students and young scholars." It turned
to the Committee because it was so active and
because the Department lacked the financial means
and administrative resources to direct the various
programs that constituted the agreement. Moreover,
Department officials recognized that the administrators and members of this league of concerned
institutions and of responsible scholars understood
many of the problems that might arise, had had
experience in the Soviet Union, and had directed a
travel program there for three years.

The Committee quickly accepted the invitation. In a series of week-end meetings it established policies, obtained $200,000 from the Ford Foundation, and accepted $10,500 from the Department of State to cover expenses of the Soviet participants for travel in the United States. It thus set out upon a far different role than its founders had envisaged.

CHAPTER THREE

The Varieties of Cultural Exchanges, 1958-75

The most remarkable aspect of Soviet-American academic exchanges, and of cultural exchanges as a whole, is that they were launched only two years after the crushing of the Hungarian revolution and have survived the major crises of the past two decades and the disagreements that grew out of the exchanges themselves. In fact, they have acquired apparent permanence and may now influence the political relationships under which they operate. Department of State statistics demonstrate that the number of Americans and Soviets visiting under the exchanges agreements has been remarkably stable, the only great leaps being those years in which large athletic teams or groups of performers have distorted the figures. Thus, the number of Americans who went to the Soviet Union in each of the first three years under all these programs exceeded those of every other year until 1972, and the large increases since then are due largely to brief visits of planning teams under the various joint research agreements signed in the 1970s. While the annual totals have been remarkably constant and many participants in later years have been repeaters or alumni, the variety of exchanges inside and outside the official agreements has slowly increased, enriching and strengthening cultural and political ties between the two countries.

The history of the exchanges reveals several
striking characteristics. Some elements, such as
the programs for both junior and senior scholars
in Russian studies and the humanities, public
health, science, athletics, and national ex-
hibitions, have been constant factors, operating
within slightly modified limits that the biannual
agreements establish. Others are additions that
are made usually after years of prodding by
American institutions and the Department of State.
These include those for language teachers,
effective in 1963; for undergraduates and university
classroom teachers allowed in 1972 and begun in
1974; and the joint research programs after 1971,
still fledglings in 1975. In addition, the size
and quality of the agreements, and even the ease
and duration of the negotiations, have been related
to the larger framework of Soviet-American relations.
Fluctuations in number of those actually exchanged
tend to lag about two years behind political
developments, demonstrating that cultural exchanges
have reflected rather than directly affected the
major changes in relations. Thus, the number of
American participants in 1971 was the second
lowest in this history, and a substantial increase
occurred only in 1973, although detente began in
1969 and the February 1970 agreement had reversed
the downward statistical trend that had begun with
the 1964 agreement.

The cultural exchange programs since the first
one was signed in January 1958 have remained a
part of the official agreements that the Department
of State has negotiated biannually, first with the
Soviet Committee for Cultural Relations with
Foreign Countries and later with the Soviet Ministry
of Foreign Affairs. The second agreement, signed
in November 1959, required only two weeks of
negotiations (the first consumed three months),
considerably expanded all the programs, provided
for direct exchanges between Harvard and Leningrad
Universities and Columbia and Moscow Universities,
and included two science agreements as appendixes.
The third, in March 1962, required five weeks but
provided a general increase of almost fifteen
percent and authorized the exchange of senior
scholars and lecturers as well as summer programs

for language teachers. This agreement reflected
the improvement in Soviet-American relations that
culminated in the nuclear test ban treaty in the
summer of 1963, and it made 1962 and 1963 the most
promising years until the early 1970s. The peak
years for Americans going to the Soviet Union on
all the exchange programs between 1960 and 1972
were 1964 and 1965.

The group of junior scholars sent to the
Soviet Union in 1963-64 was the largest and most
able the Committee had forwarded, and the number
of those who applied for 1964-65 was not exceeded
until 1974-75. The review that the participating
universities made in 1963 was so persuasively
optimistic that the Ford Foundation in August 1964
awarded the Committee $1,500,000 for the period
from July 1965 through June 1970. Moreover,
prospects were so exciting and attractive that
several universities sought responsibility for
directing the Committee's affairs during 1965-70.
The public shared this enthusiasm and confidence.
A Louis Harris national poll announcement on
December 15, 1963, revealed that sixty-nine percent
of the American nation approved the exchange of
young scholars and only twenty-four opposed. On
the other hand, only thirty-four percent favored
exchanges of scientists and engineers and
fifty-four percent opposed.

The next three agreements reflected the
changed atmosphere after the removal of Khrushchev,
growing tension over America's increasing involvement in Vietnam, pressure and crises in the Middle
East, the "spring" in Czechoslovakia, and increasing Soviet concern with ideological issues,
dissent, and dissenters. The February 1964
agreement required seven weeks of negotiations
and reduced the academic programs substantially.
The March 1966 agreement constituted still another
decline. Indeed, 1967 was the slimmest year for
academic exchanges since their establishment,
thirty percent below the average for the previous
nine years. When I visited the Soviet Union in
September 1967 on behalf of the Ford Foundation
to discuss ways of expanding academic relationships
through joint long-term and multinational research

projects, I was not even able to meet the officials
with whom I had been in correspondence. Moreover,
in 1967-68 only one American and one Soviet
performing arts group were exchanged, and no
cultural leaders visited the other country.

The agreement signed in Moscow on July 15,
1968, represented a further decline. In fact, the
Soviet draft proposals for those negotiations,
due in August 1967, arrived only on April 5, 1968,
more than three months after the period covered
had in fact begun. It reduced all the Committee's
programs, and others as well. For example, that
of major performing arts groups dropped from five
to three, national exhibits from two to one, and
technical delegations from fourteen to eleven. At
the same time, it provided for an exchange of
delegations to consider new programs for weather
control, treatment of industrial waste and
pollution, and study of solar eclipses. The atomic
energy agreement, which the Soviet government had
allowed to lapse in 1966, was also renewed, so
that 1968 foreshadowed Soviet interest in increasing exchanges in science and technology in
the 1970s.

The seventh agreement, signed February 10,
1970, after only a week's negotiation, reversed
the downward trend. All the Committee's programs
were increased, although not to their earlier
levels. The other academic exchange programs
remained stable, but the performing arts group
exchange rose from three to five, and a new
category of exchanges of delegations and information on oceanography, urban transport, air pollution, management systems, social security,
agriculture, economics, and the treatment of waste
water was added. This reversal and subsequent
expansions and improvements were apparently
directly related to the Soviet decision to adopt
the approach called detente. They reflected the
winding down of American participation in the war
in Vietnam, with growing prospects of an important
communist triumph; the fighting on the Ussuri in
1969 and the rising Soviet-Chinese hostility;
Ostpolitik and the benefits it produced for the
Soviet Union in Eastern Europe in particular; and

the desperate Soviet necessity to obtain scientific
and technical assistance from the West.

Moreover, the Soviet desire to purchase
massive amounts of grain to meet the great shortage,
represented by the meeting of Brezhnev and
Secretary of Agriculture Earl L. Butz on April 11,
1972, the day the eighth exchanges agreement was
signed, affected Soviet policy. The quick and
cordial negotiations were also no doubt part of an
effort to establish a friendly atmosphere for the
visit President Nixon was to make in May 1972. This
agreement maintained most of the academic programs
at the 1970 level but increased that for language
teachers. In addition, it finally provided that
eight American and Soviet scholars teach semester
or full-year courses in the other's universities
in fields ranging from the natural and social
sciences to language and literature. Moreover, for
the first time, junior American scholars were
allowed to bring dependent children as well as
spouses, opening the program to some otherwise
unwilling to participate.

The agreement signed in Washington on June 19,
1973, for the period from January 1974 through
December 1976 was concluded much earlier than
usual. It enlarged slightly the number of major
performing arts groups and of individual artists,
and it provided for seminars and exchanges of
educational specialists. In addition, while
the 1972 agreement provided for an exchange of
forty graduate students and young scholars, the
new one called for "at least forty." Therefore,
in the spring of 1974 each side nominated forty
persons and ten alternates, all of whom were
placed, as were all fifty-two nominees in the
summer of 1975. Moreover, Brezhnev and Nixon in
1973 renewed the agreements through 1979, with
a review scheduled in December 1976.

In short, the negotiations themselves, the
agreements, and the numbers exchanged all follow
the larger pattern of Soviet-American relationships.
They reveal that the Department of State and those
who depend on it to advance cultural exchange
programs have little authority in dealing with the

Soviet government, but also that firmness, good will, and imagination ultimately do have some influence and can be productive under benign circumstances.

The cultural exchanges have also been distinguished by variety, each program possessing its own purpose and significance, and all of them together reflecting some of the character and vitality of modern culture. These varieties, as well as those elements of our culture that are not included in these formal and restrictive agreements (such as publications), together reveal some of the limited ways in which these two states and societies now touch each other.

For most Americans, and probably for most Soviet citizens as well, basketball players and ballet dancers, sprinters and soloists are the most important elements. In fact, impresario Sol Hurok and the Soviet artists whom he brought to this country, generally within the agreement, have dominated the public image of cultural exchanges. Thus, the Bolshoi Ballet had made four tours to the United States by 1970, as had the Moiseyev Folk Dance Ensemble. The Kirov Ballet has completed two tours of the United States. Such splendid groups not only serve a Soviet political purpose, entertaining and impressing thousands, but also earn dollars. For example, on its first trip to this country, the Moiseyev Folk Dance Ensemble grossed $1,500,000 in an eleven-week tour. On the other hand, American groups perform in central cities in the Soviet Union, providing thousands of Soviet citizens some understanding and insight into the vitality and variety of our cultural life. Perhaps the most successful have been Benny Goodman, who gave thirty-one concerts in a tour in 1962, and Duke Ellington and his orchestra, who visited five Soviet cities in 1971 and attracted immense and enthusiastic audiences.

Movies constitute a less-important element in the public aspect of exchanges because Soviet films are simply not popular in the United States and because of Soviet reluctance to encourage and import our films, which they consider a projection of the United States and a corrective for their

official version of this country. For example, the
Soviet Union in 1959 purchased ten American feature
films at low prices, the first ones imported since
1949. Through 1967 it purchased a total of forty-
five. American distributors in 1959 purchased
seven excellent Soviet films, The Cranes Are
Flying, Swan Lake, Circus Stars, The Idiot, Quiet
Flows the Don, Othello, and Don Quixote. However,
our public is unfamiliar with the style and content
of Soviet movies and has no special interest in
Soviet actors or actresses. Indeed, American
distributors lost almost $500,000 on the first
seven, all of which American critics acclaimed.
Moreover, the Soviet film industry has not analyzed
the American market or studied promotional methods.
American distributors provide the Soviet Union a
percentage of the box office receipts for Soviet
films shown here. The Soviet government refuses
to adopt this system for American films. Instead
it purchases them directly at relatively low cost
and profits substantially from immense Soviet
public interest. In spite of intensive efforts on
our side, few exchanges of documentaries or film
delegations have taken place. The first joint
production, of Maurice Maeterlinck's The Blue Bird,
was undertaken only in 1975.

Privately arranged, issue-oriented efforts
outside the exchanges agreements have also
attracted a good deal of public attention and have
had some influence. The Peace Hostage Exchange
proposals, which attracted enthusiastic support in
1962, perhaps best demonstrate popular eagerness to
remove the fear and suspicion which poison relations
and the hope that the sincerity and good will of
individual Americans might change the atmosphere.
An imaginative New York advertising executive
suggested that a number of Soviet and American
leaders have their children or other close
relatives reside in Washington and Moscow,
respectively, as "peace hostages." Public response
was so enthusiastic that the group planned to lease
eight vessels from the Maritime Administration
reserve fleet to carry eight thousand volunteer
hostages to the Soviet Union. Some enthusiastic
supporters urged exchanging a million. These
dreams, like others, faded before the Soviet

failure to respond. The Citizens Exchange Corps
since then has concentrated on sending tourist
groups and on helping the rare groups of Soviet
tourists who visit the United States. In addition,
in the summer of 1975 it arranged for two sets of
conferences each year with the Institute of Soviet-
American Relations, a propaganda organization--the
first two sets in 1975 and 1976 on health delivery
services and on elementary and secondary education.

On quite a different level, but in the same
spirit, the Quakers have achieved some quiet
effects, but they have often been thwarted. The
Soviet government has long been favorably disposed
toward the Quakers, even though there are less
than two hundred thousand Friends in the world, of
whom somewhat more than half live in the United
States and Canada, and even though (perhaps
because) the Quakers come from the middle class or
upper middle class and concentrate in the
intellectual professions. Their long-term concern
for peaceful relations, understanding, discussion,
and education have clearly won Soviet respect.
Quaker relief work in Russia during and immediately
after the First World War also left a good
impression.

The postwar work of Quakers in other countries
was launched in 1947 by British Quakers, who
established the Educational Interchange Council to
exchange German, Austrian, and British students and
language teachers. They expanded this to conferences, in particular of political and educational
leaders. In 1951 the conference program included
Yugoslavia and in 1955 the Soviet Union and Poland.
The British also established programs in which
young men and women from the United Kingdom and
other countries engaged in summer work projects
in East European countries. Later they arranged
brief exchange visits of British teachers of
Russian and of Soviet teachers of English.

Interest among American Quakers in the Soviet
Union and Eastern Europe began in 1952 when they
began a series of annual seminars lasting eight or
ten days for diplomats, particularly from Eastern
and Western Europe, on "National Interests and

International Responsibilities." Soviet diplomats
participated after 1956. Seven seminars have been
held in Eastern Europe, and the 1974 seminar was
in the Soviet Union. By 1973 more than two
thousand diplomats from a hundred countries,
including seventy from the Soviet Union, had
participated.

In 1954 the Quakers established annual
seminars on East-West exchanges in Austria,
inviting six West and six East European countries
to send representatives of youth organizations. A
Quaker group visited the Soviet Union in 1955 to
establish contact with Christian and Jewish groups.
Representatives from the Soviet Young Communist
League or Komsomol then attended the 1955 and
1956 seminars, and another group visited Friends
throughout the United States in 1958. American
Quakers participated as observers in the Moscow
Youth Festival in 1957 and in a similar one held
in Vienna in 1959, but they then concluded that
these vast, highly organized spectacles were not
meetings in which they could operate effectively.

From 1960 through 1965 the Quakers maintained
a system of annual seminars for small groups of
youth leaders from the United States, the Soviet
Union, and other countries chosen on an equal basis
by the Americans and the Soviets. These lasted
three weeks and occasionally produced tense
discussions of critical issues.

In 1960 the Quakers began an exchange of four
elementary or high school teachers, each spending
from two weeks to three months in the other country.
Finally, in 1966 the American Friends Service
Committee and the Institute of Soviet-American
Relations began a series of annual seminars on
Soviet-American relations, sometimes in the United
States, sometimes in the Soviet Union (the 1974
seminar was in Moscow), and sometimes elsewhere.
These are designed for twenty participants from
each country, ordinarily men and women at mid-point
in their careers. In short, since 1955 the
American Friends Service Committee has staged a
variety of exchange programs with the Soviet Union.
These programs are small; over the first fifteen

years only 219 Soviet citizens participated. The
Quakers have faced the same problems as those
administering other exchanges, with the Soviet
Union often canceling programs just before they
were scheduled to begin. Moreover, most Soviet
participants have been more interested in propaganda than in candid discussion of different points
of view and in identifying common interests.

Private meetings of Soviet and American
scientists with scientists and public figures from
other countries to discuss major international issues have had the same goals but have probably had
much greater impact. One such series, called the
Dartmouth Conference (the first session was held
at Dartmouth College in 1960), was financed and to
some degree initiated by the International Affairs
Division of the Ford Foundation. Its meetings
bring together for about a week from thirty to
fifty Soviet and American intellectual leaders,
including a few scientists, to discuss issues
such as effective communications and the economic
problems of less-developed countries. The eighth
Dartmouth Conference, on "Problems of Detente in
the Next Five Years," took place in Tbilisi in
April 1974.

Another more important group is known as the
Pugwash Conference because it held its first
meeting in July 1957 at the summer home of Cyrus
Eaton in Pugwash, Nova Scotia. It had its origins
in the concerns of British and American scientists,
particularly those active on the Bulletin of the
Atomic Scientists, about the spread of nuclear
weapons, but Prime Minister Jawaharlal Nehru of
India and A. V. Topchiev, then Chief Scientific
Secretary of the Soviet Academy of Sciences, also
played roles. The first meeting brought together
twenty-two men, all but two scientists, from ten
countries--the United States, the Soviet Union, the
United Kingdom, Japan, Canada, Australia, Austria,
France, Poland, and the People's Republic of China.
They spent four days discussing the social responsibilities of scientists, the dangers raised
by nuclear weapons, and disarmament. Since 1957
the Pugwash group has held from one to three small
and largely confidential conferences each year in

various parts of the globe, with scientists from
twenty to thirty countries participating. Pugwash
has also organized symposia and study groups,
published several volumes, and forwarded its agenda
and occasional statements to the governments of
the major states. Disarmament and arms control
have remained the most important themes, but there
have also been sessions devoted to the role of
science in helping developing nations, the environment and the population explosion, biological and
chemical warfare, and the free flow of scientific
information.

These meetings apparently have been relatively
free from national poses and politics, but the
participants have gradually learned that the basic
problems remain national and political and that
few scientists are able to purge the national
devil within them. The sixth conference, in Stowe
in 1961, was almost destroyed when the Soviet
Union tested the largest atomic bomb at the very
time Soviet scientists at the meeting were
proposing universal and complete disarmament.
American activities in Vietnam were discussed
heatedly in meetings between 1964 and 1968. The
session in Nice in the fall of 1968 produced
vigorous discussion but no agreement concerning
the invasion of Czechoslovakia, which was not
mentioned at the conference in Sochi in December
1969.

The effectiveness of Pugwash depends on the
vigor of the group in each country; some are
energetic and productive, others are not. The
establishment of an executive committee in 1963
failed to provide continuity, and most meetings of
these busy men have been brief and hurried. Only
about a thousand different scientists attended the
conferences between 1957 and 1974, and few of
them were young.

Above all, these earnest scientists have run
directly into the main issues separating the United
States and the Soviet Union. Thus, the statement
produced at the end of the nineteenth conference in
Sochi in a quiet and civilized way summarizes
the basic disagreement concerning the free

flow of information among dedicated scientists:

>   As has been stressed repeatedly by Pugwash,
> friendly contacts between East and West in dif-
> ferent fields should be encouraged and developed.
> One aspect of such contacts is the movement
> of people, goods, and information. Some par-
> ticipants strongly felt that total abolition of
> censorship would considerably decrease the
> tension in Europe and help to promote mutual
> understanding. More particularly, when there
> is an international conflict all countries should
> make the views of other parties fully known to
> their citizens through the media of mass
> communication. Others, while fully agreeing
> with the principle of expanding in every way the
> exchange of information contributing to mutual
> understanding among the peoples of Europe, do not
> share, at the same time, the view that the
> principle should apply to propaganda for under-
> mining the foundations of peace, international
> security, and cooperation among nations. . . .
>   If contacts between East and West are to
> contribute to peace and cooperation, they should
> take into account the existing realities,
> social, political, and ideological in countries
> belonging to different systems, otherwise they
> may create additional tension and arouse
> suspicion.[1]

The Pugwash Conferences held thus far have helped
educate important scientists to the realities of
international politics, and they add a new sense
of realism both to their research and to their
deliberations. They provide an important channel
of communication among eminent scientists who have
come to like and trust each other. Above all,
many participants carry their views to their
political leaders. Thus, Pugwash may have exerted
a considerable influence at the very highest
levels of the Soviet scientific and political
communities and at the points where those groups
interact. Through the relationships established

[1]Joseph Rotblat, Scientists in the Quest for Peace. A
History of the Pugwash Conferences (Cambridge, Mass., 1972),
xiv-xv, 6.

via conferences and the information that flows from
them through the upper levels of the scientific
establishment, some eminent Soviet scientists,
including Andrei Sakharov, have acquired understanding of the need for the freer flow of
information and for political leaders who recognize
that need.

Our government has of course been especially
eager to use the exchanges agreements to improve
the flow of people and ideas, and it has given
encouragement to every public and private activity
that can assist. At the official level, the
Department of State has constantly and vigorously
sought to eliminate restrictions and to make
communications between the United States and the
Soviet Union as free as they are among Western
countries. It has therefore pressed for the
elimination of Soviet jamming of Western radio
broadcasts, of Soviet censorship, and of all
controls. This pressure helped persuade the Soviet
Union to end jamming of foreign government broadcasts in September 1973, although it still jams
Radio Liberty and resorts to jamming all foreign
broadcasts during crises, such as the Soviet
invasion of Czechoslovakia in 1968. All Western
states have been constant critics of jamming, as
expressed, for example, at the Conference on
Security and Cooperation in Europe. This serves
at least to place Soviet leaders on the defensive
and to help improve the quality of the Soviet
mass media.

The Soviet position on the flow of information
has led our government to emphasize a variety of
ways of breaking through or circumventing the
controls. While the Voice of America, Radio
Liberty, and Radio Free Europe remain the most
important American instruments against the Soviet
blockade and are remarkably inexpensive (Radio
Liberty and Radio Free Europe together cost about
$60,000,000 each year), the Department of State
considers that national exhibits promise the
greatest immediate political benefit of all the
elements included in the exchanges agreements.
Soviet reluctance to continue the exchange of
exhibits and the lack of publicity and information

about our exhibits in the Soviet Union suggest that
the Soviet government shares this opinion. The
Department uses the exhibits to display an
authentic picture of the United States at important
Soviet centers over a prolonged period, thereby
providing a wide range of contacts and countering
Soviet ignorance and misinformation concerning this
country. In a sense, exhibits are the cultural
equivalent of fleet visits or "showing the flag."
The young Russian-speaking American guides are
effective respondents to thousands of queries from
Soviet visitors, and they supplement the demonstra-
tions of our artistic, scientific, technical, and
productive skills.

The first exhibit, the American National
Exhibition in Sokolniki Park in Moscow in 1959,
attracted 2,700,000, even though the Soviet press
paid little attention and Khrushchev in particular
criticized it (as did the House Committee on
Un-American Activities). Attendance often reached
60,000 a day, and Soviet visitors "liberated"
seventy percent of the books displayed. The eight
exhibits between 1961 and 1967, on subjects such
as plastics, transport, medicine, and graphic arts,
attracted a total of 4,813,771 people, an average
of slightly more than 600,000 per exhibit.
Throughout 1972 the exhibit on research and
development attracted an average of 17,000 daily
in Moscow. In short, these exhibits, the product
and pride of USIA, greatly advance our national
interest in educating millions about the United
States and American society.[2]

Soviet exhibits in the United States have not
been quite so successful. The 1959 exhibition at
the Coliseum in New York attracted more than
1,000,000 Americans, but eight exhibits between
1961 and 1967 attracted a total of only 952,000
visitors, an average of 120,000 per exhibit.
Attendance in recent years has increased as the
quality of the exhibits and the skill with which
they are prepared have improved.

[2]Organizing exhibits is expensive. The total cost of
the 1959 exhibit, which was exceptional, was somewhat more
than $3,600,000.

In all its negotiations the Department has
sought radio and television programs, the right to
establish reading rooms, and free sale of
publications. The Soviet government has agreed
to "encourage" the exchange of publications and to
"facilitate the exchange of radio and television
programs on scientific, technical, cultural, and
other educational subjects" through commercial
channels. It has not implemented these parts of
the agreements, except for that part concerning
distribution of the two governments' journals,
Amerika and U.S.S.R., and the Department of State
has valid complaints about the restricted
distribution of Amerika.

Soviet publications are sold here in bookstores
owned by Americans, which are in fact instruments
of the Soviet publishing system and sell only books
published in the Soviet Union and Eastern Europe.
Americans of course can also purchase Soviet
publications directly and through other bookstores,
but the Soviet government maintains control over
access to information there and selectively imports
in scientific and technical fields. Soviet
publishing organizations translate and widely sell
several hundred American books each year--until
recently very rarely paying royalties, even in
rubles. The Soviet decision in February 1973 to
become party to the International Copyright
Convention may change at least the policy on
royalty arrangements, but we have little evidence
yet. Indeed, the Soviet Union thus far has
emphasized the translation and publication of
Soviet works in the United States.

France has succeeded in making arrangements
for the public sale of contemporary literature as
well as of classical and technical French books in
the Soviet Union. A 1959 protocol stipulated that
the Soviet government would allot 200,000,000
francs (about $500,000 then) for the purchase of
French books each year, largely for libraries, but
that some would be sold openly in a specified
bookstore in Moscow. However, the French have been
unsuccessful in their efforts to establish reading
rooms, such as they have in other countries, and
to arrange for the public sale of French newspapers

in Moscow. Intourist hotels set aside for foreigners since April 1968 have sold small numbers of copies of leading European newspapers kept under the counter--for hard currency only.[3]

Private travel, or tourism, is so much an assumed part of the life of the average American that including it in a formal exchanges agreement seems, and is, preposterous. However, because of the Soviet Union's position on travel, in each of the agreements the two governments have assured that they would encourage and facilitate tourist travel.

Tourists ordinarily acquire a shallow understanding of any society they visit, and the Soviet "tourist world" is carefully contrived so that most foreigners see selected parts of the Soviet Union without meeting its inhabitants. However, tourism constitutes a remarkable index to the Soviet government's attitude toward the world. From 1937 until the death of Stalin, virtually no American tourist visited the Soviet Union, and only forty-three traveled there in 1953. Approximately 2,000 went in 1956, 2,500 in 1957, and 5,000 in 1958, when the American Express Company was allowed to establish an office in Moscow. During the first four years under the exchanges agreements, approximately 35,000 Americans visited the Soviet Union as tourists; 1,200 Soviet tourists visited the United States over the same period.

Each year from 1959 to 1965 approximately 10,000 American tourists visited the Soviet Union. The figure stood at approximately the level of 20,000 per year from 1966 until the early 1970s, and then rose from about 50,000 to 65,000 annually by 1973.[4] These

[3]According to the New York Times of April 21, 1966, twenty-eight daily and forty-two Sunday subscriptions to the Times were then held in the Soviet Union.

[4]According to the New York Times of July 28, 1971, 66,365 Americans visited the Soviet Union in 1971 and 5,268 Soviet citizens visited the United States. These statistics

increases reflect not only growing interest in the
Soviet Union but also the opening of seventy cities
to foreigners, improved quality of hotel facilities,
Soviet advertising, and improved Intourist service,
although few alumni of "Skintourist" can praise it
as efficient.

Soviet tourism in the United States is quite
another matter. We know from information Soviet
tourists have provided that the police investigate
them carefully before they receive permission to
travel. Soviet tourists did not visit this country
before 1958, when sixty-six came. With rare
exceptions, Soviet tourists have traveled in groups
of twenty or thirty. In fact, the first Soviet
tourist who came as an individual arrived in 1966.

From 1958 through 1970 the average number of
Soviet tourists was 195 per year. In 1961 the
Department of State granted 183 visas to Soviet
tourists; the figure rose to 317 in 1972 and 558
in 1973. In Moscow in September 1974 a ten-day
conference of representatives of American tourist
agencies and of the Soviet Administration for
Foreign Tourism concentrated on ways of increasing
American tourism, particularly through expanding
the number of Soviet hotels and improving Soviet
service, although the Americans had hoped to
emphasize means of achieving a six-way increase
in the number of Soviet tourists.

Of all the varied elements of the cultural
exchanges, those involving education have been the
largest and the most important because of their
contributions to knowledge and understanding and
their long-term political impact. Within the
series of academic exchanges, those involving
junior scholars or graduate students and young

include visitors of all types; two-thirds of the Soviet
visitors came on official business, and others came as
members of athletic teams and other such groups. According
to Soviet sources, the total number of Americans who visited
the Soviet Union was 66,164 in 1972 and 91,254 in 1973, when
9,600 Soviet citizens, mainly officials, came to the United
States (Christian Science Monitor, April 26, 1974).

faculty, who spend a semester or an academic year
in research, have been the most constant, have
involved the largest numbers and the longest
periods of time, and have been the most significant
intellectually and politically in the eyes of both
American and Soviet officials and scholars. They
constituted the bulk and the core of the work of
the Inter-University Committee and of IREX, the
major American organizations engaged in the
cultural exchanges. Their history represents
or reflects that of the entire exchange.

The Soviet government in 1958 satisfied the
Committee's main interest by agreeing to an exchange
program for junior scholars. The Department of
State, with the eager approval of those universities engaged in the Committee's work, in turn
accepted a program between four universities--
Columbia and Moscow, and Harvard and Leningrad.
Early in 1959, therefore, Harvard sent five eminent
scholars to discuss a direct exchange with
Leningrad State University, which returned the
visit in April. In that same month three
representatives from Columbia University traveled
to Moscow State University, which replied shortly
thereafter. Within a twelve-month period, Michigan,
California, and Yale sent similar delegations to
institutions with which they wished to have direct
contact, and Michigan State, Indiana, Kansas,
Wisconsin, Cornell, and Chicago all demonstrated
great interest in direct relationships.

The exchanges agreement signed on November 21,
1959, provided for four groupings--Columbia and
Moscow, Harvard and Leningrad, Yale and Kiev, and
Indiana and Tashkent--with each group to exchange
five professors and lecturers. The agreement also
provided that other universities could establish
similar arrangements. Moscow and Columbia agreed,
for example, that each would send up to five
professors to the other university each year for
brief periods, and that they would also exchange
books, periodicals, and other library materials.

The bilateral arrangements between "sister
universities" failed utterly. Each pair of institutions exchanged ceremonial visits that were cordial

but unproductive. The visit to Indiana University
made by the group from Tashkent was both hilarious
and illustrative. The group arrived in Bloomington,
Indiana, without notice on a Friday afternoon of
a football weekend when all hotel and motel rooms
in the area had been reserved. They were without
funds because they had flown from New York to
Chicago and had spent their dollars on a taxi to
Bloomington, Illinois. Indiana received the
Ministry's letter concerning the visit after the
delegation had returned to Tashkent.

The bilaterals suffered from other ailments
endemic to Soviet administrative confusion and
political intrusions. For example, the first
Harvard professor to visit Leningrad arrived in
May 1960 during the tension created by the U-2
flight, was not accepted at the university, and
met no scholars. Both American and Soviet
scholars could have acquired the same opportunities
for research or for lecturing as tourists,
particularly since the agreement stipulated that
the visits be brief. The most serious difficulty
reflected the simple fact that Soviet university
officials enjoy no authority; the universities
are directly under the rule of the Ministry,
which was apparently willing to include bilateral
agreements but not to allow them any substance.
In fact, Harvard officials discovered by accident
that President Pusey's correspondence with the
rector of Leningrad State University went first
to the Ministry, which on occasion did not
forward it to the university. Above all, many
professors from Harvard could clearly continue
research more effectively at a number of other
institutions than at Leningrad, just as many from
Leningrad would have been more satisfied at
another American institution. The bilateral
program was therefore abandoned in 1962.

The failure of direct relationships between
universities constitutes one of the paradoxes
of the academic exchanges. Both the Department
of State and the American academic community
at the beginning insisted that the governments
should at most facilitate the programs and
encourage institutions and individuals to make

their own arrangements. Moreover, direct relations between universities have worked well for some other countries, generally those with small exchanges with the Soviet Union. They may revive when the atmosphere changes and when institutions on both sides can identify needs special to them that even the most efficient large programs do not satisfy.[5]

On the other hand, the two governments on occasion have also reversed positions on their roles. Thus, the Soviet position has been and remains that the governments should maintain control and that the agreements should identify and approve all programs. On August 31, 1961, however, the Soviet government established the Institute for Soviet-American Relations under the Union of Friendship Societies, which issued appeals to private institutions and individuals for exchanges that bypassed the formal programs. This led the Department of State in 1964 to insist that all exchanges be included in the agreements, in order to prevent the Soviet organization from making separate arrangements with individual institutions, which would have destroyed the negotiating base of the Committee and of other scholarly groups. Later, in the 1970s, both the

[5]Academic exchanges between Canada and the Soviet Union began in 1963 with exchanges between the University of Toronto and the Ministry of Higher Education. They were later expanded to include small programs between other Canadian universities, British Columbia, Carleton, and Alberta, and individual Soviet universities. In October 1971, when a cultural agreement was concluded between the two governments, the bilateral arrangements were replaced by a national program. However, the Carleton-Leningrad agreement survived as an independent arrangement within the general framework.
　　Similarly, Australian National University and Monash University in 1964 began small programs with Moscow State and Leningrad State Universities, respectively. The Soviet Union and the United Kingdom in 1968 completed arrangements for some exchanges directly between Soviet and British universities, and the agreement with the German Federal Republic in 1969 also provided for short-term exchanges of lecturers between two sets of universities.

Department and the Soviet government began to
allow direct relationships between institutions,
outside the framework of the exchanges agreement.

The so-called bilateral or sister-university
arrangements were replaced by formal programs for
senior scholars between the Committee and the
Ministry incorporated in the agreement signed in
March 1962. This provided that twenty-five senior
scholars over the two-year period could spend up
to one semester in the other country and that
fifteen scholars could be invited for lectures for
up to four weeks. The program for lecturers was
abandoned in 1966. The numbers and periods of
time for senior researchers have risen and fallen
within small limits as the temper of Soviet-
American relations has changed.

This arrangement remained small because other
programs for senior scholars were created. The
1958 agreement concentrated upon junior scholars.
The failure to include the Soviet Academy of
Sciences encouraged the National Academy of
Sciences and ACLS in 1959 and 1960, respectively,
to establish small progams within the exchanges
agreement for senior scholars interested in the
institutes of the Soviet Academy of Sciences. The
ACLS proposal in July 1959 restricted the program
on our side in the first year to twenty or thirty
specialists in Russian studies, but it also
suggested a series of seminars with the Institute
of History and the Institute of World Economy and
International Relations. The agreement signed
twelve months later for the academic year 1961-62
provided for an exchange of three lecturers for
up to one month, each on a topic posed by the
receiving side, and of five research scholars for
a total of thirty months. The first American
arrived in the Soviet Union in June 1961 and four
others by fall, and the first Soviet humanists and
social scientists came to this country in
April 1962. The March 1962 agreement raised the
figure for lecturers to seven during the two years
and for research scholars to fifteen for a total
of seventy months. Lecturers were dropped in 1966.
Since then, the agreements have provided for an
exchange of twelve scholars for from three to

ten months for a total of fifty-five months for each period.

These programs have enabled a small number of Soviet and American humanists and social scientists, of whom I was one, to carry on research in the other country. The vexations that arose were like those which the Committee endured but were less troubling because this exchange was so small and involved only senior scholars. However, this program and that of the National Academy of Sciences were important beyond their size because they increased the number of American institutions engaged in academic exchanges and enabled the centralized Soviet government in its negotiations to take advantage of our numbers and diverse interests.

Probably the most effective exchange, and that most simple to administer, has been the summer program for language teachers, which the Committee first suggested in 1956. The second exchanges agreement in December 1959 provided for negotiations for courses for twenty-five language teachers, accompanied by one or two observers or specialists, for up to twelve weeks between June and September 1960, the year in which the Soviet-French program added annual summer sessions for language teachers. In 1961 the Soviet government reached agreement with the British Council concerning a program similar to one we had proposed. However, the Committee's did not begin until the summer of 1963 because of extraordinary Soviet delays.

In this program American teachers of Russian spend ten weeks in Moscow State University, where they live in a dormitory and take courses in Russian given by Soviet professors. A Soviet group of the same size spends ten weeks at an American university that has had much experience in teaching English to foreigners. Thus, Cornell University aided the Soviet teachers in 1963 and 1964, Georgetown University in 1965 and 1966, and the University of Michigan and the University of California in Los Angeles in later years.

This program has had few troubles and has even

been praised in the Soviet press, perhaps because both governments see no hazards from such a technical project and appreciate the competence and dedication of the instructors and the participants. It was so valuable and involved so few problems that the Committee sought to raise the number of participants to forty in 1964 and to fifty in 1965. However, the maximum number in any agreement in the 1960s was twenty-five, and the Ministry reduced this to twenty in 1968. It rose again to twenty-five in 1970 and to thirty in 1972 and thereafter.

The unsuccessful small programs of short visits by senior scholars who hoped to meet with groups of specialists of course raised less-delicate problems than having Soviet and American professors teach regular courses in universities in the other country. In many fields, especially in the humanities and social sciences, American scholars held most Soviet scholarship in low regard. Both administrators and faculty also feared criticism for such appointments from parents, alumni, and legislators. Moreover, they also concluded in the 1950s and 1960s that an American invitation to an eminent Soviet scholar might endanger him. In this kind of exchange, as in others, Eastern Europe differs greatly from the Soviet Union. Since 1955 hundreds of scholars from East European countries have taught in our universities, and a smaller number of Americans have taught there.[6]

However, beginning in 1955 many universities offered visiting professorships, especially in Russian literature, to Soviet scholars, most of whom our scholars knew were eager to accept. Soon

[6]American professors have taught at Moscow State University in exceptional circumstances. Thus, Professor Nicholas Kazarinoff of the University of Michigan, who speaks fluent Russian, taught mathematics there in 1960-61. Professor Harold Berman of the Harvard University Law School taught a course in Russian in 1961-62 until obvious pressure from some official source emptied his class just as he was beginning to discuss the decisions of the Supreme Court under Justice Warren and the major issues that it still faced.

after the Committee was founded in 1956 it began
to discuss an exchange of professors for classroom
teaching in language, literature, and history,
where our needs and interests were then greatest.
In 1958 we proposed that an exchange of fifteen
experienced language teachers begin the following
year. We renewed this early in 1959. The second
agreement included a clause that the United States
would invite Soviet teachers of Russian "to occupy
positions in American universities for teaching the
Russian language," with "arrangements on positions,
transportation, salaries, lodging, and academic
benefits as enjoyed by American colleagues," and
that the Ministry would invite American teachers of
English. However, the Ministry did not respond to
the Committee's specific proposals. The Committee
renewed them in April 1961 and even identified the
Soviet scholars our universities sought, but again
it received no response. In February 1964 the
Committee proposed an exchange of teaching
assistants in Russian and English, but the Ministry
refused to discuss the suggestion. The following
year it proposed an exchange of five language
teachers and of two teachers of literature and
linguistics, each for either a semester or an
academic year. Again, the Ministry did not reply.

The eighth exchanges agreement, signed in
Moscow in April 1972, finally included exchanges of
professors to give semester or full-year courses in
the natural sciences, technical sciences, humanities
and social sciences, and language, literature, and
linguistics, "in accordance with the desires of
the receiving side." The first opportunity for
scholars to teach in the other country came in the
spring semester in 1974 when seven Americans taught
American history, American literature, linguistics,
chemistry, and chemical engineering in Moscow,
Leningrad, and Novosibirsk, while four Soviet
scholars taught statistics, mathematics, Russian,
and psychology in four American universities--North
Carolina, Tulane, Ohio State, and MIT. In the
spring semester of 1975, nine Americans taught as
Fulbright-Hays lecturers in Soviet institutions--
five in Moscow State, two at Tbilisi State, one at
Voronezh State University, and one at the Institute
of Construction and Engineering. Seven were

scientists, one a historian, and one a professor
of literature. Seven Soviet scholars, three
scientists, a historian, a specialist in history,
two in language and literature, and a professor
of journalism, taught in seven American institu-
tions--San Francisco State University, Pennsylvania
State University, the University of Chicago, the
University of Virginia, the University of Pennsylvania, the University of Montana, and the
University of Tennessee. In all cases but one,
the American scholars were accompanied by their
families. The Soviet scholars were all unac-
companied.

The exchanges agreements that other Western
states have with the Soviet Union are similar to
those which the Department of State has signed,
and the achievements and difficulties are also
remarkably similar. However, the Soviet government's policies toward other states concerning
the exchange of classroom instructors demonstrate
the particular sensitivities it has with regard
to the United States. For example, the Ministry
accepted two language teachers from the United
Kingdom as early as 1961, and since 1967 it has
exchanged from four to six instructors and teaching assistants each year. Austria since 1961
has exchanged four professors each year, ordinarily teachers of Russian and of German, and
the German Federal Republic and the Soviet Union
since 1970 have exchanged four teaching assistants
and two professors for a semester each year. Italy
and the Soviet Union in 1968 began the exchange
of three language teachers. The exchange of classroom teachers between France and the Soviet Union
since 1964 reveals the special position France
occupies in Soviet foreign policy, and perhaps also
the important role that Communists play in the
French educational system. In that year, French
instructors of French began teaching in ten
different Soviet cities--Moscow, Leningrad,
Tashkent, Minsk, Kiev, Kharkov, Erevan, Tbilisi,
Khabarovsk, and Irkutsk. The number of French
teachers in Soviet institutions rose to fifteen
in 1966, twenty-seven in 1969, and forty-five in
1972. Of the approximately three hundred men and
women from the West who have taught in the Soviet

Union since 1958, somewhat more than half have been French.

Of course, sending undergraduates to the other country for a year of study raises most delicate issues for both American and Soviet administrators and scholars. However, the December 1959 agreement provided for a summer exchange of undergraduate students of English and Russian, as the Committee had proposed that February. In 1961 the Committee suggested an exchange of 150 undergraduates, with groups of 15 to tour the host country for five weeks accompanied by scholars and a native tour guide. The Soviet government in 1959 briefly demonstrated interest in an undergraduate program, suggesting the University of Michigan for its undergraduates, but this quickly evaporated. Therefore, perhaps fortunately for us, the Committee began, and others have since continued, immensely successful one-way programs for undergraduate study in the Soviet Union that have helped lead to exchanges of undergraduates outside the official program in 1974.

The Soviet government approves of the various programs for sending undergraduates there, presumably because it obtains dollars from the participants (tuition in 1974 was $3,000 for a semester), considers increased knowledge of Russian by young Americans a political advantage, believes that the Americans return from the Soviet Union with favorable impressions, and assumes that they have minimal contact and therefore little influence on Soviet students and faculty members. On the other hand, the Ministry of Higher Education until 1974 showed no interest in sending undergraduates to the United States, where they would be welcome additions to foreign student groups on our campuses. It has also resolutely discouraged the efforts of the Experiment in International Living, which has programs in other countries in which youngsters live with families, especially in the summer months.

The Committee's summer language program for undergraduates reflected the determination of its founders in the 1950s and 1960s to strengthen the field of Russian studies as well as the expansion

of foreign language study. The Soviet Union was
seen as a "living language laboratory" that would
test traditional methods of teaching Russian. The
Committee also considered it an opportunity to
attract bright science students into Russian
language study. In fact, nine of the first twenty
students were science majors. The Committee
therefore organized a Russian language summer
study tour in 1959. The Carnegie Corporation
provided the funds (approximately $180,000) for
the first three years, and a portion of the dollars
necessary for the succeeding three years. The
Office of Education in the Department of Health,
Education, and Welfare has provided support for
this project and its successor since 1962.

In the first year, 1959, twenty-two undergraduates who had studied Russian at least two
years spent eight weeks of intensive language study
at Indiana University or at Middlebury College.
Then, accompanied by three senior language teachers,
they flew to London, journeyed to and from
Leningrad on Soviet ships, traveled in European
Russia, and spent two weeks in a summer camp, all
under a pledge to speak only Russian. The results
were immensely positive, particularly in increasing
motivation and in improving speaking skills, and
the program grew steadily.

In 1960 the 40 student participants came from
ten different colleges. In 1961 the number rose
to 105, of whom 42 were high school language
teachers. The numbers leaped so impressively and
so many colleges and universities were completing
their own arrangements that the Committee discon-
tinued its program after 1963. In 1964 Indiana
University alone sent 120 students. In 1965
approximately 500 participated, almost all in tours
organized by institutions located in the midwestern
or western parts of the United States.

As more and more colleges and universities
began to establish summer study tours (in 1972
eighteen originated on American campuses), the
Council on International Education Exchange (the
Council on Student Travel from 1947 until November
1967) became the central organization for making

summer study arrangements for many colleges and
small universities. The Council had become
involved in exchanges with the Soviet Union in
1959, when it sponsored exchange tours of student
leaders. Since 1966 it has administered growing
annual summer study tour programs for several
hundred undergraduates, as well as two other
especially exciting undergraduate ventures. In
one, between 150 and 200 undergraduates spend the
summer in intensive Russian-language study at
Leningrad State University. In the other, which
began in the spring semester of 1970, approximately
30 undergraduates, from fourteen colleges and
universities in the first year, spend a semester
at Leningrad State University. The participants
and their universities have been so satisfied that
the program has continued to grow. Many of its
alumni are now highly motivated and immensely
promising graduate students in our major universities. In fact, the program is so successful
that the principal concern in 1976 is that
Leningrad State University will establish a center
for language study for foreign students and
isolate them in a kind of ghetto.

The scholars involved in the Committee's
academic exchange were so convinced that undergraduate study in the Soviet Union under appropriate
conditions was valuable that in 1968 its Committee
on the Future proposed sending fifty undergraduates
to the Soviet Union and fifty to Eastern Europe
each year, on an exchange basis if necessary. IREX
has not carried out this proposal, in part because
it has concentrated its energies on joint research
projects and on Eastern Europe and in part because
some universities have established undergraduate
programs that supplement the work of the Council
on International Educational Exchanges. Thus, the
University of California in Berkeley in 1972
established a summer quarter program at Leningrad
State University, granting its student participants
nine credits for work in history, philosophy,
literature, and art, all for a total fee of $1,450,
including round-trip fare from London to Leningrad.

On April 18, 1974, the State University of New
York and the Ministry of Higher Education agreed

to an exchange of ten upper-division undergraduates
between the State University and the Moscow State
Pedagogical Institute of Foreign Languages--M.
Thorez to study advanced Russian, as well as
Russian and Soviet literature, and English and
American studies, respectively. The Americans in
the fall semester of 1974-75 lived in a Moscow
hotel and attended classes established solely for
them. They found the instruction excellent, met
many Soviet students, and enjoyed and benefited
from the five months. The ten Soviet participants
and the Ministry both considered their fall semester
in Albany successful, and the agreement provides
for exchanges in both semesters in 1975-76,
preferably with the Americans this time in Soviet
dormitories.

The Russian-language study tours and the
semesters in Leningrad and Moscow have been the
least troublesome programs to administer, almost
certainly because they are one-way study projects
outside the exchanges agreements and thus do not
involve reciprocity with the Ministry and attendant
problems. If the undergraduate exchange organized
by the State University of New York proves
successful, it will presumably produce increased
confidence among Soviet political and educational
leaders and may lead to most promising approaches.
In fact, it is paradoxical that the aspect of
academic exchanges both sides considered most
sensitive may help establish direct agreements
between universities and will lead toward the free
movement of people and ideas that we have always
sought.

The Soviet government is almost inevitably
more interested in opportunities for research here
in the natural and physical sciences than in the
humanities and social sciences because of its
eagerness to improve and expand its economy and
its military strengths by tapping our scientific
resources. Consequently, Soviet scientists were
among the first to go abroad after the death of
Stalin, and the vast majority of the Soviet
participants in our academic exchanges, and in
those with other countries, have been scientists.

However, our scientists were not eager in the
1950s to study in the Soviet Union or to learn more
about Soviet scientific strengths and achievements.
They believed the United States superior in most
sciences and concluded that they could learn little
from visits, research there, or combined research
operations with Soviet scholars. Few knew Russian
or were interested in learning it. Most assumed
that their knowledge of the Soviet sciences,
acquired through journals, abstracting and technical services, and publications concerning Soviet
equipment and methods, was as complete as Soviet
secretiveness would allow. Moreover, they had
been flattered by having scientists from throughout
the world come here for research, although they
had also learned that even brief visits distract.
In short, they generally lacked the motivation
that inspired our Russian specialists to create
the Committee. In consequence, formal exchange
programs between our organizations of scientists
and the Soviet Academy of Sciences and between the
Atomic Energy Commission and the Soviet State
Committee for the Utilization of Atomic Energy
began rather late.

The nature of atomic science, especially of
atomic weapons, has made exchanges of information
concerning even peaceful uses of atomic energy
between the two countries at once most important,
most sensitive, and most difficult to arrange. The
first exchanges agreement therefore did not include
the atomic field. The first Memorandum on
Cooperation in the Field of Utilization of Atomic
Energy for Peaceful Purposes was signed by the
Atomic Energy Commission and the Soviet counterpart
agency, the State Committee for the Utilization of
Atomic Energy, on November 24, 1959, and was
attached to the second exchanges agreement that
was signed three days earlier. This venture began
only in May 1960, almost two years after the
academic exchange program. It provided for short
tours or visits to high-energy physics installations
and for the exchange of specific numbers of
unclassified documents and doctoral dissertations
on the peaceful uses of atomic energy.

The Soviet government allowed this small

program to lapse in 1967 and 1968. The joint
research projects mentioned first in the 1959
memorandum did not begin until 1970, when American
and Soviet teams of scientists worked together for
several months, in 1970-71 at the High Energy
Physics Institute at Serpukhov and in 1972 at the
National Accelerator Laboratory at Batavia, Illinois.
These programs have had little significance,
although they no doubt persuaded some officials
and scientists of the advantages of increased
cooperation and of the importance of forging
additional peaceful bonds.

The exchange of senior scientists between
the National Academy of Sciences and the Soviet
Academy of Sciences also began relatively late,
although the Soviet government had proposed such
an exchange in the discussions that began in
October 1957. In April 1958, three years after
our specialists in Russian studies had become
interested in research opportunities in the Soviet
Union and three months after the first exchanges
agreement had been signed, President Detlev Bronk
of the National Academy of Sciences visited the
Soviet Union, in part at the request of the
Department of State. Bronk and his associates
were reluctant to sign an agreement because they
believed that scientists should be allowed to
travel freely and work in other countries without
the intervention of any organization. In addition,
while his knowledge of the organization of Soviet
science was limited, Bronk realized that the
Soviet Academy of Sciences has authority over
institutes carrying on virtually all Soviet basic
research. The National Academy, on the other
hand, is an honorific and advisory organization
and has no institutes, laboratories, or scholars
engaged in research, which in this country is
carried on in universities, private research
organizations, government laboratories, and
industrial installations. In short, this exchange
"matched a relatively small nongovernmental body
with what is in effect the holding company for
much of the Soviet Union's gigantic scientific
establishment."

Bronk soon learned, too, that the interests

of the two academies differed. The main purpose
of the Soviet Academy was to strengthen those
research areas in which the Soviet Union was
weakest. Through its central administration of
basic research it therefore identified the
critical fields in which visits were to be made,
and then simply assigned selected scholars to
a "mission" abroad to improve Soviet capabilities.
On the other hand, the major interest of our
National Academy, as of the Committee and of IREX,
was to assist any interested and competent American
scholar to go to the Soviet Union. In any case,
Bronk agreed to consider the draft agreement for
an exchange that Academician Alexander N.
Nesmeyanov, president of the Soviet Academy of
Sciences, gave him. Fifteen months later, on
July 9, 1959, the two Academies signed an agreement
which provided that twenty prominent scientists
from each country (half of the participants were
to be members of the Academies) might visit the
other country in 1959 and 1960 to observe, lecture,
and participate in seminars. In addition,
eighteen scientists in fourteen specific fields
might visit the other country each year for one-
month surveys. Finally, specialists in six
specific fields from each country could spend a
total of thirty-two months in research in the
other country over a two-year period.

    In November 1959, when the two governments
renewed the original exchanges agreement, the
two Academies simply agreed that their first accord
would be fulfilled over the next two years. In
their second agreement, on March 8, 1962, both
sides consented to furnish annual lists of
subjects for research and to exchange about
twenty-five scientists for from 3 to 10 months
each for a total of 150 months over the two-year
period. In addition, each side could send twenty
senior lecturers for a total of 20 months and ten
scholars for surveys for a total of 10 months. The
1964 agreement reiterated the terms of 1962. On this
occasion, on American insistence, the agreement
did not specify the fields in which exchanges were
to take place. From this time, even after the
summit agreements were signed by Nixon and Brezhnev
in 1972 and 1973, the pattern and even the size

of this small exchange of scientists remained the
same.

   Medicine, a nonpolitical and neutral field
of study in which the two countries have different
problems and resources but in which they share
common concerns and potential long-term benefits
from cooperation, constitutes probably the most
promising area for exchanges. The participation
of Soviet medical doctors in international medical
conferences, informal exchanges between medical
scientists, and the contribution of the Sabin-
applied seed virus toward controlling polio in the
Soviet Union helped to create the atmosphere in
which the first agreement was negotiated. The
United States Public Health Service was especially
eager that the Soviet Union increase its participation in international medical organizations
and work on public health problems, while Soviet
officials and medical scientists no doubt sought
also to demonstrate the progress Soviet medicine
had made and to learn from the United States.
Even before negotiation of the first agreement
began, the Public Health Service had proposed to
the Department of State a number of fields in
which it was eager to exchange information, and
the Department in October 1957 received similar
proposals from the Soviet government.

   Exchanges in the field of public health
service have therefore occupied an important role
in all the exchanges agreements. The first one,
for example, provided for the exchange of delegations of five or six medical scientists for two to
six weeks in eight specific fields, as well as of
groups of three or four for two or three weeks to
lecture in three cities of the host country.
Between 1958 and 1972 seventy delegations made
"grand tours," with a total of about 135 American
doctors and 100 Soviet doctors involved, at a
cost to this country of about $150,000 per year.
Eight joint seminars were held in that period in
the United States, and six in the Soviet Union.
Fifty-six American scientists carried on research
in the Soviet Union, and sixty-four Soviet scholars
studied here. In addition, a substantial exchange
of periodicals and books was established.

Following an American initiative in November 1970, the two governments in 1971 agreed to establish a joint Soviet-American Exchange Policy Board, headed by the designates of the Soviet Minister of Health and our Secretary of Health, Education, and Welfare, to meet annually to plan cooperation and joint research projects in the areas of viral oncology, atherosclerosis, and environmental health. In February 1972 the governments signed an agreement to pool their efforts in research on cancer, heart disease, and environmental health problems under a Joint Soviet-American Committee for Health Cooperation, which began work the next month. Subcommittees then identified areas of research, created joint research teams for common efforts, and added arthritis and the delivery of health services to the joint research subjects.

At the Moscow summit meeting in May 1972, Brezhnev and Nixon signed a five-year Agreement for Cooperation in the Field of Medical Science and Public Health. In the following two years Soviet and American medical scientists have signed work plans and protocols, created a bilingual glossary of terminology, aligned procedures and criteria, and begun the exchange of research materials. In February 1973 Soviet and American cardiologists agreed to exchange data on sudden heart attacks and to establish joint research projects on preventive medicine and emergency care. In September of that year, the Ministry of Health and the Public Health Service established telex communications so that a "health hot line" now improves communications. Consequently, in 1975 scarcely a week passes in which a Soviet doctor does not visit the National Institute of Health. At the same time, an increasing number of American doctors visit Soviet medical institutions.

Thus, the period since 1958 has produced a variety of exchange programs, largely but not entirely within the formal exchange agreements. Fruitful yet fragile, generally undramatic but nevertheless important threads now link the two societies. They reflect the initiative, good will, intellectual vitality, and eagerness of various

groups within the United States, and of our
government, to create friendly relationships
with the Soviet people and Soviet organizations
as well as the Soviet government's decision to
establish and nurture intellectual and other
relationships with its most feared rival. On
the educational side alone, the exchanges have
expanded to include programs for undergraduates
and for classroom teachers that were almost
unthinkable in 1958, and they have helped create
the atmosphere in which the joint research
agreements, all potential and little performance
as yet, have been concluded since 1971. These
various exchanges, however, do not include any
substantial flow of publications or even expanded
exchanges of books and journals, end Soviet
jamming of Western broadcasts, or ease substantially
other Soviet controls over cultural relations.

CHAPTER FOUR

The Universities, Their Scholars, and the Inter-University Committee

Before World War II American academic interest
in other countries, especially outside Western
Europe and the Middle East, was limited to a handful
of scholars in a few universities. Few scholars,
and almost no students, traveled abroad for research
or study. The professor who went to Western Europe
for casual travel on his sabbatical or who spent
a summer in the libraries of London, Rome, or Athens
traveled on his own initiative and almost always on
his own funds. Scholars were able with relative
ease to remain informed concerning new discoveries
and techniques in their fields of interest because
the enormous expansion of research and publication
of the last three decades had not yet occurred.
Few universities had formal relationships with
institutions abroad, and international conferences
were rare. Our government had no program to assist
Americans to study abroad or to help foreign
scholars and students to come here. Indeed, except
for France, which has long considered the export
of foreign culture an important element of state
policy, no government before the 1930s devoted
substantial effort to improving or expanding
cultural relations.

After World War II our study of other societies
increased enormously. Scholars and students began
to travel abroad for research, on their own
initiative but aided by their institutions and by

private foundations. Thousands of foreign scholars
came to the United States. In short, our campuses
began to extend throughout almost the entire world,
and the spirit of research and instruction changed
beyond comprehension. Our universities, sometimes
aided by private foundations and often encouraged
and supported by the government, began instructional activities abroad, especially in friendly
parts of the world. Some of these activities, like
those of the Inter-University Committee, began as
independent university functions and then became
entangled in national cultural relations policy and
in international politics because of our government's
relations with other governments, in particular
states that communists rule.

Universities should engage in academic
exchange programs with countries communists rule
when our government has civilized and mutually
advantageous relations with those governments,
principally, as Whitehead said, because "the
proper subject of study of the university ought to
be the universe." At the moment, communists
control a part of the universe. Moreover, in
order best to understand another part of the world,
our scholar-teachers should study in that country
and with qualified scholars and other citizens of
that country. Thus, one should go to Central Asia
if he wishes to know and understand that area,
just as we would hope that a Hungarian interested
in American literature or architecture or agricultural development would come here for study.
Such opportunities not only enable the scholarly
specialist to increase his knowledge and understanding, but they also assist him and his
university to help other citizens better to understand the world.

The university should also become involved
because we live in a shrinking international
community in which no nation has a monopoly of
knowledge or the best means of finding it. Our
scholars have the obligation, as chemists,
physicists, historians, or teachers of language,
to share with scholars in other countries whatever
discoveries and techniques they have mastered, and
to learn as well from them. We do indeed live in

a small world. This, of course, was clearly understood in other eras, such as the Middle Ages, which
saw the universe as a whole and which was not so
afflicted as we by nationalism. When the foundations of the modern university were being laid, the
traveling scholar was even more common than he is
today. A citizen of Christendom and a responsible
member of a universal scholarly community, he knew
several languages well, was the product of several
universities, and was at home throughout the Western
world. Moreover, he recognized and acted upon the
conviction that all share the same interests and
have an obligation to work together. As St. Thomas,
the greatest of medieval scholars, put it, "We are
all the same distance from eternity." In short,
we should distinguish between the temporary political condition and the eternal human condition. We
should be firm toward communist governments in
advocating our principles, but gentle and cooperative with genuine scholars in countries that communists rule.

For all governments, exchange programs are
essentially political. The Soviet leaders are
interested primarily in improving the Soviet
economy and in advancing Soviet political ambitions at home and abroad. Our government seeks to
advance our national interests and also to maintain ties, reduce tensions, and increase mutual
understanding. On the other hand, our universities, scholars, and students are interested primarily in improving and expanding research and
instruction. Universities should therefore become
active in academic exchange programs to defend
themselves from external pressures, particularly
from government, and to prevent others from as-
suming their functions. They should also assume
responsibility simply because the immense political
importance of exchanges makes intellectual integrity
and high quality paramount.

Paradoxically, as Secretary of State Dean
Rusk noted, the program that had the greatest
impact within the Soviet Union in the 1960s was
that for academic exchanges, established and
administered by scholars whose goals were academic,
not political. Thus, the nature of the program,

which emphasizes academic quality and eschews politics, is directly responsible for its political impact. If the universities should abandon their primary goal and seek a political effect, or if they should allow the government or another outside agency to control their functions or to alter their goals, they would not only violate their own principles but also greatly reduce the program's political importance.

This university engagement produces numerous problems. The most important derives from the conflict raised or the tensions caused by the nature and function of the university. Ideally, the university is to some degree isolated from society, or at least able to maintain a calm spirit and atmosphere in which scholars can carry out serene and unhindered research and make independent judgments. Ideally, outside forces, particularly political forces, do not affect or influence this effort to increase knowledge and understanding. In short, the university should be an independent institution, in a society and of a society, but free. However, a university that participates in academic exchanges with countries which communists rule becomes to some degree a ping-pong ball of domestic political factions and of international politics. At the same time it is attacked from the right on the ground that it is aiding communists, it is attacked from the left, especially the student left and the neo-isolationists, for serving "American imperialism."

The creation of a league to serve as the instrument of all individuals and universities interested in academic exchanges with the Soviet Union was an elemental and important development, but not inevitable. It reflected the national and international perspective, the good sense, and the vision of the men to whom this volume is dedicated and others who promoted the study of Russia and Eastern Europe before and immediately after the Second World War. Others with less imagination and insight might have launched institutional rivalries that would have been destructive. The small group who founded the Committee had the foresight to recognize that union would assist individual scholars and also provide strength for all institutions that would participate.

Their sensible decisions were of course much influenced by the way in which Russian studies had grown. Moreover, most of these scholars had received their graduate training at Columbia or Harvard, and the group was highly concentrated on the East Coast. They had begun to cooperate in the late 1930s, had shared experiences in the Second World War, and in the 1950s had served together as members of advisory groups and selection teams for the Ford Foundation, the Foreign Area Fellowship Program, the ACLS, and the SSRC.

These men also appreciated that an association of private and state institutions could provide some security for those chosen to study in the Soviet Union, and for their universities, both from the Soviet security police and from American politicians convinced that some professors were communists or were sympathetic to the Soviet regime. All those interested in even brief trips to the Soviet Union in and after 1956 understood the Soviet totalitarian system, its emphasis upon police control, and its hostility toward foreigners. They believed that the regime would be particularly suspicious of specialists who knew Russian and who had had government or military experience. Almost all those interested in travel to the Soviet Union when the Committee was founded, young and old, had served in the government during either or both World War II and the Korean War. Most senior scholars had naturally been engaged in work that involved Soviet affairs. Most of the young had served in the military forces, many of them in military intelligence.

The years in which the Committee was established were also those in which dislike and fear of communism and of the Soviet Union were especially powerful because of the Soviet Union's repressive domestic system, its control over the peoples of Eastern Europe, its apparent sponsorship of the invasion of South Korea, and the threat it offered in many areas of the world to hopes for some sort of stable peace. Some scholars, many of them

distinguished emigrés, opposed travel to the
Soviet Union and Eastern Europe because this
seemed to imply both acceptance and approval of
Soviet authority in Eastern Europe and would
weaken the spirit of resistance in Eastern Europe
and the Western world as well.

Scholars and administrators recognized also
that formation of a league of universities would
enable them to deal effectively with the Department
of State, which might seek to influence the
behavior of institutions engaged in an exchange
program with the Soviet Union. They also realized
that programs involving Soviet universities would
almost inevitably involve relationships with the
Soviet government. Moreover, although the founders
hoped that the Committee would be temporary and
that its activities, when routine, could be assumed
by individual institutions, they also appreciated
that an organization with experience in dealing
with communist regimes might be helpful one day
in arranging exchanges with the People's Republic
of China. In fact, they chose a colorless name,
the Inter-University Committee on Travel Grants,
omitting a reference to Slavic, Russian, or East
European, in part to forestall sensational newspaper stories that would attract those wildly
opposed to any relationships with the Soviet Union
and in part to eliminate any obstacles a title
might create for the Chinese communists or the
Cubans.

Finally, financial costs were important
factors. The Committee was established originally
to send scholars to the Soviet Union as tourists.
The costs were so great (Intourist then charged
$30.00 a day in advance for the thirty days
allowed, and travel to and within the Soviet Union
was also expensive) that few scholars, especially
young ones, could consider financing such a venture.
The scholars also came from rival universities
that were competing for faculty, graduate students,
and financial support, and all were therefore
eager to avoid competition in obtaining travel
funds from private foundations.

After two years, when the program involved

exchanges of Soviet and American scholars, the
financial aspect became even more central. It is
difficult to define the true costs of education,
especially of programs involving scholars from
countries with different educational systems,
because they carry hidden costs, in the time and
energy of scholars, administrators, and foreign
student offices. Administration of a program with
a suspicious rival state is particularly expensive.
However, the Committee estimated in 1958 that
sending a junior scholar to the Soviet Union for
an academic year would cost approximately $10,500,
the equivalent then of four graduate student
fellowships. Moreover, the estimate quickly proved
to be low because the Committee underestimated the
costs of maintaining the participants' families.
No universities then or now could sustain such a
program.

The universities' financial contributions to
academic exchanges have been much greater than
even the most prudent administrators anticipated
in 1958 or appreciate now. Each university waives
tuition and fees for any scholar it accepts. Approximately eighty percent of the Soviet scholars
have been scientists who require expensive laboratory space and equipment. Consequently, throughout the period from 1958 through 1969 our universities contributed about one-third of the total
cost of the programs. This share has probably not
changed substantially under IREX.

In addition, the universities serve scholars
who come to the United States on programs administered by the ACLS, the National Academy of Sciences, the Ford Foundation, and other organizations.
They serve as hosts for all kinds of visiting cultural groups. This substantial contribution is
often not appreciated, especially by organizations
that assist foreign scholars to come to the United
States and then, often with little warning, ask
our educational institutions to provide space, facilities, and instruction.

The institutions interested also realized
that the foundations would reject a flood of
applications from individual universities but

might consider favorably an application from a
league of institutions that promised important
subsidiary benefits from cooperation. In short,
the universities therefore felt profound forces
pressing them toward creating a league that would
enable them to defend their interests and meet
new responsibilities.

Alternatives, of course, existed. One was
that each major institution establish a program
of its own, as the Soviet government originally
proposed. Another was administration by the
Department of State, perhaps through an expanded
and revised Board of Foreign Scholarships.
Professional organizations, such as the American
Historical Association, might have established
their own programs. Academic exchanges might also
have been administered by a "friendship society,"
an organization of communists or of those sympathetic to the Soviet Union, that would have
placed a political stamp on them, wrecking them
almost irretrievably. Finally, they might have
been coordinated by a weak new organization that
then accepted funds and functions from the CIA,
as other needy groups did in the 1950s and early
1960s. This would have poisoned academic exchanges
for a very long time indeed.

The principles on which the Committee was
established were simple. It was, first of all, a
national league of universities, not a grouping
of specialists in Soviet affairs. The universities
agreed to share responsibilities, opportunities,
hazards, and costs, and to choose one institution
to serve as administrator, representative, and
spokesman. Thus, Columbia University volunteered
as the administrative agent in 1956. Dean
Schuyler Wallace of the School of International
Affairs was chairman, and David Munford served as
his deputy. The university as a whole then
provided outstanding leadership during the
formative years. In the fall of 1959, when
Wallace and Munford were totally exhausted by
their splendid efforts, the participating
universities chose Indiana University to administer the program from 1960 until 1965. In
January 1964 the universities invited Indiana

to serve another term "from three to five years."

Administration of the Committee's program was centralized in a small office on a university campus. Day-to-day operations were in the hands of the chairman and the deputy chairman, advised by a committee of local administrators and scholars.[1] They managed the program, sent participating institutions all available information, and administered the selection of our participants and the placement on our campuses of Soviet and East European scholars.

The general administrative principles devised between 1956 and 1960 have remained in force for both the Committee and IREX, with minor changes and improvements as circumstances changed and experience produced new ideas. The principal administrator was deliberately called chairman, not director, and the organization operated entirely on the committee system. All member institutions participated in reaching policy decisions at the annual meetings, held in a New York or Chicago hotel the first years and then on a different campus each year. Each institution ordinarily sent one senior administrator, usually the dean of the graduate school, and one faculty specialist on the Soviet Union or Eastern Europe; the meetings were therefore expensive for the universities in administrative time and travel costs. At the same time, this approach produced a significant subsidiary benefit: it helped to bring together senior administrators and area specialists, educating both. The administrator increased his understanding of the need for study of foreign areas and of the special difficulties those studies face, and the specialist understood better

---

[1]The deputy chairmen were central figures. The Committee was extremely fortunate in the intelligence, skill, and dedication of these men and women: David Munford, 1956-60; Stephen Viederman, 1960-65; Howard Mehlinger, 1965-66; E. Willis Brooks, 1966-68; and Miss Patricia Lambrecht (now Mrs. Richard Gordon), 1968-69. Since 1969 Allen Kassof has been the Executive Director of IREX, with Daniel Matuszewski his deputy for the Soviet Union and John Matthews for Eastern Europe.

the complexities of university affairs and the need
to put his interests in the perspective of larger
university concerns.

At the annual meetings the chairman provided
complete and candid information on all issues,
particularly difficulties, which the representatives then discussed fully and frankly. The
university representatives also elected a policy
committee of scholars and administrators; this
group chose the selection committees and ordinarily
met once or twice a year to review issues as they
arose.

Influenced by the qualities and positions
of those who had founded Russian and East European
studies and by their knowledge of the conflicts
that wracked Chinese studies in the 1950s, those
who established and helped administer the Committee
emphasized its national character and ensured
that all interested universities shared in its
work. Its meetings and the work of its committees
helped to spread knowledge of the strengths and
weaknesses of university programs throughout the
United States. University parochialisms began to
collapse, while friendly and knowledgeable
relationships grew. Eastern scholars began to
appreciate that institutions beyond the Alleghenies
have respectable resources, while scholars from
other parts of the country came to understand the
dedication and time required to create the great
Eastern institutions. This spirit of cooperation
naturally expanded beyond academic exchange
programs. In fact, the Committee was only one
of a series of national cooperative endeavors that
have helped to bring our universities closer to
each other.

From the beginning of the exchange program
any university interested in sending scholars to
the Soviet Union or accepting Soviet scholars
on its campus could participate. The number of
university members rose gradually from the original
seven in 1956 to twenty-two in 1960, forty in
1964, fifty-six in 1969, and ninety-one in 1975.
By 1960 every part of the country was represented.
In 1960-61 the Committee received junior scholar

applications from only twelve institutions. In 1968-69 it received applications from forty-one institutions and chose participants from twenty-one. Between 1958 and 1967 the Committee placed Soviet and East European scholars in sixty-two American universities, not all of which were formal members of the Committee; the number rose to eighty-seven by 1975. In each of the last five years of the Committee's operations and throughout IREX's administration, junior participants every year came from twenty to twenty-six institutions in various parts of the United States, demonstrating that specialists on the Soviet Union and Eastern Europe are now scattered throughout the country and that interest is now truly national.

The history of academic exchanges is one of impressive achievement by a group of universities and scholars inexperienced in dealing with powerful, centralized states. However, these years of achievement have been marked by one important failure, the inability of the universities and the other organizations to create even a loose federal system to define and advance their interests. This has wasted time and energy and has created unnecessary squabbles. It has enabled the Soviet government to take advantage of the disunity and the disagreements on our side to "justify" denying us research opportunities to which we are entitled. It has also delayed a careful, rational appraisal of American long-term interests in academic exchanges.

At the outset no one in the government, in the universities, or in other organizations interested in academic exchanges considered establishment of an independent public corporation or national organization to direct or coordinate the various programs. The organizations involved all acted independently of each other and often in almost complete ignorance of each other's interests. The absence of a national organization, or even of a proposal for one until 1964, reflects our stupor in the 1950s concerning relations with the Soviet Union and the fear that Soviet policy would soon switch again. It also demonstrates the

disorganization of higher education, the isolation
of humanists and social scientists from the
natural and physical sciences, and the relative
backwardness of those interested in education
and in international politics in establishing
organizations to serve their needs.

The founders of the Committee from the
beginning planned to surrender its functions as
soon as they became "sufficiently routine."
However, Wallace and Munford soon realized from
the complications which arose in negotiations
with the Soviets that an organization something
like the Committee would remain necessary for some
time. In addition, the ACLS and the National
Academy of Sciences exchanges, the direct exchanges
authorized in 1959 between two sets of Soviet and
American universities, and the Ford Foundation
programs for some of the East European countries
demonstrated the need for a common strategy, a
confederation of some sort, or a new master
organization. The requirement became especially
serious when Wallace and Munford realized that
Committee scholars were being restricted to Soviet
universities, generally in Moscow and Leningrad,
and denied access to the institutes of the Soviet
Academy of Sciences, which the Ministry argued were
"beyond our competence." Finally, the Committee's
experiences were strongly supplemented by its
knowledge of the British Council's system and its
admiration for the way the Council coordinated
all British academic exchanges and indeed all
British cultural activities abroad.

The Department of State also encouraged
coordination or even consolidation. Its officers
naturally appreciated that establishment of one
organization for all academic exchanges would
simplify the Department's work, but they also
recognized that such an organization would be able
to mobilize heavy support from the academic
community if the Department and scholars should
disagree. Above all, they saw that the Soviet
government was taking advantage of American
disunity. The Soviet Academy and the Ministry of
Higher Education were no doubt jealous of each
other and competed for opportunities to send their

scholars abroad, a great privilege then as now.
However, the Soviet government used its centralized
system for establishing broad policies and for
coordinating the activities of its institutions to
flood the exchange programs with scientists, to
reject a substantial number of scholars whom the
Committee nominated, and to deny Committee nominees
access to the research institutes of the Soviet
Academy. The Department therefore urged our various
organizations at least to negotiate with the Soviet
government as a unit. However, the 1961 conference
it called at Yale for this purpose was unsuccessful.

The Ford Foundation also urged that the
various organizations combine their efforts, not
only to enable us to negotiate more effectively,
but also to assure the most rational use of Ford
funds; the Foundation was a major contributor to
the Committee and to the ACLS, helped support the
National Academy, made substantial grants directly
to some of the universities, and supported other
organizations interested in study abroad, such as
the Foreign Area Fellowship Program. That initiative was also unsuccessful.

Between 1959 and 1965 the Committee made five
proposals to the other organizations engaged in
exchanges. These ranged from a common application
form, through coordination of plans and policies,
to establishment of a public corporation to direct
all the academic exchanges. The last would have
provided an administrative center and a protective
umbrella for all exchanges of scholars with
countries that communists ruled. It would have
significantly reduced administrative costs,
simplified fund raising, represented all academic
interests in discussions with the Department of
State and with all Soviet institutions and agencies,
and provided a national forum for discussion of
issues. It would have helped to neutralize or
sanitize government grants by creating a buffer
zone between any government organization that
provided support and the scholars. It would also
have helped to separate political from scholarly
issues.

The ACLS and the National Academy rejected

these proposals, pointing out that the arrangements in effect, though cumbersome, worked, while
the proposed one might not. Moreover, they noted
that creating a new organization might confuse the
Soviets with whom we dealt and damage all
programs. They agreed only to establish inter-
locking or overlapping advisory committees.

The Committee's willingness to dissolve may
have reflected its newness and its founders' hope
that it would be only temporary. The ACLS, on
the other hand, was a half-century old. It has no
direct relationship with universities but is a
federation of organizations of scholars in the
humanities. It properly felt that humanists
require special attention. It feared that some
large organization which scientists might dominate
would neglect research in the humanities.
Finally, providing direction and support for
research on the Soviet Union and Eastern Europe
had been an integral part of its total program for
more than two decades, and it naturally was
reluctant to surrender such an important segment
of its activities.

The National Academy of Sciences seeks to
advance research in the sciences by senior
scientists. Its members found it difficult to
understand the plight of humanists and social
scientists, because they had much greater funds
for research and because Soviet scientists are so
eager to cooperate with them. It did not wish to
entrust the goals of a prestigious institution
that had approximately a thousand members and its
relationship with the Soviet Academy of Sciences
to a large organization in which these concerns
might be neglected or used to others' advantage.
It even rejected a "single unifying agency for
negotiations" with Soviet authorities, which would
probably have strengthened the position of the
humanists in obtaining access to archives and areas
denied them. Moreover, it approved the proliferation of administrative organizations because it
saw great virtues in any arrangement that increased
the number of Americans in contact with Soviet
administrators and scientists.

By agreement from the beginning, the responsibility for administering the Committee's
programs was to rotate among universities. The
discovery that jealousies were growing among some
of the universities as exchanges prospered
suggested that transferring administrative
responsibility away from a campus would restore
harmony. At the same time, Indiana University and
those of its faculty engaged in the Committee's
work were tired by the administrative chores,
which had earlier exhausted Columbia faculty and
administrators. Moreover, these men proposed
several promising new programs, especially multinational research projects on problems of common
concern that would almost certainly require new
staff and fresh energies. Second, the Committee's
long-term grant from the Ford Foundation was due
to expire in 1970. Redefining programs and
negotiating an extended grant, perhaps even an
endowment, from the Foundation clearly would
require a great amount of time. Moreover, the
Committee would have to coordinate discussions with
the Foundation and with the Department of State,
particularly because the Foundation's willingness
to commit itself to a large long-term award rested
on assurance that the Department would continue its
substantial support. In short, by 1967, as by
1960, the very progress of the Committee suggested
the need for a careful review, for identifying new
leaders, and for outlining new administrative
arrangements.

Fortunately, at that time President Burkhardt
of the ACLS concluded that obtaining funds for and
administering its small program were too demanding
for his staff, and that this generally successful
operation should be transferred. Finally, the
officers of the Ford Foundation, who had always
regretted the proliferation of exchange organizations, decided in 1967 to review its efforts in
international studies and in international affairs
in order to eliminate or reduce these activities and
transfer some resources released to other interests.

The universities at their annual meeting in
March 1967 therefore established a Committee on the
Future, chaired by Ivo Lederer of Stanford

University. This group, which through its subcommittees involved more than a hundred scholars,
carried out a thorough review of the previous
twelve years and, above all, collected ideas
concerning new programs and organizational
arrangements. It informed the universities, the
Foundation, and the ACLS of its views as they took
shape. The national advisory committee then
unanimously supported its proposals when it met in
San Francisco in March 1968, and the member
universities acted with the same unanimity at
Seattle on April 20.

In brief, the Committee on the Future proposed
establishment of IREX under the aegis of the ACLS
and the SSRC. In July 1968 IREX accepted responsibility for the exchange programs of the ACLS and
the bulk of those of the Ford Foundation and a
year later those of the Committee. The creation
of IREX as the single American organization for the
exchange of humanists and social scientists with
the Soviet Union and Eastern Europe increases
efficiency and strengthens American leverage in
negotiating with organizations in other states.

IREX has continued the principles and
procedures that the Committee's founders established, although its relations with the member
universities are much less close and its reporting
less detailed and candid. However, moving the
administrative headquarters from a campus to an
office in midtown Manhattan has reduced university
control and has made IREX in some ways just another
one of the many national educational organizations
with headquarters in New York or Washington. Allen
Kassof, whose title is executive director (not
chairman) of IREX, is no longer a full-time member
of a university faculty, and the staff is almost
inevitably more remote from the interests of
individual scholars and more bureaucratic than the
much smaller Committee group. IREX retains
university participation and support, but the
universities no longer have the authority they
once enjoyed. Indeed, the paper that defined the
power and procedures of IREX noted that its
director would consult as necessary with representatives of participating universities, which

reflects an important shift of authority. The
annual meetings are now reporting sessions, not
discussions of policies, and they are not held
independently but in conjunction with the annual
meetings of the American Association for the
Advancement of Slavic Studies. IREX held no
meeting in 1974 because the AAASS met in Banff.
Some universities no longer send representatives,
in part because they are not so directly involved
as earlier, in part because their interest has
declined, and in part because of the expense. As
their importance has withered, that of other
organizations, such as the American Historical
Association and the Council on Foreign Relations,
has risen.

In recent years the national character of
IREX has declined somewhat, and Eastern campuses
have begun to dominate it and its important
committees. Thus, in 1974 sixteen of the twenty-
four members of the five selection committees
came from the East, defined here as that part of
the country under Eastern Standard Time. All the
original American members of the Joint Commission
on Collaboration in the Social Sciences and
Humanities established in 1974 were from the East:
two faculty members from Harvard and one from
Columbia, the president emeritus of the ACLS in
New York, the executive director of IREX in New
York, and the executive secretary of the American
Historical Association in Washington, D.C. In
the spring of 1975 four other members were added,
three from New York and one from Philadelphia.

Perhaps the Inter-University Committee's
most impressive achievement was the skill and
efficiency with which it placed Soviet scholars
in our institutions. At the very beginning the
universities quickly agreed that each institution
would give careful consideration to any nominee
whose papers the Committee forwarded and that they
retained authority to admit or reject any Soviet
scholar who might wish to study on its campus.
They agreed that the Committee should place the
Soviet scholar at the institution most qualified
to assist him and that he should be treated as any
other scholar. They recognized that nomination

of an American scholar to study in the Soviet Union
did not involve his university's accepting a Soviet
scholar, just as a university's accepting a scholar
did not affect the application of one of its own
faculty or graduate students. They also waived
tuition and fees as well as the physical examinations and English-language competence examinations
that many institutions required for foreign
students.

     Some administrators in 1958 and 1959 were
concerned that the presence of communist scholars
on their campuses would cause criticism from
parents, alumni, and other concerned citizens.
This fear proved to have no foundation. Similarly,
the belief that these scholars would cause great
excitement was also mistaken; the participants
from the Soviet Union and Eastern Europe had
surprisingly little impact, perhaps because so
many were laboratory scientists and studied on
large campuses accustomed to the presence of
hundreds of foreign students, perhaps because they
were so much older than most American students,
even graduate students.

     The principles and procedures adopted in
1958 have survived almost unchanged. Until 1963
the Committee forwarded the papers of every
scholar that the Ministry of Higher Education
nominated to each member institution, as well as
to any other institution mentioned in the
application. After 1963 Committee and IREX
administrators sent the papers only to those
universities mentioned and to any other institutions that the staff thought might provide
outstanding service to the Soviet scholar. When
more than one university indicated that it could
provide effective service, the administrators,
with the advice of scholars in the field concerned
and of the universities involved, chose that
university most qualified and interested to assist.

     This system served the universities and the
foreign scholars remarkably well. Most mistakes
were the Ministry's responsibility because it
provided such inadequate data. Moreover, when
later information revealed that a more helpful

placement could be made, the universities involved
were generous and quick in transferring
participants. The Ministry and Soviet participants
sometimes questioned placements because they
thought that research of high quality was
concentrated in just a few institutions. In
addition, the Ministry in the first decade insisted
that no Soviet scholar be placed alone, even
though the second Soviet scholar might have been
better served at a different university. The
issues that arose were therefore minor and on
occasion amusing. For example, in 1969 the
Ministry protested at great length against the
assignment of a specialist in oil drilling to
Tulsa University, which proved the most competent
institution, rather than to Stanford or Harvard,
neither of which had specialists in that field but
both of which have deservedly high reputations in
the Soviet Union.

Selection of American nominees was a far more
sensitive and rigorous process, but the Committee
handled it just as effectively and fairly. The
principles and procedures it adopted in 1958 were
based on those that the Ford Foundation and its
Foreign Area Fellowship Program developed in the
1950s and that the Committee tested further on its
original travel grant program. First, the
decisions were made through a careful national
selection system, rather than by allocating a
certain number of awards to each major institution
and allowing its faculty to designate the fellowships. The Committee therefore announced the
opportunities to universities throughout the
country. Its policy committee each year appointed
a select committee of several men and women from
several disciplines in different universities and
in various parts of the country to choose the most
qualified candidates. No scholar served on the
selection committee more than three years.

This system provided a subsidiary benefit
because the selectors learned about principal
research trends throughout the country from reading
applications and interviewing applicants. Thus,
the selection process helped make the Committee
a kind of intellectual center for Russian and

East European studies. Most important, it created
a sense of participation in a genuinely cooperative
national enterprise.

The 1958 exchanges agreement provided that
participants on both sides should be candidates who
had not yet completed their doctorate. After the
first year, postdoctoral candidates up to thirty-
five years of age were included. This limit was
raised to forty in 1964, as the Ministry continued
to nominate candidates quite mature by our graduate
school standards. The universities decided that
all those nominated in the first year should be
specialists in Russian studies, because their
capabilities and interests would enable them to
profit most from the experience and because the
natural sciences were "not peculiar to the Soviet
Union." However, the Committee requested and
received from the Ford Foundation permission "to
select persons other than fully qualified specialists on Russia." Moreover, the Committee in the
second year sent three graduate students in sciences
as well as four foreign language teachers, so that
transforming the program from one for specialists
into one for education in general began very early.

Except for two experimental years--1959-60,
when the Committee nominated four graduate students
working for the M.A. degree rather than the Ph.D.,
and 1965-66, in which it nominated two first-year
graduate students--each candidate in this program
was expected to pass his general examinations for
the Ph.D. before leaving the United States. In
addition, he should have completed research on all
materials available in this country before going
to the Soviet Union to use sources available only
there. All candidates except those in science
were expected to have some knowledge of Soviet
society and culture. All were required to have
sufficient knowledge of Russian so that they could
live and work in the Soviet Union with no difficulty. Before 1967 the Committee required those
whose language ability was inadequate to attend a
special intensive summer language program in the
United States. The Ministry of Higher Education
then finally accepted its proposal that the host
country establish intensive language programs late

in the summer for all participants for the forth-
coming academic year.

The selection process emphasized professional
ability and promise, then maturity and stability.
At the minimum, the Committee expected those
selected to demonstrate the intellectual quality
required for a fellowship in a major university or
in an intensive national competition. It sought
to identify truly cultivated young men and women
of exceptional ability and promise whose careers
would significantly expand our knowledge and
understanding. In the early years especially, the
selection committees employed the most careful and
demanding selection process because they feared
that the Soviet government might reverse its
policies, end the exchange program, and deny us
a precious opportunity to increase the number who
had lived and worked there. Particularly since
1969, standards for both intellectual quality and
maturity have relaxed somewhat as our need for
specialists has been satisfied, our understanding
of the Soviet Union has increased, and Soviet life
to some degree has relaxed.

The procedures were like those of the ordinary
fellowship process. Every member of the selection
committee read each application, and the committee
as a whole then decided which candidates had
survived the first step. At least two members of
the committee, neither of whom knew the candidate
or had taught in his institution, then interviewed
each of these candidates, seeking answers to
questions that had arisen earlier and to measure
the applicant's ability, promise, and maturity.
The full selection committee then reached a
decision concerning those whom it would nominate
for study in the Soviet Union.

The concern of everyone engaged in the
Committee's work with maturity and stability led
the Committee on February 22, 1958, to adopt two
additional steps in the selection process. First,
it obtained the university's endorsement of any of
its faculty or graduate students under consideration. In fact, it made the award to the sponsoring
institution to ensure that it would assume full

responsibility for its scholars. Therefore, after
preliminary selection of the superior candidates,
the Committee forwarded the name of each applicant
to the president of his university, asking the
institution to accept full responsibility for
"the applicant's political and emotional stability."

     This step was based on practices established
by the Foreign Area Fellowship Program, which
Wallace also headed and which sent young Americans
to other parts of the world. Wallace believed
that "we must know whom we are sending in order
properly to weigh the risks we are taking." In
the letter sent to the university president, the
Committee indicated it wanted "to know from the
central administration of each university whether
there is anything in the student's file of a
psychiatric or behavioral disciplinary character
which would make you hesitate to send him into an
environment where stability and emotional maturity
are of great importance." On occasion a university
refused to sponsor a faculty member or graduate
student. Thus, one president wrote that the
"applicant has all the intellectual qualities to
rank him among the very best on our campus, but
is sufficiently lacking in emotional maturity and
common sense to force us to conclude that we
cannot sponsor him as our representative overseas."

     In April 1970, in part because of the uproar
in the late 1960s against university scrutiny of
the qualities and activities of its scholars and
students and in part because university approval no
longer seemed necessary, IREX dropped the requirement of university sponsorship. However, the proper
concern of the Committee's founders with this issue
was demonstrated in an important new program in
1973, when the Committee on Scholarly Communication
with the People's Republic of China established a
small exchange of senior scholars in delegations of
twelve for short periods of time. This organization
announced that selection would be based on
"scholarly merit, reputation in the field, maturity
and good judgment, and diplomacy." Moreover, it
did not accept applications; for each delegation,
it appointed a chairman and two advisers to
recommend a slate, from which the executive

committee made the selections. In short, the group responsible for exchanges of senior delegations with China is even more prudent concerning maturity and responsibility than the Inter-University Committee had been.[2]

The second additional step was the Committee's decision to send to the Department of State the names of those who had survived the first stage in the selection process, at the same time it forwarded the name of each applicant to his university for sponsorship. This enabled the Department to complete a "name check," a low-level review it used when considering applications for all of its cultural exchange programs and that federal agencies use for positions which do not involve access to confidential information and are not "sensitive." The other private organizations that administered academic exchange programs with the Soviet Union and Eastern Europe and that accepted federal funds, the ACLS and the National Academy of Sciences, later followed the same policy. This procedure survives in 1975, although the Department plans to end it. It came under heavy attack in the late 1960s, when many questioned all structures of authority and national policies, especially our policy in Southeast Asia.

From the beginning, both the universities and the Department of State realized that selecting Americans for study in the Soviet Union would be a delicate task. They agreed that the academic quality and promise of the participants were central, that scholars should make the decisions, and that these scholars should follow the same principles and procedures used when they granted fellowships for study within the United States. They also agreed that the Soviet Union is a special country, as the very existence of a government-negotiated exchange program demonstrated. They therefore concurred that those selected should be men and women of "political maturity and emotional stability," "steeped in the American tradition," and "good representatives of American higher

2Harrison Brown, "Scholarly Exchanges with the People's Republic of China," Science, LXXXIII(January 11, 1974), 52-54.

education." They agreed, too, that in the first years at least the Committee would not nominate anyone "born within the present limits of the U.S.S.R." or who had defected from the Soviet Union.

The Department naturally had a special interest in the quality of those selected in this first exchange program with the Soviet Union, one which it had negotiated, to which it contributed financial support, and for which Congress would hold it responsible. Department officers believed that the successes or failures of the program might have an important influence upon the total Soviet-American relationship. Moreover, the Department in 1947 had established an autonomous Board of Foreign Scholarships composed of eminent and responsible citizens appointed by the president, which had full authority to select American participants for study abroad under the Fulbright program and other educational programs for which government agencies provided funds. The Board reviewed applications similar to those used in all fellowship competitions and followed the same principles and procedures. It also had access to classified information, which was held secret for reasons of national security. It reviewed this material in the same scrupulous way as the rest of the application before reaching its decisions. In particular, the Board at its first meeting in 1947 had adopted the "name check" review.

The Department, the universities, and the great majority of interested scholars accepted and approved this system for applications for Fulbright awards. However, two or three prominent scholars created a fearful row when they charged that the Board had rejected them for political reasons. This situation was exacerbated when the Board then refused to explain its decision, a policy that all fellowship-granting organizations properly follow. In general, however, most scholars and officials thought that this solution to a complicated problem was sensible and successful.

The Committee, however, would not yield its authority to the Board of Foreign Scholarships. It insisted instead that its own selection committee

have full authority to choose its participants.
In a most important decision the Department of
State recognized the special character of this
exchange program, agreed that the Committee and
the participating universities should select the
American participants, and yielded the authority
that the 1947 legislation had given the Board of
Foreign Scholarships. In turn, the Committee
agreed that it would send the Department the names
of the applicants who had survived the first step
in the selection process.

The Committee announcements indicated that its
programs were part of a formal agreement negotiated
by the Department of State. Its administrators
and selection committees made clear that the
selection committees alone chose the nominees,
and letters to applicants who had survived the
preliminary screening informed them of the
"name check."[3]

In the first year, 1958-59, no problems arose
because the Department encountered no information
which suggested that any individual under consideration be denied this opportunity. In the spring of
1959, however, the Department informed Wallace that
its information suggested that one candidate should
not be allowed to participate. In response, the
selection committee and the university involved
completed another full review of the data they
possessed. They concluded that the candidate did
qualify. The Department reiterated its position
but informed Wallace that the materials on which

[3]Other Western countries escape this thorny problem
because their governments control and administer the academic
exchange programs and bring university scholars into the
process. Thus, the British Council invites each British
university to nominate several graduate students or scholars
for the appropriate program, thereby creating a preliminary
selection process within each institution. The Council
selection committee contains a number of academics and has
full access to all data, including those in the government's
possession. In addition, on the exchange program with the
Soviet Union and Eastern Europe, the Council works closely
with the vice-chancellors and principals on applications on
which questions arise.

its views were based could not be divulged. In
turn, the Committee refused to share its information or open its files to the Department, which
asked for access only in this initial case.

In this situation, Wallace and Department
officials reached an extraordinarily sensible
solution. Except for the first individual in
1959, about whose identity the selection committee
had already learned, and the controversial case
in 1967 discussed later, they arranged that the
selection committee not be informed, so that
Department reservations did not affect its
judgment. They agreed that a member of the
academic community, whose judgment both the
universities and the Department respected and who
had obtained the appropriate security clearance,
would read the Department's material in those
instances where the Department had reservations.
Both parties would then accept whatever decision
he reached. Thus, if he concluded that the
applicant should be allowed to participate, he
would be nominated, if he survived the selection
committee process. If he reached a negative
decision, the applicant would not be nominated,
whether or not he survived the selection process.

This procedure resolved the issue in 1959;
the candidate under consideration was nominated,
accepted by the Ministry, and spent a successful
year in the Soviet Union. In the following years
the Department of State indicated that its evidence
suggested that the Committee should not nominate
13 of the 1,777 applicants. In each case, a
member of the academic community read the Department's materials. In nine cases he recommended
that the candidate participate; eight survived the
selection process, were nominated, and then went
to the Soviet Union. In one of these cases, all
three of the senior American ambassadors who had
served in the Soviet Union, as well as the heads
of the Bureau of European Affairs and the then
Office of Soviet Affairs in the Department,
recommended against this decision; nevertheless,
the applicant did go to the Soviet Union.

In four cases the scholar concluded that the

applicant should not be nominated. In one instance the Department possessed published information that a court in a democratic European country had convicted the applicant for serving as a spy for the Soviet Union. In a second case, the candidate had served as a courier between the Soviet Communist Party and a revolutionary party in another part of the world. In a third case, which was particularly complicated, the scholar who reviewed the materials consulted with two colleagues who had reviewed Department files on similar occasions. All three then met with the candidate; all four agreed that he should withdraw his application because a visit to the Soviet Union would be most hazardous. The fourth instance, also quite complicated, will be discussed later. In none of the four cases had the applicant completed the selection committee's screening process and won nomination.

In short, this agreement, in which the Department of State surrendered an important part of its authority to a private organization, worked successfully, guaranteeing the rights of the individual candidate as well as those of the Department, the universities, and the program as a whole. In fact, if the Department of State had retained authority to make the final decision, the universities would have surrendered an essential responsibility and eight candidates ultimately selected would not have been nominated for study in the Soviet Union.

In the winter of 1966-67, when the Department of State raised a question concerning an applicant, the Committee followed the procedures used effectively on twelve other occasions. As the responsible academic in this instance, I read the papers of the candidate, an outstanding young scholar who had participated earlier and had requested another grant. I decided it would be unwise for him to return, largely because a report he had written after the earlier occasion revealed in great detail that Soviet security officers had shown a special interest in him and that American officials in Washington and Moscow and the individual himself then believed that his remaining

in the Soviet Union would be hazardous. He had not
kept a copy of his long report and had forgotten
its substance, so we reviewed it together. He
then accepted the decision, and the issue seemed
settled.

However, the applicant reversed his position
and asked his friends and associates at other
universities to protest. Perhaps inevitably,
because of the intellectual climate in those years,
the campaign shifted from a complaint concerning
rejection of an applicant to a general attack on
the Committee, its procedures, and its relations
with the Department of State. A review committee
of three senior scholars quieted the storm when
they upheld the rejection and found that "the
chairman of the Inter-University Committee had had
a reasonable basis for his action in recommending
rejection and that, in his place, they would have
come to the same judgment."

As often occurs in controversies of this kind,
the incident was engulfed in ironies and paradoxes.
Far from collecting and making available confidential information concerning applicants, as its
critics alleged, the Committee's staff had created
a special sealed file containing all such information, set aside so that no one should have
access. Thus, not even the members of the
selection committee saw the report that was the
foundation for the decision. In fact, I was not
aware that the Committee had a copy, and I read the
copy in the Department of State's file. Moreover,
the Committee concealed the unsuccessful candidate's
identity, but he and his friends exposed it. Some
of the critics had themselves urged that the selection committees be most restrictive in selecting
candidates. The ultimate irony was that one of
those who strongly urged that the Committee have
no relationships whatsoever with the Department
of State later that year asked the Department for
some kind of semi-official status while he traveled
to the Soviet Union on another fellowship.

After this incident the Committee made two
changes in procedure. First, although it had
always informed applicants of the Department of

State's role, it also sent a formal letter to each
person interviewed stating that "Since Department
of State funds are involved, final selections are
made with the authority of the Board of Foreign
Scholarships, in accordance with the provisions
of the Fulbright-Hays act. The names of all
applicants and accompanying wives therefore have
been forwarded to the Department of State." In
addition, instead of having one specialist in the
field of Russian studies review the Department's
materials, the Committee established a committee
of three senior scholars, one from the West coast,
another in a Midwestern university, and the third
a physicist in an Eastern university who had long
participated in the Committee's work. In 1967-68
the physicist read the materials concerning four
applicants "flagged" by the Department of State.
He then discussed the information, but not the
names or circumstances, with his two colleagues.
One applicant's university refused to sponsor his
application, so the committee needed to make no
decision in his case. The three scholars then
decided unanimously that the other three applicants
should participate. As in earlier circumstances,
no identities were revealed. All three whom these
scholars approved did in fact go to the Soviet
Union.

     In the spring of 1968 the universities
approved a further revision establishing a Board
of Review of three from outside the academic
community and outside government acceptable to
the Department of State and the Committee to
review the materials concerning any candidates
about whom the Department raised a question and to
interview the candidate if he wished to appear.
The Board retained authority to permit candidates
to go to the Soviet Union. However, it did not have
authority to reject a candidate; it simply warned
any who faced exceptional risks and advised others
that they should not participate. In short, the
decision in some cases was left to the individual,
after he had been fully informed of any peril to
him and to the program. The Department of State
then retained final authority to deny the applicant
permission to go to the Soviet Union. I considered
these steps a surrender by the universities of a

responsibility they should have retained, one that
reflects the emotional madness which affected some
members of the academic community in those days.

Since 1969 IREX has continued to submit the
names of applicants to the Department of State for
review. When the Department raises a question
concerning a candidate's participation, it notifies
a referee from the university community acceptable
to IREX and to the Department from a discipline
other than those from which most participants
come. Neither the selection committee nor anyone
associated with IREX is informed. The referee,
after reviewing the Department of State materials,
discusses their content, without revealing the name
of the candidate, with two consultants chosen by
IREX from the university community who have
participated in the exchange program, are familiar
with conditions in the Soviet Union and Eastern
Europe, and have no association with IREX or the
selection process. The three vote, with their
decision binding on all parties.

Even during the most nervous years the
Committee had the good sense and courage to keep
the need for political maturity in perspective.
Thus, it sent to the Soviet Union one or two
young men who had been communists, others who had
worked for intelligence agencies or the National
Security Agency, and an officer of Students for a
Democratic Society (SDS), all enjoined, like their
colleagues, to concentrate on their research and
to engage in no intelligence or political warfare
enterprises. In the late 1960s, after exhaustive
study, the Committee nominated a young man who had
innocently participated in a small exchange program
administered by the National Student Association
in the early 1960s but secretly financed by the
Central Intelligence Agency (CIA). At about the
same time, after similar careful scrutiny, it
endorsed a young scholar who had traveled to the
Soviet Union in the summer of 1962 on a grant from
the Program for Intercultural Communication, which
neither the applicant nor the Committee knew the
CIA had founded.

In general, the selection system worked

remarkably well, although the Committee made several horrendous errors in selection and, no doubt, erred also on rejection. The membership of each selection committee varied because of the rotation system, and some committees naturally had more insight and better judgment than others. Usually, the selection committee followed the principle that "when in doubt, do not send the applicant," but various committees did gamble concerning impressive candidates who had apparent flaws or presented problems of one kind or another. Some gambles were successful, others were not. Comments were constant concerning the selection system, but proposals for raising the standards were balanced by those suggesting that we lower them.

The selection process and the entire exchange program has taught us much about the Soviet Union and Eastern Europe and about higher education. We have also learned a good deal about the willingness of some scholars and graduate students to violate most central professional canons in order to obtain a coveted goal. The dishonesty of a few applicants and their sponsors would depress anyone who participated or who reviewed the history of the selection process. Thus, some scholars who understood the particular conditions of life in the Soviet Union failed to mention that applicants they were recommending had psychological problems and were under psychiatric care, although they were fully informed. Some candidates concealed debilitating psychiatric stresses, and others concealed physical health problems. Several participants sought to conceal other fellowship awards, and others cheated on the grants that they received for expenses, particularly travel. Three applicants, with the approval of their mentors, proposed research projects other than those in which they were in fact engaged and therefore went to the Soviet Union under false pretenses. The Ministry of Higher Education, to the participants' and the Committee's chagrin, discovered this trickery and arranged for the participants to leave.

The relationship between any fellowship-granting organization and its Fellows has certain competing elements imbedded in it. The granting organization has high expectations of performance. When the program is new and offers a rare and especially valued opportunity, expectations are correspondingly lofty. On the other hand, the Fellow, who has demonstrated outstanding qualities in a national competition, comes to believe that his opportunity is a right. This attitude was especially common in the 1960s, when fellowship funds were vast and many graduate students lived in comfort for several consecutive years on substantial grants. The relationship was especially complicated because living and working conditions in the Soviet Union differ considerably from those with which we are familiar.

Throughout the history of the academic exchange, those responsible for its administration have fretted over relations with participants and with alumni. They discussed it annually at meetings of university representatives and at policy committee meetings, and they sought to revise the relationship as Soviet policy changed. Moreover, they also discussed this with administrators of the British Council and of the Deutsche Forschungsgemeinschaft. They were always relieved to learn that these organizations were concerned about the same issues and adopted similar policies.

During the early years the administrators of the Committee, the selection committees, and the university representatives as well may have overestimated the strains life in the Soviet Union place upon our participants, although most alumni urged raising the standards for maturity and stability. One participant and veteran described the circumstances as "more severe than in the Army." Some participants and senior scholars believed the tensions so great that they recommended a psychiatrist participate in the selection process. The Committee therefore allowed each participant to visit Finland or Western Europe for a week or two around Christmas, a tradition IREX continues. In addition, it arranged that the chairman, accompanied by one or two other scholars, visit the Soviet Union in January, a custom IREX also follows.

These visits, and similar ones British Council
representatives make, were designed to overcome
the isolation most participants felt by January
and to help them obtain access to Soviet archives
and study-related travel.

For most participants the Committee and IREX
ceased to exist after they reached the Soviet
Union. Most gloried in their confident independence
and made their way in the Soviet Union with
seriousness, tact, and humor. They acted precisely
as their mentors and sponsors had hoped they would,
and they enjoyed a fruitful experience. For those
who were baffled by the Soviet bureaucracy and
especially frustrated by its endless skills, the
Committee, and later IREX, became distant and
powerless agencies responsible for but unconcerned
about their desperate front-line plight. These
men and women often nurtured resentments, as
veterans remember the contrast between their
hardships and the comforts of those back home.

The nature of the evidence concerning the
activities and experiences of American participants
in the Soviet Union and Eastern Europe is
inevitably fragmentary. The Committee and IREX
sought and obtained only brief reports from
participants. They urged each participant to send
a letter within a month after his arrival,
providing the chairman and his professor in the
United States with his address and telephone number,
the name of his Soviet rukovoditel' or director of
research, and information concerning his first
weeks of work. They also urged him to send a
further report in December, identifying problems
so that the chairman might be of assistance during
the annual January visit. After the participant
had completed his semester or year of study he was
expected to write a report, with particular emphasis
upon suggestions that might help future participants.
The reports to the Committee, which I have
carefully studied, were often brief and incomplete.
In fact, many participants in the various exchange
programs filed none.

The great majority proved to be men and women
of exemplary professional ability and promise,

maturity, and personal integrity. In fact, they
reflect great credit on themselves and their
institutions. The contributions their publications
and their teaching have made to improving the
quality of research and instruction concerning
the Soviet Union and Eastern Europe are already
immeasurable and constitute the supreme justification for the exchange program. However, perhaps
as many as five percent acted in a fashion that
discredited them, often placed them in some
jeopardy, and of course gave Soviet critics of
American scholarship and of the United States
splendid ammunition. Three unfortunate
participants, overwhelmed by the pressures of
Soviet life, indicated to American friends in the
Soviet Union, to relatives at home, or to their
mentors that the strains were becoming intolerable.
However, after the Committee had encouraged them
to leave because of these declarations, they became
"bold cowards" and charged it with improperly
recalling them. A small number wasted this
opportunity, failing to work or even to enjoy the
cultural life, as a good number do at home.
Unfortunately, these dilettantes aroused Soviet
suspicion concerning their activities and those
of their fellows. Others behaved in more
reprehensible fashion. One clipped articles from
Soviet newspapers and magazines of the 1920s.
Several engaged in the black market, selling
American goods to Soviet speculators. Two were
arrested for consorting with drug addicts and
speculators, although they were not guilty of
selling or using drugs and were not themselves
involved in illegal activities.

Perhaps more serious, because these activities
endangered Soviet citizens who could not leave the
country, some kept diaries, relating in detail
political conversations with Soviet students and
professors, some of whom they identified. In fact,
one participant some days wrote twelve or fifteen
pages concerning his conversations. The Soviet
police read some of these diaries, and Soviet
citizens were thus needlessly exposed to danger.
Others were similarly careless and indiscreet in
correspondence with Soviet citizens, in telephone
conversations that they learned later had been

monitored, and even in their publications, which
is especially inexcusable. Some scholars whom the
ACLS and the National Academy of Sciences sent
were just as irresponsible.

In the eleven years the Inter-University
Committee administered its several academic
exchange programs, it withdrew nine American
participants from the Soviet Union or Eastern
Europe, in every case but one with the advice and
approval of the participant's supervising professor
and his university. IREX has withdrawn at least
one in the years it has administered its programs.
It has also refined and made more cumbersome the
conditions and procedures for withdrawing a
participant for breakdown of physical or mental
health, academic nonperformance, "evidence of
voluntary or involuntary involvements in intelligence activities of any kind whatsoever, whether
by the participant or by an accompanying family
member," or gross misconduct.

Perhaps the most surprising discovery these
programs have revealed about American academic
life has been that the majority of the youngish
specialists on Russian affairs have not sought
an opportunity to study in the Soviet Union.
For example, only twenty percent of those who
obtained the Ph.D. degree in any one of the
fields of Russian studies from 1960 through 1964
had by 1969 applied for an opportunity to study
in the Soviet Union. Only one-eighth of the
Foreign Area Fellowship Program Fellows in
Russian studies over a longer period, from 1952
through 1965, had sought that opportunity by
1969, even though they had proved in national
competition that they were the most promising
young men and women in the Russian field. In
only six of the Committee's eleven years did
the number of junior candidates selected equal
the number the agreement allowed. Indeed, the
average number of applicants for the period from
1958 through 1969 was slightly less than 100,
only three times the number of nominations
possible. Under IREX the number of applicants
slumped from 123, the figure for the last year
under the Committee, to 104 in 1969-70, 98 in

1970-71, and 86 in 1971-72. In the succeeding three years it rose to 95, 120, and 140, before slipping to 135 for 1975-76. The number of applicants for the exchange of senior scholars that the Committee and IREX have administered between 1962 and 1975 never rose to 60.[4]

This disinterest is especially remarkable when one considers the spectacular growth in the number of Russian specialists throughout the 1960s and the dedicated and imaginative efforts the Committee and IREX made to announce these splendid fellowship opportunities. Whatever the cause, many of the hundreds of specialists on the Soviet Union educated in the 1960s and early 1970s clearly lacked the dedication to their profession and the interest in studying in the Soviet Union that our handful of scholars had demonstrated in the 1920s and 1930s and that a large percentage possessed in the 1950s.

A number of factors are responsible for this. They include the unpleasant, uncomfortable, somewhat tense life in the Soviet Union. Some decided not to apply because they believed they lacked the intellectual or related qualities the exchange program required. Others refused to accept Soviet influence or control over their choice of a research subject. Others were turned away by their knowledge of Soviet inefficiency and by Soviet delays in reaching decisions concerning admission. Some did not apply because of the unwillingness of their spouses to participate. The refusal of the Soviet government until 1972 to admit children forced many to choose between going to the Soviet Union and staying home with their families. Some young scholars, particularly in the sciences, were eager to accept academic or other appointments and to enter directly a productive life of teaching and research, rather than delay by spending a semester or a year in the Soviet Union. In addition, some faculty members discourage their students from applying

[4]The number of junior applicants rose gradually from 60 in the first year to 127 in 1964-65. It then declined to 104 the following year, 98 in 1966-67, and 84 in 1967-68.

until they have completed the Ph.D. At that time,
the young scholar often has a spouse and children
and concerns about his future that persuade him
not to apply.

Other significant factors are our national
attitude toward learning foreign languages and the
continuing acceptance of inferior command of
languages throughout our system of higher
education. Our graduate programs on the Soviet
Union and Eastern Europe generally have higher
language requirements than do most graduate
departments, but most still emphasize reading and
tolerate low performance in understanding, speaking,
and writing. Few seek to make a period of study
in the Soviet Union or a part of Eastern Europe an
essential part of the planned curriculum of even
their most promising graduate students or to insist
that these students prepare to spend a semester in
the country in which they are most interested.
Most graduate students therefore arrange their
study programs and research projects so that they
can complete their degrees without study abroad.
The quality of our research and instruction is
therefore lower than it need be.

No graduate program can require its degree
candidates to study abroad or can provide
assurance that even its most highly qualified
students will be able to study in the Soviet
Union or Eastern Europe. Moreover, no national
organization seeks to or could impose language
standards. In addition, many inspiring teachers
in Russian and East European studies have not
mastered the languages necessary for living or
doing research there, and raising language
requirements for such men and women would not
be productive.

Perhaps the best solution to this shortcoming
would be reviving the Committee's original
program, enabling young scholars and teachers
to travel a month or two in the Soviet Union and
Eastern Europe. This would not only increase
their knowledge and understanding, but it would
motivate some to increase their own abilities.
But raising this issue and proposing a return to

the 1956 travel program, established to enable
enthusiastic scholars to visit the country of
their special interest, reveal that Russian
studies have lost some of the qualities that
its founders possessed and that created the
Inter-University Committee. It should also
remind us that academic exchanges constitute
an unsatisfactory and temporary means and that
free and unfettered opportunities for research
and study by scholars in all countries still
remain our goal.

CHAPTER FIVE

The Committee and the Department
of State

The relationships between the scholar and
the university, on one hand, and the government,
on the other hand, are different in the United
States than in other democratic countries because
of ancient and honorable American beliefs and
practices. Americans since the early 1930s have
turned more and more to our central government
for services that earlier generations believed
were the responsibility of individual citizens
or of private organizations. However, the skeptical,
critical intellectual and his fellow citizens in
all walks of life believe that the influence of
government over intellectual life and over
individuals should be limited, because each of
us has "an ethic of individual independence and
idiosyncracy, a distrust of ideas and rulers, and
an inbred suspicion of too close an association
with governments."[1] On the other hand, anti-
intellectualism has often played a profound role
in American life, and some have sought to direct
government pressure against scholars and other
intellectuals. Even today, when most people
understand the contributions scientists have made

[1]Charles Frankel, The Neglected Aspect of Foreign
Affairs. American Educational and Cultural Policy Abroad
(Washington, 1966), 39.

118

to the quality of American life and to our role
in world affairs, the public attitude toward the
highly educated and toward those who engage in
intellectual activities retains a strain of
suspicion. The outbursts that have marked our
public life since the end of World War II, in
particular the crusade Senator Joseph McCarthy led,
simply reflect this deep-seated popular feeling.

The relationships between the scholar and
the government have changed considerably in the
twentieth century as the scholar has provided a
growing number of services to the government
and has also relied upon it increasingly for
financial aid and other forms of support. Members
of the academic community began to serve the
government more frequently as our economic and
social life became more complicated and as our
involvement in international politics increased.
While educated men and women have always constituted
a high percentage of government employees and
of elected officials, the service in Washington
of scholars began only during World War I. Their
participation in federal government service
increased rapidly in the early years of the New
Deal and again throughout World War II. During
the administration of President Kennedy, the
visible role played by intellectuals leaped
significantly. In short, in the last fifty
years scholars from colleges and universities
and other intellectuals have served in increasing
numbers as consultants and officials in many
government agencies. Indeed, probably the
majority of today's faculty members in major
universities have worked in government agencies
or have served as consultants at one time or
another.

Our institutions of higher education have
remained closer to public service than have those
in other Western countries. At the same time,
both our scholars and our universities are
suspicious of government and are eager to restrict
its influence, though not its financial aid.
Universities consider themselves privileged
sanctuaries of freedom and are accustomed to
their own ways. Small colleges and great centers

of learning, private institutions and state
universities all believe they must conduct research
and instruction as they see best, inviolate against
all outside interference.

Thus, everyone agrees, first, that the
university cannot be removed from the society in
which it functions and which it serves and, second,
that it must remain true to its primary educational
goals if it is to remain truly independent and
serve society effectively. Neither the universities nor the government wants Washington to
become St. Petersburg-on-the Potomac.

The reserved relationship between the
universities and the federal government began to
shift during World War II and has changed
considerably in the past thirty years. During
that war, when the country sought to mobilize its
resources and when most young men were in the
armed forces, our colleges and universities
provided special training programs, preparing
young men and women for service overseas in
different cultures. They also contributed the
work of their scientists and laboratories to
increase our military capabilities. The development of the atomic bomb is just one indication
of this effort.

Since the war, our universities have become
an ever-growing resource for the federal government, particularly in research. Practically all
government agencies, in particular the Departments
of Agriculture and Defense, support research on
our campuses. Most government agencies involved
in work overseas, particularly the Department of
State, turn to universities for training institutions, administrators of programs, advisors, and
consultants. The various agencies that have
brought thousands of foreign students and scholars
here rely upon universities for educational
services.

Moreover, the funding of higher education has
changed considerably in the last three decades.
Federal funds now constitute an important
percentage of the resources available for research

in the sciences in many major universities. The
government has also provided massive financial
assistance in the humanities and social sciences.
Indeed, fellowships provided by the National
Defense Education Act of 1958 and other programs
directed and administered by the Department of
Health, Education, and Welfare and other direct
grants from the Office of Education helped continue
the rapid expansion of Russian and East European
studies, and of instruction on other foreign areas
as well. However, while our universities have
welcomed government financial support and indeed
plead for more, they want government influence
reduced or even eliminated. In short, since World
War II the assistance the universities provide
the government and government financial support
for the universities have drastically changed the
nature and character of the relationship.

Even so, the universities themselves have
provided the great bulk of the financial support
for our foreign area programs, with private
foundations the second largest contributor. The
most complete analysis of the growth of foreign
area studies in the United States concluded in
1973 that universities contributed about eighty
percent of the total costs in 1971.[2] The government
had contributed less than thirteen percent of the
funds for the major university Russian and East
European area programs through 1969, when both
foundation and Department of Health, Education,
and Welfare support dropped sharply. Thus, the
Ford Foundation between 1952 and 1969 spent almost
$300,000,000 to expand international studies in
this country and abroad, almost double the amount
the Department of Health, Education, and Welfare
awarded all language and area centers between
1958 and 1969 under the National Defense Education
Act, the main source of government funds in these
fields. Moreover, the Ford funds were available
early in this period and were essential for
launching these programs, while NDEA funds began
later and supplemented programs already under
way.

[2]Richard D. Lambert, Language and Area Studies Review
(Philadelphia, 1973), 299-311, 345-49.

Ford Foundation support for the Inter-
University Committee and for IREX has also exceeded
that from the Department of State and the National
Endowment for the Humanities, the government
agencies that have provided financial assistance.
Thus, between 1958 and 1974 the Foundation gave
the Committee and IREX almost $7,000,000, while
at the same time awarding the ACLS and the
National Academy of Sciences smaller totals.
Department of State funding for the same period
amounted to somewhat less than $5,000,000, and
generous National Endowment grants from 1971 to
1975 to IREX amounted to less than $2,000,000.
Moreover, Department of State support began at
only $10,500 for 1958-59, rose to $64,500 and
$101,000 the following two years, and then averaged
about $200,000 annually throughout the 1960s. It
then leaped to $400,000 for each of the following
two years, to $460,000 for 1972-73 and 1973-74,
and to $614,730 for each of the subsequent years.
Thus, the Department contributed about four
percent of the Committee's total budget in 1958-59,
twelve percent the second year, twenty-four percent
the third year, and approximately thirty-three
percent for subsequent years until 1974. However,
the Ford Foundation after a quarter of a century
of constant support is withdrawing all but token
aid for foreign area programs and may end its aid
to IREX, or reduce it very drastically, when the
grant for 1975-76 expires. The Department of State
may therefore contribute more than $1,000,000 for
1976-77, more than half IREX's budget. IREX may
soon become completely dependent upon government
funds to maintain the academic exchange programs.
It would then in fact become a government
instrument.

The flow of publications between the United
States and the Soviet Union is another element in
the relations between our government and universities. Neither has been able to overcome the
blockade against the flow of Western publications
into the Soviet Union, but they have combined to
expand that from the Soviet Union and Eastern
Europe into the United States. In the early 1950s,
in particular, the universities were annoyed when
customs and post office officials occasionally

interfered with their efforts to acquire Soviet
and East European publications. Ironically,
government officials conducted these actions
under the Foreign Agents Registration Act, passed
in 1938 to require registration of foreign agents
and identification of propaganda materials
distributed by Nazi Germany and Fascist Italy.
Similarly, in the mid-1950s, the Immigration and
Naturalization Act of 1952, as amended, raised
difficulties when it required that scholars
invited from the Soviet Union and Eastern Europe
be fingerprinted when applying for visas. The
Department of State in September 1957 succeeded
in having this act waived for those who came at
university invitation.

The beginning of the exchange program with
the Soviet Union and the surfacing of these
problems led the Joint Committee on Slavic Studies
in December 1958 to establish a subcommittee on
relations between universities and the government.
Paradoxically, Soviet officials interpreted this
group, established to increase the flow of
materials essential for scholarship, as a conduit
through which our government exercised control
over Russian studies.[3] However, the sessions
between scholars and senior government officials
improved the flow of research materials and of
government-financed translations to university
libraries and helped educate both groups concerning
the problems any kind of relationship with the
Soviet Union created.

For the Inter-University Committee, IREX, and
the universities they serve, the Department of
State is the most important government organization.
Their relations have been remarkably amicable and
effective, because all involved have so well
understood each other's purposes and qualities.
In fact, the skill and candor with which the
Department and the universities have defined their
positions, respected each other's responsibilities

[3]Ivan M. Krasnov, "Izuchenie istorii SSSR v SShA.
Nekotorye tsifry i fakty" [The Study of Soviet History in the
USA. Some Figures and Facts], Istoriia SSSR, Number 6
(November-December, 1964), 166-83; Pravda, March 1, 1967.

and privileges, and cooperated to preserve the
special qualities of our system and to advance the
national interest have been a tribute to both.
However, some tension concerning specific issues
and procedures was inevitable, particularly in
the early years when both sides were dealing with
new problems and were especially sensitive.

From the beginning, both the Department and
the universities have been anxious to establish a
free flow of scholars and publications. Both were
reluctant to participate in a formal exchanges
agreement because they saw that it allowed some
flow of scholars, but also controlled it. Both
were fearful, and with reason, that the principles
of the 1958 agreement would survive and would
restrict rather than encourage the kind of
relationships familiar to Western society. At
the same time, the Department's relative in-
experience in cultural relations with other
countries and its dealings with authoritarian
states in the previous two decades persuaded it
to seek some influence over such explosive matters.

The United States had paid almost no attention
to cultural exchanges until just before World War
II. The Smithsonian Institution's activities
abroad and the use of reparation funds from the
Boxer Rebellion to bring Chinese students here
constituted the only federal government activities
in the cultural exchange field before 1938, when
the Division of Cultural Affairs was established
in the Department of State, largely to combat
Axis propaganda in Latin America. During World
War II, the Office of War Information emphasized
countering Nazi propaganda. After the war our
interest in cultural affairs and educational
exchanges increased enormously. We helped to
organize, and joined as well, a number of
international organizations, such as UNESCO,
UNICEF, ILO, and WHO. The Fulbright Act, passed
in 1947, and the Fulbright-Hays Mutual Educational
and Cultural Exchange Act, enacted in 1961,
enabled more than 100,000 intellectuals, of whom
approximately two-thirds were from 110 other
countries, to visit the United States or other
countries. In 1968 alone, the Bureau of Educational

and Cultural Affairs enabled 8,500 men and women
to travel abroad or to visit the United States for
educational and cultural purposes. The Department
of State has established enormously successful
programs in other countries to increase and
improve the teaching of English, to expand
American studies, and to establish libraries and
schools, while the United States Information
Agency, its Voice of America, and its information
centers and libraries have become known throughout
most of the world. The onset of the cold war and
the necessity to create defenses against Soviet
propaganda and to advance the democratic cause in
other parts of the world have led to increased
attention to forms of cultural relations in which
the shared advantages envisaged in the other
programs were not so visible. USIA in particular
has concentrated on spreading news and information
concerning this country and the West in general
through radio and television programs, publications, and other accepted mass media forms.

Our government seeks to encourage the free
flow of people and ideas across national frontiers,
as a matter of vital principle and of mutual or
shared advantage. We believe that this free
exchange will advance our foreign policy and will
contribute toward establishing peaceful conditions
everywhere, which is profoundly in our national
interest. We seek to learn about and from other
people, as many others seek to learn about and
from us.[4]

In the 1950s our foreign policy sought to slow

[4]American purposes in cultural exchanges are perhaps
best expressed in the Fulbright-Hays Act: "to strengthen
mutual understanding . . . ; to strengthen the ties which
unite us with other nations by demonstrating the educational
and cultural interests, developments, and achievements of the
people of the United States and other nations, and the contributions being made toward a peaceful and more fruitful
life for people throughout the world; to promote international
cooperation for educational and cultural advancement; and
thus to assist in the development of friendly, sympathetic,
and peaceful relations between the United States and other
countries of the world."

down the Soviet effort to expand, to reduce Soviet forces in and Soviet control over the peoples of Eastern Europe, to strengthen and unite the other peoples and countries concerned about Soviet power and policy, and to move the Soviet Union from an intransigent position into one accepting a peaceful framework of international politics under the principles posed by the United Nations for resolving international disputes.

Department officials consider academic exchanges a significant element in this total relationship with the Soviet Union, particularly because they maintain ties at times of great tension and hazard as well as in more calm periods. In the Department's view, this opportunity for dialogue reinforces the tendency within the higher levels of the Soviet government to engage in relationships on peaceful grounds under conditions of mutual advantage, a practice that is regularly condemned in the Soviet Union as "ideological coexistence." Department officials also appreciate that academic exchange programs advance the national interest by increasing Soviet understanding of the United States. Thus, in the long run they contribute to reducing misunderstanding and fear on both sides, and they help the Soviet elite to see more clearly and appreciate the wider world in which we all live.

In addition, identifying or defining Soviet policies and the considerations underlying them is a difficult task, complicated by lack of information and by the difficulties we encounter in penetrating the Soviet mind. The Department therefore considers the exchange program a kind of index or barometer of larger Soviet policies and of the atmosphere in which Soviet decisions are made. Thus, decreasing KGB harassment of American scholars reveals a change of the temperature or atmosphere within which all Soviet policies are decided.

Department officials, like all informed observers, see foreign affairs as "a complicated and disorderly business, full of surprises, demanding hard choices that must be based on

judgment rather than analysis." In part because
foreign relations are their responsibility,
in part because the Department considers academic
exchanges important, and above all because the
exchanges are conducted under an intergovernmental
agreement, some tension arose between the Department and the Committee and exists between the
Department and IREX. On their part, the universities were determined to retain control of
university programs and to remain independent of
politics. They were therefore eager to defend
their own interests against all outside influence.
They feared that the Department might not be
capable of protecting their concerns against
critics and Congressional pressures.

Department of State officials naturally
believed they possessed the professional competence
required for conducting our foreign policy and
defending the national interest in all the
country's undertakings abroad. They had access
to far more complete information than scholars.
The Department's responsibilities involved our
relations with all countries throughout the world,
and policies on many issues and toward many
countries were closely interrelated. Our relationships with the Soviet Union were particularly
complicated and delicate, involved many interests
and government agencies, and inevitably affected
our relations with other parts of the world.

From the Department's point of view, the
Committee and IREX represent a special interest
group, similar to businessmen whose main concern
in trade with other countries is their own profit.
The Department recognized that both scholars and
businessmen have a sense of the national interest,
but it believed that these groups tend to place
their own interests first and often confuse
personal or professional ambitions with national
objectives. Its officials almost inevitably saw
university representatives as ivory tower amateurs,
poorly informed and inexperienced in dealing with
the Soviet Union. In the early years in particular
they were concerned lest one mistaken judgment by
the Committee or even by a participant should wreck
the academic exchange program, throw into disarray

the entire exchanges agreement, and significantly affect Soviet-American relations.

Relations with the Soviet Union were so central, and cultural exchanges so sensitive, that President Eisenhower, in establishing the Office of East-West Contacts in the Bureau of European Affairs in 1955, also appointed a special assistant to the Secretary of State for East-West Exchanges, Ambassador William S. B. Lacy, and a special assistant to the President, William H. Jackson, whose assignments included reviewing cultural exchanges with the Soviet Union. He gave the new office responsibility for coordinating the Department's position on all exchanges with the Soviet Union: negotiating with the Soviet government, with the aid of other interested agencies; administering and monitoring the exchanges programs; and locating and persuading private organizations and institutions to participate. Its officials worked very closely with the Bureau of Educational and Cultural Affairs, created in 1961 from a number of organizations within the Department that had dealt with such issues since 1938. Committee and IREX administrators handled these two offices so harmoniously that they considered them one. Departmental financial support to the Committee and to IREX comes through the Bureau of Educational and Cultural Affairs after informal and amiable discussions, and the scholars' organizations also deal with the Bureau on proposals for revised or new programs.[5] When Committee and IREX representatives have discussed proposals with Department of State officials, they have been completely candid and forthright and have accepted or rejected Department advice as they have that of members of the academic community.

From the very beginning, the Committee and the universities and scholars it represented sought to

[5]The Office of East-West Contacts, later the Soviet and East European Exchanges Staff, was disbanded in 1974, when its personnel and functions were transferred to the Office of USSR Affairs, which has responsibility for advising the Secretary of State on all our relations with the Soviet Union, and to the desks that deal with each of the East European countries.

maintain their independence from the Department of
State and all government agencies, just as the Department remained aloof from the Committee's work.
No government officials at any time saw any applications to the Committee or to IREX. In 1957, when
the Committee was making grants for thirty-day
trips to the Soviet Union and Eastern Europe, it
declared highly competent applicants from the RAND
Corporation ineligible, because they had a substantial connection with the government.[6]

However, because they recognized the nature of
the Soviet system and the political significance of
sending scholars to the Soviet Union, the founders
of the Committee from the beginning informed Department officials of its plans and programs. Thus,
Dean Wallace sent a copy of the application for
funds submitted to the Carnegie Corporation in
October 1955 to the Department of State. He invited it to send representatives to the meeting
reviewing the work of the Committee in November
1956, a tradition that later administrators of the
Committee and IREX have since followed. Department
officials have attended these annual meetings since
November 1960.

After the cultural exchanges agreement was
signed in January 1958 and the Inter-University Committee accepted responsibility for the first academic exchange program with the Soviet Union, the chairman sent to the Department of State an information
copy of each of his letters to the Soviet Ministry
of Higher Education. He also sent a copy to the
American Embassy in Moscow, as well as to the Soviet
Embassy in Washington, largely on the assumption
that the American Embassy would often represent the
Committee's interests in Moscow when no Committee
representative could be there and when the Ministry
seemed slow in responding to its queries, and that
the Soviet Embassy in Washington would often represent the Ministry's interests. IREX has continued
the practice of sending copies to the American and
Soviet Embassies, although probably not systemati-

[6]IREX in 1975 made travel grants to RAND employees, thus
reversing this long-standing policy and revealing how much it
has drifted into the government sphere.

cally to the Department itself. Moreover, IREX
now has direct telex contact with the American
Embassy in Moscow and often communicates with the
Ministry of Higher Education through the Embassy.

The establishment of the Committee in 1956 was
a blessing for the Department because the universities and scholars involved by 1958 had had experience in directing a complicated national program
and had some understanding of the difficulties involved in dealing with the Soviet system. Indeed,
the Committee constituted an ideal private, autonomous, and independent agency to undertake administrative responsibility for one of the essential
elements of the entire exchanges agreement.
Similarly, the Committee was deeply grateful to
the Department for the essential services it provided. The principles and pattern their offices
together established in the early years survived.
Thus, the Department negotiated the original agreement with the Soviet government, identified a
responsible instrument for administering academic
exchanges, and gave it full responsibility. After
the November 1959 renewal of the first agreement,
the Committee and, later, IREX officers joined
Department officials in negotiating the section of
the exchanges agreement that concerned them.

On the other hand, a number of important issues have disturbed relations between the universities and the Department. The basic problem, one
that sensible and skillful action has kept within
bounds, has been the determination of each party to
maintain its independence and integrity and to
achieve a satisfactory division of responsibilities.
In the early years, Committee representatives
sometimes felt that the Department used the academic
exchange program, which they believed of particular
value to the Soviet Union, as a lever for obtaining
advantages in other parts of the exchanges agreement,
particularly national exhibits, in which the Department had a special interest. The Department and the
universities have also disagreed on occasion concerning the nature and size of the programs and the
most effective way to negotiate with Soviet officials. The first disagreement rose in December 1958
when the Committee realized that most Soviet

participants would be in science and technology, and so encouraged young American scientists to participate. It therefore sought to add the California Institute of Technology and the Massachusetts Institute of Technology to the seven original member institutions. However, the Department urged the Committee to limit the number of universities to seven until the Soviet government had allowed American participants to study outside of Moscow and Leningrad. In this case the Department yielded, and the Committee surrendered advantages to the Ministry without reciprocal benefit.

The next disagreement arose because of the euphoria of "the spirit of Camp David" from the fall of 1959 until the early summer of 1960, when the Department was under considerable pressure from President Eisenhower and other political leaders to expand exchanges. It also sought increased numbers of exhibits. The Department in the fall of 1959 therefore proposed to the Ministry that the two countries exchange eighty-five scholars each year. The universities through the Committee sought to delay expanding the program until Soviet performance had improved and had helped stimulate increased interest among qualified candidates. They believed expansion "could be achieved only by taking a firm line," preventing the Ministry from exploiting our facilities while restricting our participants' access to archives and travel. The Department then considered establishing a noncompetitive program of its own, designed to attract young men and women who would choose careers beyond the academic community, perhaps as Foreign Service Officers. Some officials thought this especially attractive, because fewer than half of the Department's fifty-six specialists on the Soviet Union in 1961 had received any graduate training and because the British Council was sending young men and women to the Soviet Union who had no interest in Russian studies or in an academic career. Moreover, the Department thought such a program might enjoy broad geographic representation and help soften Congressional criticism.

This deeply divisive issue died quickly after the U-2 flight, cancellation of the invitation to

President Eisenhower to visit the Soviet Union, and continuing tensions over West Berlin. However, the Department in March 1962, over university opposition, again sought to raise the number of scholars exchanged, this time to seventy-five each year.

Another problem arose when important public leaders and Congressmen became deeply critical of the Department of State over academic exchanges. Thus, in August 1962 George Meany of the AFL-CIO ridiculed the Department for believing cultural exchanges could bring progress toward peace. Congressman Michael Feighan of Ohio, a member of the House Judiciary Subcommittee, and Congressman John Rooney of Brooklyn, Chairman of the House Subcommittee on Appropriations for the State Department, often denounced the Department because "the Soviets send scientists who work on important problems in American laboratories, while we send scholars to work in ancient Russian history in Soviet libraries." Feighan also suggested that "for all practical purposes our students are confined to a sanitized vacuum and tolerated as the price which must be paid for the training of Russian scientists by the United States." He urged that the exchange program should be curtailed or abolished because he thought the Soviet Union obtained great advantage "by penetrating into the vitals of our scientific life."

The Department of State, accountable to Congress for its appropriations, was sensitive to these criticisms and pressed the Committee to increase the number of scientists sent to the Soviet Union. In fact, it urged that fifty percent of our participants and no more than fifty percent of the Soviet participants be scientists. The Committee rejected this because quotas were a violation of its principles, few American scientists were qualified for or interested in research in the Soviet Union, and the Ministry would use such a proposal to place additional restrictions.

The Department and the universities on occasion also collided over the Department's decision to deny visas to Soviet scholars whom the Ministry of Higher Education nominated and whom the universities were

willing and able to assist. When the Department's
denials were based on national security grounds that
specialist members of the Committee understood and
accepted, the denial stood. However, on some other
occasions, when Department of Defense explanations
were not convincing, the Committee and the universities were able to persuade the Department to admit the Soviet scholar.

The Department, the Committee, and later IREX
were in agreement in many instances, that were
often reiterated for several consecutive years, in
which the Ministry nominated scholars in fields
then considered sensitive to the military security
of both countries, such as gas dynamics at very
high speeds, high energy physics, computer technology, and micro-miniaturization in radio-elec-
tronic microwave solid state devices. In the first
year the Department issued a visa to a Soviet scholar whom the Committee placed at the Livermore
Laboratories at the University of California in
Berkeley for work in high energy physics. The
following year the Soviet Union denied a visa to a
young scholar from that laboratory who wished to
work in the Soviet Union in the same field. The
Department in an aide-mémoire on August 7, 1961,
then offered to accept Soviet nominees in that
field if the Ministry would provide assurances of
placement for a similar number of our nominees.
The Ministry failed to respond, so the Department
maintained a denial, with full support from the
universities.

In addition, the Department on occasion has
denied visas to Soviet scholars when the Ministry
has sought to use the academic exchange program
to bypass another part of the exchanges agreement
that it was refusing to honor. For example, in
1962 the Department denied admission to a Soviet
scholar in the field of computer technology after
the Soviet Union had refused to fulfill a part
of the agreement that provided for the exchange
of delegations in that field. Finally, on occasion
the Department has denied visas to Soviet nominees
whose past activities as intelligence agents or
political officers indicated that they were not
genuine scholars or that their activities within

the United States might extend beyond the academic world.[7]

After the Department had issued a visa, the Committee and the Department only rarely had disagreements concerning placement of Soviet participants on particular campuses. The Department sometimes sought to dissuade the Committee from placing a Soviet scholar in a department where important classified research was under way. The Committee and IREX have both given careful consideration to these protests, and they have on occasion decided then to place the Soviet scholar in a department of equal quality about which the Department of State had no concerns.

Similarly, little friction occurred concerning access of Soviet participants to closed areas and to travel throughout the United States. Since 1937 the Soviet government has closed most of its territory to travel by foreigners, and it has placed very tight restrictions on travel even within the other areas. Its restrictions on Americans, particularly diplomats and journalists, were so severe that the Department of State in 1955 closed (that is, listed areas that Soviets could visit only with

[7]Soviet nominations of graduate students and young scholars for 1964-65 represented this problem at its most acute stage. The Department that year rejected sixteen of forty-six Soviet applicants. Six were engaged in nuclear research; the State Committee for Utilization of Atomic Energy should have proposed them to the Atomic Energy Commission, but the Soviet government, which allowed the atomic energy exchange to lapse the following year, apparently wished to bypass that program. Five wished to study advanced computer technology and automatic control systems, very sensitive fields at the time and areas in which the Department had denied opportunities in previous years. Five others were in areas of electronics that were also sensitive and in which the Department had also rejected Soviet applicants in earlier years. Some of us concluded that the Ministry nominated these men with the assumption they would be rejected, but hoping that the Department for one reason or another would accept one or two. The Ministry may also have been creating justification for its rejections of American nominees: it rejected twelve that year.

the Department's permission) a number of areas to
Soviet officials and journalists and to representatives of other communist regimes as well. On occasion the university most qualified to assist a
Soviet nominee was located in a closed area. Ordinarily the Department of State accepted placement
in that institution.

The travel of Soviet participants constituted
a minor problem because most of our scholars understood and supported the Department's policies. In
1958 the Department of State waived all travel restrictions for Soviet participants within a twenty-
five mile radius of the university in which they
were studying. It allowed travel elsewhere after
the Soviet scholar had requested permission in
writing from the Department four working days before
his travel was to begin and described his itinerary,
mode of travel, and overnight places of residence.
The Department in August 1957 and twice in 1958
offered to reconsider its restrictions if the Soviet
government would liberalize its travel controls and
the arbitrary manner in which it administered them.
On January 6, 1961, the Department again proposed
to the Ministry of Foreign Affairs mutual abolition
or reduction of travel restrictions. On July 6,
1962, the Department eliminated closed areas for
tourists and Soviet exchange participants, reduced
them for other Soviet citizens, and again offered
to end all restrictions if the Soviet Union would
reciprocate. No response has been received to this
offer, which has been frequently reiterated. Thus,
Soviet scholars travel with remarkable freedom and
regularity throughout the United States, and they
are denied access only to industrial and scientific
installations and conferences that the Department
of Defense declares sensitive. In fact, a good number of Soviet participants have purchased second-
hand automobiles and toured the United States.
Thus, American security restrictions have gradually
faded and their administration has progressively
relaxed--to the consternation of some appalled by
the hundreds of Soviet officials and commercial
representatives who flood our research and industrial
installations in the 1970s.

Our scholars and officials both regret restrictions of any kind on travel by Soviet participants, because lessening the rights of a visitor weakens the rights of all. Moreover, we all regret the impression that limitations produce upon Soviet visitors. On the other hand, the extraordinary control over American travel in the Soviet Union and the inability of the Committee, IREX, and the Department to persuade the Soviet government even to allow easy study-related travel creates support for these limitations. The alumni of the various exchange programs, whom the Soviet government has often prevented from making even short trips essential to their work and for whom all but a tiny fraction of the Soviet Union has been a closed area, generally believe the Department of State should place some restrictions on Soviet travel in this country.

However, some scholars, who are generally scientists not informed concerning Soviet practices or the larger framework of which academic exchanges are a part and who are often personally interested in a particular Soviet scholar, have protested bitterly concerning these simple rules and the occasional denials of travel to security areas. Some, ordinarily with some fanfare, denounce the Department for policies that seem to them "petty and senseless." One eminent scientist even criticized the Department for denying a Soviet scientist permission to visit sensitive industrial installations, although the scholar from September through March had already completed thirteen trips, one of three weeks' duration, and had planned another of sixty-nine days' duration.

Cooperation between the Committee, IREX, and our government is best illustrated by the relationship between officers of our Embassy in Moscow and the hundreds of participants in the exchange programs. Throughout the first year, Committee officers and Department officials agreed that participants should visit the Embassy on their arrival and then avoid it as much as possible and that our officials in the Soviet Union should maintain a similar reserve. Munford instructed the first participants that they rely on the Embassy for no assistance whatsoever. After he visited the Soviet

Union in December 1958, all again agreed that the
Embassy should play no role.

By the summer of 1959, new policies and new
relationships were established. The participants
had learned that Soviet officials opened some of
their mail. They felt reluctant to mail reports to
their professors or private letters through what
they came to call the "opened mail." They also
learned that Soviet officials assumed they had close
relations with the Embassy and that nothing they
could do to establish an aloof or reserved position
influenced that view. Finally, when Munford visited
the Soviet Union again to negotiate with the Ministry of Higher Education, the Embassy was so helpful
in providing transportation, interpreters, typing
services, and general assistance that the reserve of
Committee officials quickly broke down.

Since the summer of 1959, American scholars
have benefited enormously from assistance Embassy
officers provide. They make extensive use of the
Embassy reading room, where they find current
American newspapers, journals, books, records, and
films. The snack bar, where they can purchase
familiar American food, has become a meeting place.
Indeed, some scholars have spent too much of their
precious time every day in the snack bar, and have
made it a kind of clubhouse. Participants use the
Embassy commissary to purchase food, except perish-
ables, and staples difficult to obtain in the Soviet
Union. They are allowed to receive mail and to
mail private letters, notes, and draft manuscripts
through the diplomatic pouch, a practice that all
Western governments have followed for their citizen-
scholars.

The Embassy has also proved enormously helpful
in advising and assisting participants during times
of emergency--when they need an exit visa quickly
or the advice of the Embassy doctor, or when they
are provoked or harassed by Soviet agents. Indeed,
the marked good sense and generosity with which
Embassy officers have assisted American participants
constitute a shining page in the history of this
program. As one cultural affairs officer wrote,
"The Embassy was a firm but kindly uncle who has a

genuine interest in their well being, who stands
ready or willing to offer assistance if requested,
but who would be very pleased to have them solve
their own problems and make their own decisions in
the Soviet Union independently and intelligently."

This relationship and life in the Soviet Union
have helped American participants acquire a high
understanding and appreciation of the qualities of
Embassy officials, of the difficulties the Department has in dealing with the Soviet Union, and of
the nature of Soviet-American relations. They have
considerably affected our scholars' view of the
Soviet system and reduced the likelihood of a gap
in understanding and approach between the Department and American specialists on the Soviet Union.

Problems have inevitably occurred, particularly
in the 1970s, as American Embassy officials and
Leningrad consulate officers have been overwhelmed
by the relative flood of businessmen seeking advice
and assistance. A few participants have resented
occasional advice Embassy officers have given concerning behavior. Some complained about early limitations concerning purchases in the commissary.
Others "seemed to feel that the United States established diplomatic relations with the Soviet Union
in 1933 in order to prepare for and facilitate the
student exchange program." This led one wise officer to suggest that "the participants should simply
ask themselves where else in the world an exchange
student could expect an official of the United States
government to travel several hundred miles [to
Leningrad] specifically for the purpose of deliver-
ing their mail and a new supply of peanut butter,
Kleenex, bouillon cubes and Finnish chocolate."

The simplest but at the same time the most
delicate problem facing institutions of higher
learning in their relationships with the federal
government is that posed by security and intelligence agencies, which exercise important responsibilities in the Soviet-American contest. The Committee's administrators and the universities from
the beginning were convinced that they must retain
their independence and integrity and that the contamination of one scholar or institution by improper

relationships with security and intelligence agencies would taint the integrity of all. In addition,
they were aware that the personal safety of any
American who served one of these agencies would be
threatened while he was in the Soviet Union. Finally, scholars and government officials agreed that
any relationships between organizations such as the
Committee or IREX, or any of their participants,
and intelligence and security organizations might
destroy the entire exchange program, thereby denying future generations of scholars the opportunity
to study in areas of their special interest, substantially reducing our knowledge and understanding
of the Soviet Union and Eastern Europe, and, of
course, throwing a shadow on the total Soviet-
American relationship.

     Many American scholars are deeply critical of
our security and intelligence organizations, in
part because they do not accept their importance
in this unsettled world. Moreover, these agencies
are relatively new in our life, involve great secrecy, and have on occasion acted most improperly.
This attitude became increasingly censorious in the
late 1960s and 1970s as views and moods changed, as
the nature of the contest between the rival states
and systems seemed to shift, and as some of these
agencies' less-scrupulous means of collecting information and influencing affairs in other countries
became known.

     Relations with the Federal Bureau of Investiga-
tion (FBI) have constituted no problem. Before September 1958, when the first academic exchange program
began, the FBI, alerted by the success of men such
as Klaus Fuchs and by the skill of Soviet agents in
subversion, paid particular attention to the few
Soviet scholars who visited our campuses. It carried out obvious surveillance of Soviet employees
of the United Nations or representatives in the
Soviet Mission to the United Nations who attended
classes on the campus of Columbia University. In
1957 it persuaded the newly established Office of
East-West Contacts in the Department of State to
request that the universities meet the first few
East European scholars at the airport, keep a record
of their residences, and report their travel plans.

The universities rejected these requests emphatically, refused to play any role in surveillance, and urged the FBI to stay off their campuses. These vigorous decisions were immensely important in establishing policies both for the universities and also for the government agencies.

The institutions involved in founding the Inter-University Committee agreed that it should undertake no activities for the FBI, which ended surveillance of Soviet scholars on university campuses in August 1958. To ensure that no connection whatsoever existed with the FBI, the Committee discouraged FBI inquiries concerning either Soviet or American participants or Committee activities. Whenever consultation was necessary because of KGB interventions against American participants in the Soviet Union, or on the two or three occasions when the FBI had evidence that a Soviet participant was not a genuine scholar and was engaged in improper activities, the chairman of the Committee discussed that incident with responsible security or intelligence officers. The Committee's decision and experience helped persuade IREX to establish a policy under which no member of the staff except the executive director may discuss any IREX matter with either the FBI or the CIA. Both of these organizations have thoroughly understood this position and have sought information only in these restricted circumstances.

The founders of the Committee probably exaggerated the interest that intelligence officers would have in the exchange programs. They believed that the relationships of the Committee and its participants with the CIA would be more difficult to control than with the FBI, largely because the FBI is generally restricted to the United States while the CIA has worldwide responsibilities. Moreover, the CIA was established only in 1947, it grew rapidly, and its procedures and controls were not so clear and tight as those of the Bureau. Above all, it was eager to obtain information concerning the Soviet Union and Eastern Europe, about which its knowledge and understanding were much less profound than now.

The Committee's administrators in the early
years understood the desperate need at that time
for reliable information concerning the Soviet
Union, and they had some knowledge of how intelligence organizations operate because many of them,
like me, had served in the Department of State, the
Office of Strategic Services, or some intelligence
service during World War II or the Korean War.
They showed great foresight in prohibiting all contact with all intelligence agencies and in announ-
cing the automatic rejection or recall of any participant who engaged in intelligence activities.
Their major concern was that an unwary or foolish
young scholar might agree to collect information
or to carry out some other function for an intelligence agency while in the Soviet Union.

Throughout their history the Committee and its
successor organization have remained exclusively
interested in scholarly activities and have had no
ties with the CIA or any other intelligence or
security organization, except when discussing KGB
interventions and activities with responsible intelligence officers. They have received no funds
from any such organization, they have provided them
no information, and the CIA has had no influence
whatsoever on their policies or actions. Because
of their determination to prevent any improper contacts, the Committee and IREX have warned every
applicant not only to reject any approach that
intelligence or other government agencies might
make, but to report any incidents that occur. The
selection committee interview teams asked each
applicant specifically if he had had any government
employment, particularly in intelligence, as well
as one or two other questions designed to test his
integrity and sophistication in handling an attempt
by American or Soviet intelligence agencies to
engage him in improper activities.

Every participant in the main programs administered by the Committee and IREX signed a
pledge that he would undertake no activity other
than the scholarly one for which he was selected.
From the first year of the program, this pledge
read: "Participation in this program carries an

obligation for full-time graduate study during the tenure of the participant. This precludes any work for others, with or without pay, except as is called for by virtue of your undertakings with your degree sponsor in your university." The Committee was so convinced of the centrality of this issue that the universities reviewed it in detail at each of the annual meetings until 1965, when it apparently had faded away.

The senior administrators of our security and intelligence agencies shared our scholars' concern about the need to protect the integrity of the academic exchange programs. As a matter of policy, the CIA and these other organizations have refrained from trying to use the institutions that administer the exchange programs or the participants themselves for intelligence purposes. These intelligence officers quickly understood the long-term national need for a program which increased the number and quality of those engaged in research concerning the Soviet Union and that an effort to use this program for clandestine activity would jeopardize an essential educational function. Moreover, they appreciated that most young Americans are skeptical of relationships with the government and would not only refuse to serve an intelligence organization but would probably publicize any approach to them. In addition, humanists and social scientists in Soviet dormitories for a semester or an academic year would learn little, if anything, of value to the CIA. Moreover, intelligence officers no doubt considered both hazardous and unproductive the use of unskilled young scholars resident in the Soviet Union for a prolonged period for some kind of sub-versive activity. They must believe, too, that the KGB would quickly identify any young scholar who unwisely accepted intelligence functions.

The interest of the universities and of the CIA in avoiding contact was sharpened in 1956, the first year in which scholars were sent to the Soviet Union for thirty days as tourists, when a new and ambitious West Coast employee of the CIA sought to persuade one of these scholars to be alert for in-formation of interest to intelligence officers. The scholar not only rejected the suggestion, but he

informed the Committee chairman. Wallace arranged
that a senior scholar explain to Allen Dulles, then
Director of the CIA, the necessity that there be
no relationships whatever between the CIA and participants. Dulles quickly agreed that the Agency
would under no circumstances seek to use scholars
on this program. This agreement was renewed in
1960, and it was reviewed and renewed annually
thereafter until the need for it had ended.[8]

The Committee knowingly nominated young men
and women who had worked in military intelligence
or for the National Security Agency, the CIA, or
other such organizations while fulfilling their
military obligations. The selection committees
judged these applicants as they had any other and
concluded after careful review that the service had
been open and honorable and that it had ceased.
They saw no reason to discriminate against a young
man or woman who had served his country creditably,
even though they recognized the interpretation
Soviet officials, especially the KGB, would inevitably reach.

The Committee and IREX have been so scrupulous-
ly careful that no participant has engaged in intelligence activities in the Soviet Union or Eastern
Europe, so far as anyone engaged in the Committee
or IREX has been able to determine. It is reassuring that the Soviet government in its attacks in
the press has produced no evidence to demonstrate
that the Committee, IREX, or any of their partici-

[8]After 1960 this commitment by the CIA applied only to
the exchange of graduate students and young scholars and to
the summer program for language teachers. The former of these
has always been the principal activity of the Committee and
IREX, and it remains the most important single element in the
academic exchange program. The CIA has refused to commit
itself from contacting senior scholars. However, I have no
evidence that the CIA has in fact asked any senior scholar to
undertake activities of any kind. Moreover, the reason against
the CIA's asking a senior scholar and against his accepting
any assignments are at least as impressive as those against a
younger scholar's doing so. Both the Committee and IREX
have obliged all scholars to report any attempt by an intelligence agency to contact them.

pants did in fact serve any intelligence purpose,
or that the CIA sought to use any of the organizations engaged in the academic exchange programs.
Moreover, so far as I have been able to determine,
the Soviet Union has never complained that any
American intelligence organization sought to sub-
vert a Soviet participant.

I did learn years afterwards that the Committee in one of its first years had sent to the
Soviet Union a young man who had concealed from the
selection committee that he had worked for several
years for an intelligence organization. His dis-
honorable action in suppressing information he
knew to be significant casts doubt on his good
sense and integrity. The Soviet press later attacked him, suggesting that his trip to the Soviet
Union was made "at the instigation of the CIA."[9]
However, many scholars have been similarly attacked,
and we have no evidence he acted improperly while
in the Soviet Union. Moreover, he has since traveled to the Soviet Union on a number of occasions
and maintains excellent relations with leading
Soviet intellectuals. It seems unlikely that he
would have returned to the Soviet Union if he were
or had been an agent, or that the Soviet government
would have admitted him and then allowed him to
leave if it believed so.

Annually, through 1965, an applicant each year
reported an inquiry by a CIA employee. The Committee after careful study concluded that each incident
was the responsibility of an over-eager officer
whose function was interviewing Americans who had
traveled to parts of the world on which intelligence
is limited. These new officers, located far from
Washington, were unaware of the agreement made by
Dulles and renewed later, and they were often not
well informed concerning the Committee. The CIA
immediately reprimanded them. So far as I can tell,
these incidents ended in 1965.

One incident, an applicant's report that a
fellow graduate student had asked her to serve the
CIA while in the Soviet Union, illustrates the

[9]Pravda, March 1, 1967.

fascination with secret intelligence, the Committee's determination to defend its integrity, and
the alacrity with which applicants reported improper approaches by intelligence officers. The
Committee, university administrators, the FBI,
and the CIA conducted independent inquiries. We
all learned that the graduate student had no connection with any government organization and was
simply trying to impress the young lady with his
importance. I have been told that such incidents
are not rare and that self-appointed agents are a
common plague for intelligence agencies.

Participants, particularly those who expect
to return for further study, face a quandary after
they have returned from the Soviet Union. The
Committee's information was not precise or complete,
simply because it did not inquire concerning the
activities of participants after their return. However, in the early years, when knowledge concerning
life in the Soviet Union was less common than now
and when judgments concerning insights participants
could acquire were exaggerated, intelligence or
security officers sought to interview some participants after they had returned. The Royal Canadian
Mounted Police and other national security organizations have also interviewed some of their nationals,
presumably concerning political, social, and economic developments and perhaps concerning friends
and acquaintances. The Committee informed participants that this might happen and explained the
dilemma this raises for some scholars, who are
tempted to assist a responsible government agency
engaged in an important function but who are determined to preserve their integrity to shield
Soviet friends and the program from contamination,
and to return to the Soviet Union with their record
and conscience absolutely clean. My impression
from random, informal conversations with some participants is that such interviews were quite in-
frequent. Some participants responded, others
refused.

Some of the CIA's other activities that became
public knowledge in the mid-1960s, and that then
ceased, led the Committee to protest because they
threatened the fundamental integrity of all study

of the Soviet Union and the relationships on which
the Committee's work was based. Moreover, they
strengthened Soviet suspicion of all organizations
engaged in cultural exchanges. Thus, in the late
1950s in particular, the CIA persuaded some youngish
Americans to travel to the Soviet Union as tourists,
to take photographs, and to obtain information in
other discreet ways. The Soviet police apprehended
some, if not all. Some were students or graduate
students, and their activities threw suspicion upon
all students and universities, and upon the exchange
program.

Some other CIA activities also threatened to
poison the academic well. For example, American
newspapers disclosed in 1967 that the CIA had
covertly subsidized extensive research and publication in the social sciences on a number of campuses,
without its role being known in many cases, even
to many of the scholars assisted. For example, it
provided a substantial part of the financial requirements of the Center of International Studies
at MIT from 1951 through 1966. They also revealed
that the CIA had provided financial support to the
National Student Association, which from 1959
through 1963 exchanged two young scholars with the
communist youth organizations of the Soviet Union
and of Poland and which in 1966-67 administered a
small exchange of graduate students with Poland.

Finally, in the late 1950s and early 1960s
the CIA established several temporary phony foundations, such as the Northcraft Educational Fund and
the J. N. Kaplan Fund, which made available a small
number of grants to "students" for travel in the
Soviet Union as tourists. The Program for Intercultural Communications, designed to assist young
scholars to visit the Soviet Union and converse
with Soviet students, was so skillfully established
in 1962 that the official organization of scholars
interested in Russia and Eastern Europe published
its advertisements. It also fooled two senior political science specialists on the Soviet Union, who
served on its board of directors. Later, the CIA
apparently acquired control of one or two organizations that private individuals began and which
foundations then helped by providing scholarly

books to Soviet visitors and by mailing additional volumes after they had returned to the Soviet Union. Corrupting a thoroughly good cause with clandestine financing thus enabled the Soviet government, which considers even scholarly books instruments of ideological aggression, to denounce all efforts to improve the flow of information as an intelligence plot.

The history of American academic exchanges with the Soviet Union and Eastern Europe helps identify some of the new challenges to the independence and integrity of our educational institutions which Soviet-American relations have created. They also illumine the changing role of our institutions of higher education in international politics and the complexity of the relationships this enlarged function creates for these institutions in their relations with agencies of our government, which are facing problems new to them. Finally, it reveals the ways in which these changes involve our educational institutions in negotiations with the Soviet government and its instruments, which again complicates the relations between American universities and the American government.

CHAPTER SIX

Negotiating with the Russians

The relationships between the Committee and
IREX and the Soviet government inevitably reflect
the fact that the American and Soviet governments
are rivals, in competition or collision at almost
every level of human endeavor in almost every part
of the world. In fact, they constitute a deadly
conflict between the ideas of Thomas Jefferson and
Woodrow Wilson and those of Karl Marx and Vladimir
Lenin over the way a society should organize, or
should be organized, and over the character of relations among states. A special sharpness therefore
occurs because the United States is a political and
social democracy, while the Soviet Union is authoritarian. One country has a pluralistic, open political system and is relaxed and free, while the other
is centralized and closed and treats all foreigners
as suspect agents of a hostile power. One, at the
moment the most advanced country in the world,
struggles with the problems of social change in an
industrial society and also serves as the unprepared
leader of a part of the world in a new and confusing
era. The other, still fettered by the Stalinist
system, struggles to catch up in economic power and
at the same time to extend its influence beyond its
frontiers and those of neighboring states that it
dominates. In addition, the capabilities of the
two countries for exchanges are not equal, which

raises problems on both sides because sharing resources and opportunities among unequals is complicated, in trade as in scholarship, even when
the two sides share a common culture and have similar goals. Both governments are naturally interested in advancing their own interests and are
dynamic in different ways, and they find measuring
success in academic exchanges difficult; the benefits are often invisible, and each side perceives
its own and the other's advantages in a different
way. Above all, academic exchanges are especially
sensitive for the Soviet Union because the free
movement of people and ideas strikes at the very
heart of the Soviet system.

In these relationships the two countries
therefore tend to be critical of each other, rather
than affectionate or appreciative, because "freedom
and the application of freedom" separate them the
most. The exchanges are thus not a cooperative
process but a competitive one. Both sides try to
take advantage of, not assist, the other. The
process of negotiation is therefore especially
tense.

Relations with the Soviet government and with
its controlled universities involve our institutions
in highly organized exchange arrangements with a
totalitarian government, which takes advantage of
the great discrepancies in power and authority.
While Soviet policies and practices have become
more relaxed and flexible in the 1970s than they
were in the 1960s, each agreement still tends to
fix views and patterns on both sides. One of the
dangers is that we accept this primitive system of
barter as a permanent practice (in 1975 it is already
seventeen years old), in violation of the ways in
which we live and believe scholars ought to work,
and we accommodate ourselves to the oppressive
Soviet negotiating position. Thus, in June 1975
IREX urged those junior scholars accepted by the
Soviet Union for 1975-76 to swallow their disappointment on assignment and access to archives in
the following words:

> Needless to say, there are a few cases
> in which political considerations may have

been of primary importance in the Soviet
placement of individual American students.
In such cases it is important to weigh
the imperfections of the placement re-
sulting from such a situation against the
overall potential benefits which the student would still be able to obtain from
exchange participation, even under what
may be unsatisfactory conditions.

The intrusion of political issues illustrates
another difficulty facing American universities,
which try to isolate research and teaching from
politics. For example, in the summer of 1960, during the trial of Captain Francis Powers, the pilot
of the U-2 plane shot down over Sverdlovsk, the
Soviet government expelled two Americans, three
British, and one French exchange participant. The
Ministry delayed the placement of American and British participants for that fall semester, and the
Soviet Academy of Sciences postponed the visits of
Americans in its program. Professor Seymour Slive,
who arrived in Leningrad then as a participant in
the brief exchange between Harvard and Leningrad
State University, never set foot in the university.

Similarly, in 1967-68, when the Soviet government was visibly upset by the "Czechoslovak Spring,"
it allowed the exchange with the Atomic Energy Commission to lapse for two years. In January 1971 the
Ministry canceled its small exchange program with
the University of Toronto and recalled its participants when Toronto maintained the nonacademic appointment of a Soviet physicist who had defected
from the Soviet Union in 1966. In 1973 the Ministry
delayed discussion of placement for twelve weeks
because of the visit of Brezhnev to the United
States. Thus, Ministry officials were due in New
York on May 12, but IREX and the American Embassy
in Moscow received no information concerning their
arrival until July 9. Assignments were then settled
in mid-August, very late indeed for scholars scheduled to leave that month.

The primacy of our scholars' interests in the
program for junior scholars rather than for research
and travel for senior scholars who had already lived
and studied in the Soviet Union helped shape the

framework for the academic exchange program, since
Soviet representatives have simply responded to our
proposals. This emphasis, the founders' under-
standable ignorance of Soviet institutions and practices, and the circumstances in which the negotiations took place led to a most unfortunate arrangement for the junior exchange, one that became permanent, as well as to supplementary procedures for
senior scholars that have always been complicated.

During the 1957-58 negotiations, both governments were determined that prospects for agreement
not be spoiled by premature disclosures. Consequently, the Department of State did not fully inform the universities and private organizations ultimately involved, although they did provide some
information. It even proposed an exchange of one
hundred junior scholars each year, without asking
the universities whether this was feasible. The
Committee, for example, assumed that the agreement
would engage Moscow and Leningrad State Universities
and seven or ten American universities. In fact,
the agreement asserted that "both parties will
provide for an exchange of students between Moscow
and Leningrad Universities, on the one hand, and
the United States universities on the other hand."
The records of the Committee's meetings in the
winter of 1957-58 show that its members assumed
that the major American and Soviet universities
would arrange their own exchange programs and that
the Committee would have only two functions, providing a clearing house for information and assisting small institutions whose faculty members had
had no experience in the Soviet Union.

However, the Committee learned, too late, that
American universities would not be directly involved
and that the Committee would deal with the Ministry
of Higher and Specialized Secondary Education. It
then learned that this Ministry has very little
authority in the Soviet government, that it controls
all Soviet universities and many other institutions
of higher education in a highly centralized system,
that these institutions are primarily concerned with
teaching, and that the Ministry has no influence with
the Soviet Academy of Sciences in whose institutes
most Soviet academic research is concentrated. Since
the Soviet government has refused to revise the 1958

arrangements, the exchange of junior scholars has
always operated under inequitable conditions; Soviet
junior scholars enjoy access to our universities, in
which most research is undertaken, while American
participants are denied access to the institutes
that could best serve their research interests.

It is curious that none of the Americans involved in founding the academic exchange program
suggested that the Soviet Academy of Sciences be
engaged. They learned only as the second year
began that the Academy of Sciences should participate if our junior scholars were to have opportunities equivalent to those Soviet junior scholars
received in this country. Indeed, only in the
fourth year did the Committee appreciate that its
proper correspondent was the Soviet Committee for
Cultural Relations with Foreign Countries, then
often called the Romanovsky Committee. Until
December 1967, when the Cultural Affairs Division
of the Soviet Ministry of Foreign Affairs assumed
responsibility, this institution coordinated all
Soviet cultural exchange activities and controlled
access to all institutions of higher learning,
including the universities, the Academy of Sciences,
the Academy of Medicine, the Academy of Pedagogical
Sciences, and all the institutes of the Ministry
of Culture.

The weakness of the Ministry of Higher and
Specialized Education may explain some of its
inefficiency and casuistry. Thus, on four occasions,
after the Ministry had accepted an American for
study, the Ministry of Foreign Affairs denied him
a visa. In one of these instances the Ministry
explained that the equipment which the American
expected to use was being overhauled. Then it informed the Committee that a scholar from the People's
Republic of China was working in the same laboratory.
It then proposed assigning the American to another
institution. Finally, it abandoned explanations
and simply did not answer inquiries. In 1966 the
Ministry of Agriculture withdrew three participants
from the United States without the knowledge or
consent of the Ministry of Higher Education. In the
fall of 1967 the Ministry was not even able to provide housing for American participants in the Moscow

State University dormitories to which they had always been assigned because they had been commandeered for the celebration of the fiftieth anniversary of the November Revolution. In addition, the Ministry had no influence with the Main Archival Administration, which was under the KGB until 1960 and then was placed under the Council of Ministers.

However, the Committee and IREX were especially concerned because the Ministry has little influence with the Soviet Academy of Sciences. Thus, while the institutes of the Academy could arrange that the Ministry nominate their scholars for research in American universities, the Ministry rarely was able, or perhaps did not attempt, to persuade them to accept our junior scholars. When American universities invited senior Soviet scholars who had appointments in an Academy institute as well as in a university to lecture, the Ministry usually rejected the invitation, without informing the scholars, on the grounds that they were doing "fundamental work in the Academy of Sciences" and therefore were not eligible.

After the Ministry refused in 1959 to assign a young American geographer to the Academy institute he requested, the Committee arranged the insertion of an appendix to the November 1959 exchanges agreement declaring that each participant's study plan "can, where appropriate and possible, include work in research institutes which are outside the system of higher education establishments." However, its efforts to use this declaration were unavailing.

The Deputy Minister of Higher Education, S. A. Yudachev, in Bloomington, Indiana, in March 1961 agreed that the Ministry "will take measures necessary to expand the number of institutions of higher learning" open to Committee scholars. However, after he had returned to Moscow he forwarded a translation that indicated instead that the Ministry "will consider measures necessary to expand the number of institutions of higher learning." In subsequent biannual negotiations, the Ministry of Foreign Affairs continually rejected American efforts to incorporate in the agreement phrases such as "opening the whole range of scholarly institutions"

of both sides to all junior participants. Unfortunately, American universities would not endorse
a 1962 proposal to resolve this issue by denying
access to our universities to scholars from Academy
institutes closed to American junior scholars.

The establishment of IREX in 1968 to administer the ACLS and Ford Foundation programs, and
those of the Committee as well in 1969, has
strengthened the American bargaining position by
creating one instrument to deal with both the
Ministry and the Soviet Academy of Sciences in
the humanities and social sciences. Persistent
pressure and imaginative IREX policies have contributed to some relaxation of restrictive Soviet
policies but little substantive progress. Thus,
IREX in the 1970s has encouraged and supported
colloquia bringing together small groups of
American and Soviet social scientists and historians from our universities and from Soviet
universities and Academy institutes. It has established direct connections with important
institutes, particularly the Institute of the USA.
It has financed invitations from Soviet institutes
to American university scholars in fields in which
the Soviet Union is especially interested, such as
Chinese studies, and it has supported visits to our
universities and to international conferences by
Soviet scholars from both universities and institutes. In 1973 it proposed to the Ministry and
the Academy of Sciences the establishment of an
American coordinating office in Moscow and of a
Soviet coordinating office in New York. If such
offices should be established and if our National
Academy of Sciences should agree to participate,
IREX might succeed in further blurring the distinc-
tion between the Ministry and the Academy. In
September 1974 IREX and the Soviet Academy established a Commission on the Social Sciences and
Humanities to facilitate joint research projects
on problems of mutual interest. Its first meeting,
in New York in the spring of 1975, planned cooperation by Soviet and American research institutes in
the application of quantitative methods to historical studies and symposia on subjects such as edi-
torial principles in editing classics, Soviet and
American foreign trade laws, and local government.

This agreement enlarges our universities' ties
with Soviet Academy institutes, but years will
no doubt pass before it produces substantive
cooperative work and aids the junior scholar.

For whatever reasons, of the thirty-eight
young scholars whom the Ministry accepted for
1973-74, it placed one in the Academy of Sciences,
one in the Academy of Pedagogical Sciences, and
one in the Uzbek Academy of Sciences. The following year, when it accepted fifty, it placed
two in institutes of the Academy of Sciences,
one in an institute of the Academy of Pedagogical Sciences, and three others in other institutes outside its jurisdiction. However, when
it accepted fifty-two for 1975-76, it placed only
one in an Academy institute, so the problem
remains.

Before reviewing the specific difficulties of
negotiating with the Ministry of Higher Education,
and other Soviet agencies, one must recognize that
the Committee inadvertently created problems for
Soviet officials. Its character must have baffled
them because it was an organization of private and
state universities, united for this purpose only
and cooperating with the Department of State, but
at the same time quite independent of it and on
occasion in disagreement with it. An organization
utterly unthinkable in the Soviet Union, it also
differed from the British Council and the Deutsche
Forschungsgemeinschaft, public corporations established by the British and German governments to
administer their cultural programs abroad.

Our cultural habits, particularly our interest
in efficiency, neatness, and dispatch, also created
problems. Committee requests for detailed information concerning Soviet applicants, including transcripts, confused them, as did its sending quantities of materials concerning American scholars. In
May 1960 the Committee forwarded a hundred pages of
materials concerning twenty-eight nominees, in addition to their academic transcripts. One especially long letter in 1963 that complained about a
number of Soviet actions was ten pages in length,
single-spaced.

The independence of American universities
puzzles Soviet officials. They simply cannot
comprehend the inability of the Committee and
IREX to assign a Soviet scholar to a particular
university or to move him freely from one to
another. American insistence on university principles, even such an elementary one that a university select Soviet scholars to lecture on its campus rather than have the Ministry appoint them,
constantly puzzles them.

Finally, the quality and character of our
participants no doubt worries Soviet officials
because most are different from others with whom
they deal. Only ten percent of the American participants from 1958 through 1975 have been scientists. Most have been particularly interested in
history, government, and literature, all quite
sensitive subjects in the Soviet Union. They
usually speak Russian well and have had excellent
training concerning Russian history and culture.
These young scholars are eager to work in archives,
which Soviet scholars ordinarily do not enter until
they are in their mid-thirties. Their purposeful-
ness, individualism, tempo, and casual behavior
clearly make Soviet officials uncomfortable, particularly those in organizations such as Intourist,
which generally deal only with groups or delegations.

Finally, many Soviet professors who have not
had knowledgeable foreign students in their seminars
or working under their direction are wary because of
the danger that close contact with foreigners may
one day create. While some professors "radiated
intelligence, modesty, good-will, and humanity" and
won the admiration and affection of the American
participants, others remained frightened, reluctant
to establish close relationships, and devious.

Traditional Soviet negotiating practices constitute the most obvious difficulties. Soviet
officials have a clear and narrow definition of
Soviet interests. They have little concern for the
goals of othe other party or for the long-term
relationship. They see every issue as a battle,
and they are practical and tough in seeking their
goals. They try to take advantage of every strength

and opportunity, especially our concern with
reducing international tension and our efforts
to persuade the Soviet government to relax its
policies. In their relations with Americans they
rely on our giving full consideration to legitimate Soviet interests and to larger permanent
international concerns and on our reluctance to
risk ending relationships. Thus, for every step
toward a wider and freer exchange, they insist
upon a specific Soviet advantage. In short, Soviet
officials represent a very intractable government
that has a parochial view of the world and that is
not generous or understanding in its relations
with others.

Claiming virtuous triumphs in negotiations
with Soviet authorities is a silly practice and
often conceals basic failures. The Committee and
IREX have both made errors and suffered defeats.
These reflect basically the nature of negotiations,
especially with the Soviet Union, as well as our
own shortcomings. Thus, the Committee's founders
were well-informed specialists with considerable
insight into the Soviet political system and the
difficulties involved in negotiations with Soviet
officials. They recognized that no community of
aims existed, and they made few "fatuous gestures
of good will." At the same time, especially in
the early years, Committee officers lacked experience, and were perhaps too anxious to reach
agreement. Soviet officials took advantage of this.

The relationship is far more complicated
than it appears because our powers for dealing
with the Soviet government are so limited. We
cannot force it to allow American scholars the
freedoms necessary or to treat our scholars as we
treat theirs. At the same time, we cannot inflict
similar restrictions on Soviet scholars whom our
universities have admitted, because this would be
a violation of our own values and would in the long
run harm us even more than it would the offending
country.

The Committee kept the program under continual
review and remained prepared to close exchanges
whenever Soviet performance was irresponsible or

vicious and whenever no sign of progress was visible. The Committee and IREX have sought to be firm and fair in advancing American interests, while at the same time giving full attention to those of the Ministry and seeking to understand and remove Soviet misconceptions. They have sought reasonable equity, not mathematical equality. In dealing with the Soviet government, they have attempted to advance our interests vigorously, while remaining courteous and candid. They have been persistent and forthright in providing information and views and in executing policies, and they have pressed the Soviets to act as responsibly. Appalled by the time and energy required by minor issues that seemed settled but are forever revived, they have sought to move our relationships into productive channels. In fact, the American actions that have most impressed Soviet representatives have almost certainly been the flood of proposals for new kinds of exchanges and new ways of ending squabbles over issues in themselves trivial but important to both sides as matters of principle.

At the same time, the Committee issued warnings and vigorous protests against unjustified actions by the Ministry, the KGB, or the Soviet press. In November 1963, when the Committee learned that the KGB had without justification arrested and detained Professor Frederick Barghoorn of Yale University, it was prepared to recall its scholars from the Soviet Union and to close its universities' campuses to Soviet scholars when Barghoorn was released. It ended the bilateral arrangements between four sets of universities after two years had revealed their futility, and it terminated the exchange of lecturers in 1966 when efforts to make it effective proved unsuccessful. It reduced the number from fifty to forty in the main program in the 1964 negotiations because the Ministry denied admission without persuasive reasons to many nominees and restricted our participants so tightly to Moscow and Leningrad. It gave a moratorium to the summer language teachers' program in 1968 when the Ministry would not confirm its participation by an agreed date. Similarly, when extraordinary Soviet tardiness in responding to nominations of senior scholars reduced American nominations over a three-

year period from sixty-nine to forty-four to
thirty-seven, IREX indicated it would terminate
that exchange unless the Ministry was more efficient. The Soviets responded by "reasonably prompt
acceptance of all of our 1974-1975 nominees." In
January 1975, when the Ministry announced that
American married couples would have to pay an
additional thirty rubles a month for their rooms,
IREX declared it would deduct these costs from
those available for Soviet participants in the
United States, and the Ministry retreated.

The Ministry's refusal to grant admission to
1 of every 7 junior nominees and 1 of every 9
senior nominees of the Committee and IREX from
1958 through 1974 has been a fundamental issue
because it involves the central purpose of the
program. The 1958 agreement noted that each side
was responsible for choosing its participants.
The Department of State apparently believed that
nomination would guarantee a candidate's admission
to the other country. However, from 1958 through
1969 the Soviet government denied admission to 55
of the 390 Americans nominated in the program for
junior scholars, an average of 5 each year for the
entire period and of 8 for the years after 1965.
The number of rejections after 1969, when IREX
assumed responsibility, averaged 4 per year until
1974-75, when the Ministry for the first time since
1962 accepted all junior nominees.

The Soviets have rejected nominations from
other American organizations in the same fashion.
Thus, between 1961 and 1975, the Soviet Academy
of Sciences rejected twenty-four ACLS nominations,
while the ACLS rejected only two Academy nominations. The Soviet Academy rejected three of
fifteen ACLS nominations in 1969-70 and six of
nineteen in 1972-73. It rejected one ACLS nominee,
and the Ministry of Foreign Affairs denied a visa
to another of the eight nominees in 1974-75,
when two senior IREX nominees were also rejected.
Some of the Soviet actions were especially annoying
because the Ministry of Foreign Affairs without
explanation simply denied visas to scholars whom
the Ministry of Higher Education or the Academy
had accepted.

About as many Soviet nominees have been denied
the opportunity to study in the United States, but
for different reasons and in different ways. From
1958 to 1969 American universities were unable to
accept 39 Soviet nominees, almost all because none
was capable of directing the proposed research
projects, such as construction of railroad engines.
However, most denials were the responsibility of
the Department of State, which, under the Immigration and Naturalization Act of 1952, as amended,
has to recommend a waiver of "inadmissability"
before it can authorize a visa enabling a Soviet
citizen to enter this country. From 1958 to 1969
the Department of State denied admission to 47
scholars of the 457 nominated. Since 1969 the
Department has denied admission to 17 of the approximately 250 nominated, all because they wished to
study in scientific fields closely associated with
national security.

The Department of State consults with the
Department of Defense before it concludes that
granting a visa is in the national interest. On
occasion the Department of State has then rejected
Soviet scholars in fields of study critical to
national security or in which the United States
had achieved significant advances of a break-
through nature beyond those of Soviet science and
technology. In many of these cases even an American
scholar interested would have needed a security
clearance. The Department has also denied admission
when the Soviet government sought to use the academic exchange to obtain entrance in fields in
which it was failing to honor obligations under
other agreements. For example, the Soviet government allowed the nuclear energy exchange agreement
to lapse and then tried to place a scholar in
nuclear energy through the academic exchange program.
Similarly, the Department rejected a Soviet participant interested in metallurgy, in which the
exchanges agreement provided for an exchange of
delegations that the Soviets were delaying and
preventing. The Committee and the universities
reviewed each of the Department's actions carefully
to make certain the decisions were sound and on
occasion persuaded the Department to reverse its
position. The Soviet government never protested

these decisions, presumably because it understood
them fully.

The reasons for which the Soviet government
has denied admission to American scholars clearly
illuminate the differences between the two systems,
their levels of development, and their definitions
of "security" and "sensitivity." Basically, the
Soviet government has denied admission to nominees
who wished to study subjects it considered politically sensitive: modern history and politics;
Russian and Soviet foreign policy and Russia's
relations with other states, even in the nineteenth
century; the Soviet economy; various religious
sects, even long before 1917; and relations between Russians and Poles or between Russians and
any national minority. For example, no American
has been admitted to study the organization and
operation of the Soviet central government, the
Soviet Communist Party, or relations between the
government and the Party. The Ministry denied an
application to study the international communist
youth organization from 1919 to 1943 because it was
a "non-state organization." It rejected the various applications to study Russian foreign policy
in the nineteenth century because these involved
"relations with other countries." In 1964 it informed an American who wished to study "differential land rent and related questions of price
formation in the collective farm sector" that he
could not study in the Soviet Union and instead
"should read carefully the speeches of Premier
Khrushchev in order to understand differential
rent." Between 1958 and 1969 five of the twelve
Americans who wished to study the Soviet economy
were denied admission; this particularly annoyed
the Committee, which placed all twenty-six Soviet
economists interested in similar subjects in the
United States.

On occasion Soviet rejections simply baffled
the Committee. For example, the Ministry in 1964
denied admission to a scholar to study the work of
Victor Shklovsky on the grounds that Shklovsky was
a "second-rate writer" who did not deserve scholarly attention and that "the American side did not
have enough time to spare in the exchange program

to devote to study of second-rate topics." On
another occasion the Ministry refused to accept a
nominee who wished to study Russian political
theory in the sixteenth century because it was a
religious subject and therefore unworthy of study.
It rejected an application to study the Revolution
of 1905 because so much research had been published
that nothing new could be discovered.

The Committee and IREX considered these rejections of crucial significance because they violated
the foundation on which the exchange program is
based as well as the principles essential for research. Moreover, we placed Soviet scholars in
every field of research, including those that dealt
with our most painful social problems, in those
institutions best qualified to serve them. Indeed,
the Committee and IREX have placed every Soviet
scholar nominated in the social sciences and
humanities.

American institutions and scholars also protest
because this Soviet practice exerts an important
influence upon the direction of American scholarship
and, in the long run therefore, on the way in which
we look at the Soviet Union. It also helps to
create an imbalance among the fields of study
within our universities that may become permanent,
since scholar-teachers tend to reproduce themselves.
American research concerning the Soviet Communist
Party, foreign policy, economic development, and
political dissent will no doubt remain of high
quality. On the other hand, those who will publish
and teach about these important subjects would
surely have acquired greater knowledge and insight
if they had been allowed to study in the Soviet
Union. Moreover, the number of scholars engaged
in research on these central subjects would clearly
be greater if opportunity for research in the Soviet
Union were assured.

Thus, in the first seven years of the junior
exchange program the Committee sent eighty-three
historians to study those aspects of Russian history
acceptable to the Soviet government (the Ministry
sent only seventeen in American history), but it
sent none to study issues that were recent or

sensitive. Similarly, it nominated a number to
study local government, but none (even now) to
analyze Soviet foreign policy or relations between
the Party and the government. Because of known
Soviet restrictions, no American has even applied
for research on the lives of Soviet leaders; the
purges; critical Soviet political and social problems, such as anti-Semitism; the place of religion
in Soviet life; or agricultural or industrial
productivity. In 1971-72 none of the thirty-five
IREX participants was in political science or
government, and only four had projects that dealt
with the twentieth century. In 1972-73 only thirteen of the thirty-nine were engaged in projects
involving the twentieth century, while nine were
working in periods before the nineteenth century.
In 1973-74 twenty-four of the thirty-eight accepted
were interested in the history of Russia before
1917.

Committee scholars and university representatives discussed these rejections and their effects
frequently, and IREX officials also continually
review the issues. The problems they pose and
the response of the Committee, IREX, and our universities constitute a splendid sample of the difficulties involved in negotiating with the Russians
and of the limited number of alternative actions
open.

Each year the universities at the Committee's
annual meeting considered these rejections and
other abuses before deciding to continue, while
pressing hard for substantial improvement. They
did not even consider the adoption of reciprocal
practices, such as denying Soviet scholars the
right to study recent American history. They also
agreed that they should not penalize Soviet scholars
in this country for actions their government took.

A third option, which the Committee and the
Ministry used in the first two years, was providing
alternate nominees for those who might be denied
admission for one reason or another. The Committee
in the 1960s allowed the Ministry to nominate alternates by receiving and seeking to assign a
larger number of Soviet nominees than the number

the agreement then provided. IREX followed this policy in 1974. In 1961, for example, the Ministry nominated sixty-three candidates, and in 1962 fifty-eight, for fifty places. The Committee sought to place all these nominees, and it did place forty-seven for 1961-62 and forty-six for 1962-63. In addition, the Committee, after long consideration, proposed in 1965 that each side nominate five or ten more candidates than the agreement provided. Curiously, the Ministry rejected the proposal.

American scholars are of course accustomed to selecting alternates for fellowships and positions. However, the Committee and IREX were extremely reluctant to accept a system that included alternates because they and the universities are determined to retain control of selection. Giving the Ministry a list of fifty names for forty places in effect would give it a role in selecting our candidates, a power neither the Committee nor IREX would grant the Department of State. Second, the Committee was convinced that the Ministry would continue to reject those interested in Soviet affairs and would use the system to eliminate others who would be bothersome or those who the Ministry thought might benefit the most.

In short, the Committee and IREX have responded by insisting on reasonable equity of opportunity, pressing for admission for all qualified scholars, and informing the Ministry we would place approximately the same number of Soviet scholars as the number of Americans the Ministry was willing to admit "on a rational placement basis." Thus, in June 1961, after the Ministry had denied admission to an American nuclear physicist, it nominated two Soviet nuclear physicists. The Committee, with the approval of the Atomic Energy Commission and the Department of State, indicated it would accept the two Soviet nominees if the Ministry would accept an American the following year. The Ministry did not respond, so the Committee denied admission to the two Soviet scholars. The following year the Ministry placed all of our nominees.

In June 1963, when the Ministry denied admission to three nominees for clearly untenable

reasons, the Committee refused to admit three
Soviet nominees in similar fields unless the
Ministry changed its position. The Ministry stood
firm, so none of the six was able to enjoy a year
of study in the other country. In 1965 the Committee offered to admit a Soviet specialist in
mathematical economics if the Ministry would
accept an American nominated in the same field.
The Ministry accepted this proposal but rejected
a similar one in 1969. In 1966, when the Soviet
Ministry of Foreign Affairs in late August denied
a visa to an American whom the Ministry had accepted, the Committee denied admission to a Soviet
scholar already accepted in a field that would
have required large expenses for research materials.
It adhered to this position, even after the Ministry withdrew another Soviet nominee and sought to
replace him with the denied Soviet scholar.

    In its response to Soviet rejections of
American nominees, and to Soviet policies that
hampered our participants in any way, IREX since
1969 has followed basically the same negotiating
practices as did the Committee. However, it has
been less firm in its defense of principles and
rights than was the Committee and has used more
"la douce parole" of Philip the Fair in its
negotiations with Soviet officials and in its
other actions. Thus, the 1969 report referred
to the invasion of Czechoslovakia as "distressing
developments" and "the difficulties of 1968."
Annoyed in 1971-72 by Soviet rejection of five
junior and two senior nominees, in particular for
the first time of some "whose writings on the Soviet
Union have been judged by the Soviet authorities
to contain unacceptable interpretations," IREX
rejected a Soviet nominee, only to reverse the
decision at the request of American scholars. In
the spring of 1975, when the Soviet government
denied a visa to a scholar whom the Academy of
Sciences had accepted, it took the same two steps
and finally became more firm, until the Soviet
government reversed its position. Thus, it first
declined to request a visa for a Soviet scholar on
the same program, only to admit him upon the urgent
request of his Soviet institution. It then chose
to decline to receive a Soviet scholar whose

behavior on a previous visit had destroyed his
prospective hosts' willingness to receive him
again. The Soviet Academy then rejected two more
senior American scholars, leading IREX to suspend
that program. Finally, the Soviet Academy accepted
the two Americans and the program was reinstated.

     In 1973-74 the Soviet government quite dramati-
cally began to relax its restrictions against admitting Americans interested in some subjects it
previously considered most sensitive. Thus, the
Ministry, while rejecting a sociologist who wanted
to study the impact of new workers from the country-
side and a specialist in Lithuanian folklore, accepted subjects similar to those it had systemati-
cally rejected in the past: the province of
Erevan under Persian and Russian administration
in the eighteenth and nineteenth centuries, the
Social Revolutionaries from 1901 to 1917, the role
of the police before World War I, and several subjects dealing with Soviet life, hitherto sacrosanct--
the impact of sociological research upon urban planning, ideology and technological innovation, the
attitudes of Soviet and American youth toward work,
and Soviet and American day care centers. For
1974-75 the Ministry accepted five specialists in
Soviet literature, a historian interested in change
in Soviet Central Asia, eight political scientists,
three sociologists, and even two economists. Many
of these young scholars failed to obtain the materials they requested, and the economists in particular
were restricted, but they were at least admitted.
For 1975-76 it placed historians and political
scientists interested in subjects such as nationalism in Galicia, which previously would have received
no consideration. However, it did not grant access
to essential archival materials. Moreover, a young
American scholar on his arrival in August 1975
learned that he had been assigned to Leningrad, not
Lvov, the central city in Galicia for his research
in which the Ministry had assured IREX he would be
placed.

     Another series of problems involved restric-
tions placed on American participants admitted to
the Soviet Union, which disturbed many so deeply
that they urged ferocious retaliation upon Soviet

scholars here. The continual dissatisfactions and
frustrations these exercised deeply affected the
view of everyone who dealt with Soviet officials
and therefore influenced all policies.

Most participants were not especially bothered
by the living conditions, which are those that
Soviet citizens experience. Thus, the quality of
the food, the size of dormitory rooms, the rare
availability of hot water in Leningrad and other
cities except Moscow, the long waits for elevators
and for all services, the hazards and annoyances
raised by the KGB, and all of the other discomforts
associated with Soviet life were not significantly
disturbing. In fact, most reveled in overcoming
the challenges and have described the semester or
year in the Soviet Union as an immensely valuable
and stimulating period. Many returned full of
admiration and respect for the Soviet scholars with
whom they had worked. Some lived and worked in
Moscow and Leningrad as they would have in an
American institution, and many were untouched by
police activities.

However, other handicaps and restrictions
bothered almost all. The first involved the status
the Ministry gives American junior participants.
The Committee in the winter of 1957-58 had decided
to send young scholars at the postdoctoral level,
but the exchanges agreement restricted the program
in the first year to graduate students, which produced permanent unfortunate consequences. In
general, rank and status are more important in the
Soviet Union than in the United States. Practices
once established there also become fixed, because
Soviet officials are reluctant to change or even
to challenge accepted principles or procedures.
Moreover, the Ministry of Higher Education and Soviet
universities are principally interested in instruction rather than in research, and they are more
accustomed to deal with students and graduate
students than with research scholars. Consequently,
since all American participants during the first
year were graduate students, as were most in the
second year, the Ministry has always defined each
of our junior participants as aspirant stazhër, which
can probably be translated best as special graduate

student. The junior participants have thus been
subject to the direction and controls customary for
foreign graduate students, even if they were established young scholars with impressive publications.
In this status, each has had to submit a detailed
study plan to the Soviet professor to whom he had
been assigned, although his principal responsibility
remained to the professor in the United States
directing his thesis. Above all, he has had to
obtain the Soviet professor's support to gain access to libraries and archives and permission to
travel, even for study-related purposes. This has
often been difficult and sometimes impossible to
obtain, even for the most innocent topics. Most
Soviet professors are reluctant to recommend or
support access to archives, which were under the
administration of the Ministry of the Interior from
1939 until 1960 and which, in their minds, remain
a province of the KGB. The Ministry of the
Interior also controls travel.[1]

The participants' status and the genuine
shortage of housing in the Soviet Union contributed
to another strain, the Ministry's reluctance in the
first decade to allow American wives to accompany
their husbands.[2] The Committee insisted spouses be
encouraged to accompany their mates so that they
would share their professional experiences. Moreover, the Ministry's policy and its refusal to
allow children on the program for young scholars
until 1972 significantly reduced the number of
Americans interested, because a high percentage of
our graduate students are married and have families.
The Committee pressed constantly on this, always
assuring the Ministry that it would pay all costs

[1]The Ministry does grant one important special privilege:
it allows young American scholars in the Lenin Library in Moscow to use Reading Room Number 1, which is reserved for senior
scholars and is more quiet, comfortable, and efficient than
the other reading rooms.

[2]The Ministry was also most reluctant to allow wives
from other Western countries. For example, although it had
agreed to accept the wives of Canadian participants, the first
five and their wives in 1964 had to wait in Western Europe for
several weeks before they were admitted.

and even that it might pay the expenses of Soviet
wives the first year. It later invited the Ministry
to send both wives and children (almost no Soviet
participants have been women). Beginning in January
1967, it urged that the Ministry allow four married
couples to bring their children.[3]

At first the Ministry refused to allow any
wives, but it finally agreed in the early fall of
1958 to permit four of the twelve wives to accompany
their husbands, only to reverse its position on two.
It then raised obstacles for those wives who sought
visas for a month in the spring. For the second
academic year the Ministry agreed that it would
accept up to ten wives. In 1961 the Committee and
the Ministry reached an informal agreement that
the Ministry would allow approximately ten wives
each year to accompany their husbands, but in 1964
the Ministry sought to restrict each wife to only
four months. Moreover, Leningrad State University
would not accept married couples until 1964-65,
and it resisted even later accepting a participant
and his wife. However, Soviet acceptance of
spouses was complete by the end of the first decade
of this program.

Persuading the Ministry to admit children was
also a long struggle, but the Soviet government finally yielded in 1972-73 when it placed in Moscow or
Leningrad one couple with one child, three couples
with two children, and one couple with three children.
The Ministry in addition accepted a couple with two
children who withdrew. It rejected a family with
four children. For 1973-74 it accepted sixteen wives
of participants and three husbands of participants.
It placed two couples with two children each in Moscow (each family in one room), and one with one child
in Tashkent. In 1974-75 it accepted twelve husbands
with wives, two wives with husbands, four husbands
with their wives and children, and three wives with

[3]The National Academy of Sciences in its small exchange
program for senior scholars does not encounter this problem
because few of its participants remain more than a month.
Moreover, the Soviet Academy of Sciences has apartments, and
now a hotel of its own, for visiting scholars and their
families.

their husbands and children. The 1975-76 record
reveals even more clearly that the old restrictions
have been destroyed: participants include sixteen
husbands with wives, one wife with her husband, four
wives with seven children, and a total of eighteen
children.

No Soviet spouses have accompanied their
wives or husbands on Committee or IREX programs.
However, in December 1968 a Soviet participant
in the exchange between the Soviet Academy of
Sciences and the National Academy brought his
wife for a few months. Seven high energy
physicists were accompanied by their wives
when they arrived at the National Accelerator
in January 1972 for several months of experi-
ments arranged by the Atomic Energy Commission
and the State Committee for the Utilization
of Atomic Energy. By the fall of 1975, wives
of three senior Soviet participants in the
exchange between the ACLS and the Soviet
Academy of Sciences had accompanied their
husbands for the entire period of their stays.
In 1972-73, five; in 1973-74, seventeen; and in
1974-75, thirty-two Soviet wives paid visits
of one or two months to their husbands on the
junior scholar exchange. In short, Soviet
policy on this important human aspect of the
academic exchange program may be mellowing
in a most significant way.

The Ministry's decision to assign almost
all our participants to just two universities,
those in Moscow and Leningrad, has constituted
another annoying restriction, especially because
the Committee and IREX have assigned Soviet
participants to universities throughout the
United States. In the first five years the
Ministry placed only one American outside of
Moscow and Leningrad. Two hundred ninety-
five of our first three hundred participants
were assigned to those two cities. Between
1958 and 1969 the Committee placed Soviet
participants in sixty-two institutions in
thirty-four cities, while the Ministry placed
all but eleven Americans in Moscow and Leningrad. In 1974-75 IREX placed Soviet parti-

cipants in thirty universities, while ours were
concentrated in five Soviet universities.[4]

The Committee was naturally interested in
the organization and operation of that part of
the Ministry responsible for placing American
participants in Soviet institutions. So far as
the Committee could learn, the Ministry controls
all information, assigns the American participants, and also defines the system for choosing
Soviet participants. In the first few years
the Ministry simply assigned the Committee's
nominees to Moscow State and Leningrad State
Universities. It now distributes a few to other
cities. The Ministry ordinarily completes these
placements without discussion; it simply informs
university officials, sometimes several months
after it has reached its decision and has informed the Committee or IREX. The defects of
this system, both for American participants and
for the Soviet institutions and their faculty,
are obvious. Thus, in May 1969 the Ministry
was unable to name the advisors of American
participants for the next academic year, even
after it had assigned them all to Moscow and
Leningrad State Universities. Some participants
learned even in 1975 that the Ministry had not
informed their advisors of their coming. An
eminent Soviet scientist who has directed the
work of several junior scholars told an American
colleague in 1975 that he had never been asked
or informed of a participant's coming to work
with him; the American simply appeared at the
opening of the semester.

Substantial reasons did and do exist for
assigning most American participants to Moscow
and Leningrad. The original agreement identi-

[4]The British Council administered its placement system
under the same principles as we. In the first year of its
exchange program, it placed the twenty Soviet participants
in eleven British universities. Similarly, the Deutsche
Forschungsgemeinschaft in its first year placed Soviet
scholars in eight German cities, from which they traveled
freely throughout the Federal Republic. All German and British
participants were also limited then to Moscow and Leningrad.

fied Moscow State University and Leningrad State
University as the Soviet institutions to which
American participants would be assigned. Most
Americans have requested Moscow and Leningrad. In
fact, our fifty nominees in 1961-62 requested only
Moscow and Leningrad. Even in 1973-74 more than
forty of our fifty nominees proposed Moscow or
Leningrad, and forty-six of fifty requested one of
these two cities in 1974-75.

These two universities presumably have the
most distinguished Soviet faculties. Moscow and
Leningrad contain the most important libraries
and archives. In 1962, only four universities,
those in Moscow, Leningrad, Kiev, and Tashkent,
had foreign student offices and experience in
dealing with foreign students. Most other universities have primitive dormitory facilities,
and all are overcrowded. Indeed, the first participant assigned to Kiev was placed five miles
from the campus, shared a room with five other
men in a building that had one telephone for
460 students, and deeply resented the Committee's
success in getting him to Kiev, which he had
requested.

Moreover, some Soviet universities are in
areas closed to all foreigners. While the Committee and IREX have placed Soviet participants
in universities located in areas closed to Soviet
diplomats, the Soviet government has resolutely
denied our participants access or even travel to
closed areas in the Soviet Union. Finally, the
Soviet police would naturally prefer to have a
group of educated Americans who know Russian concentrated in the two cities where they have the
most experience in observing foreign visitors.

At the same time, other universities have
eminent scholars, who are in some cases better
known to foreigners than those at Moscow and
Leningrad. Moreover, Kiev naturally is a better
base for the study of Ukrainian literature, Tbilisi
for studying Georgian history, and Tashkent for
studying Uzbek than either Moscow or Leningrad.
Finally, the majority of our participants are
preparing to be Soviet specialists. They know

that Moscow and Leningrad do not constitute the
Soviet Union, and some seek to live in other
areas of that vast and varied country in order
to increase their understanding of Soviet culture
and Soviet society.

However, the Ministry remains most reluctant
to allow Americans to study in institutions outside
of the two principal cities. In fact, it has been
slow to permit Committee and IREX representatives
to measure the quality of other university faculties and facilities. Thus, in spite of sustained
efforts, no one from the Committee or IREX was
ever able to visit Saratov, which is known to have
a strong faculty in Russian literature. The
Ministry granted Committee representatives permission to visit the university in the academic
city near Novosibirsk after five years of requests,
and even then it gave less than twenty-four hours
notice. Americans interested in studying in cities
such as Irkutsk and Alma Ata have been denied
those opportunities. Similarly, our Public Health
Service administrators have noted that the groups
of American doctors traveling to the Soviet Union
have generally visited the same institutions in
just a few cities. By 1964 twenty-eight delegations had visited the Institute of Experimental
Pathology at Sukhumi.

Increasing pressure finally led to placement
of an American interested in Ukrainian literature
at Kiev in 1961 and a mathematician in the same
institution in 1965. Erevan was opened to a scholar
interested in Armenian history in 1965, when two
other Americans studied in Kiev. In 1967 the
Ministry placed a specialist in Lithuanian history
in Vilna and a physicist in Novosibirsk, the first
year the Soviet Academy of Sciences placed a
National Academy of Sciences nominee there. In
1968 a student of Uzbek was placed at Tashkent,
and in 1969 the Ministry on its own initiative
placed two Americans at Rostov and three at
Voronezh, both particularly suitable because of the
nominees' research interests. In 1973-74 the
Ministry placed only twenty-nine of the thirty-
seven IREX nominees in Moscow and Leningrad State
Universities. In 1974-75 it placed individuals in

Erevan, Kiev, Kharkov, Tashkent, Tbilisi, and
Voronezh. In 1975-76 it assured placement of
three in Tashkent, Lvov, and Dushanbe, only to
revise the promise on Lvov when fall came. However, much remains to be done to achieve the access to institutions throughout the Soviet Union
that Soviet scholars have always received in the
United States. Thus, in 1972-73 the thirty-eight
Soviet nominees came from nineteen different
institutions. The Ministry had placed Americans
in only nine of the nineteen and had denied access to many of the others.

Everyone in the exchange program has learned
the truth of the observation Adam Olearius made
in 1634: "Foreigners are allowed to travel in
Russia only with extreme difficulties and are
carefully watched during these travels. Because
of this reticence and general suspicion, foreigners
in Moscow can see only each other." American participants have learned that it is easier to obtain
permission to go abroad for a holiday than to
travel from Moscow to Leningrad, even though they
are entitled to an annual komandirovka, that is,
one study-related trip, with expenses paid. The
Committee and IREX, and above all our participants,
have been thoroughly annoyed not only by the
strict control over travel, but also by the arbitrary manner in which restrictive measures are
administered.

In an effort to provide participants from
both countries an opportunity to see substantial
parts of the host country, the Committee and Ministry in the first year arranged for end-of-the-year
group tours of two or three weeks' duration. A
private organization, the Committee on Friendly
Relations Among Foreign Students, administered
this for the Soviet participants, and Intourist
managed, or mismanaged, that in the Soviet Union.
Even these tours raised annoying problems. For
example, in 1958-59 the Committee paid the tour expenses of both the Soviet and the American participants. In 1962 and 1963 the Ministry sought to
eliminate Tashkent, Bukhara, Samarkand, and Erevan.
In 1964, after the Committee and the Ministry had
agreed on a fixed limit to their contributions

toward tour expense, the Ministry insisted that our
participants pay the balance for their expenses in
American currency. Finally, our participants were
not allowed to travel by themselves. In 1964 the
group in Leningrad even had to delay its trip for
two weeks until the professor assigned was able
to leave. After that year, at our insistence, the
annual tour was abandoned.

The Ministry of Higher Education has not only
refused to recognize the principle of travel for
recreation, but it insists that American participants follow a four-step procedure for even study-
related travel. The participant first has to
obtain approval from his academic advisor, then
of the foreign student office in the university,
then of the Office of Visas and Registration, a
police organization that processes internal pass-
ports, and, finally, of Intourist, which controls
tickets for public transportation and hotel reservations. The Ministry requires a minimum of ten
days' notice for obtaining permission even for
overnight travel.

A few participants have traveled with remarkable ease, perhaps because their academic
advisors were interested and powerful, perhaps
because they were more enterprising and energetic
than their colleagues, perhaps because the foreign
student offices and Intourist happened to be
particularly efficient in their cases. However,
travel in general is tightly restricted. Thus,
a Canadian scholar writing about Sholokhov was not
allowed to meet him or even to visit the Don country
during his year in the Soviet Union. One participant who documented his difficulties spent more
than forty hours obtaining the permission necessary
to make a study-related visit from Moscow to Leningrad, even though the Ministry had expressly approved that trip when it accepted him. I know of
only two Americans who were able to spend weekends
with classmates and of a very few who were able
to enjoy the kind of relaxed informal travel that
we take for granted in the United States. Even
in 1974-75, American participants found it very
difficult to transfer from Moscow to Leningrad, or
vice-versa, for two or three months of study.

Married couples had to organize exchanges of rooms with couples in the other city, or to separate during the travel period. More than half of the short tours to historical centers near Moscow and Leningrad were cancelled that year, and participants could visit Central Asia only when they organized a group of twenty-five foreigners. Even so, travel is generally easier than in the past.

Another problem involves access to archives open to Soviet scholars, but closed to ours. For most American participants, especially those in history and literature, research in government documents and the papers of important officials or intellectuals is a principal purpose of their trips. Being denied the opportunity to use essential sources is therefore a bitter disappointment. In fact, these denials led to the Committee chairman's annual January visit, a tradition that the British Council and IREX have followed. In the late 1960s the Soviets opened some archives just before the chairman arrived in January or just before the American participants had to leave in June.

The KGB administered these archives until 1960, when they were transferred to the Main Archival Administration of the Council of Ministers, but presumably with the same men and women responsible and with similar policies and procedures. The archives for the period after 1917 have always been closed, and access to many archives for periods before that, even for Russian medieval history, is often denied. The Ministry informs some before they arrive that they may not use pertinent archives, and it denies others permission to come to the Soviet Union on the grounds essential archives would be closed to them. Many Soviet academic advisors have refused to support applications for access to these source materials. On the other hand, others have been extraordinarily helpful and have even arranged for use of provincial archives and for the transfer of materials from closed archives to institutions in which our scholars were able to work. In 1958-59, only one of six who sought archival material was successful, and he only very late in the academic year. Two

years later, only six of ten succeeded, and the
following year none obtained access. Very often,
when our scholars have been allowed admission,
Soviet authorities have withheld the inventories
of the collections in which they were interested.
Even in 1973-74 those in Leningrad did not obtain
archival materials until late in March.

   The Ministry has responded to complaints by
suggesting that few Americans were qualified to
use archives and that some had not used the archival
materials to which they had been given access. On
occasion it has declared that a Soviet scholar was
using the materials sought or that the papers were
being reorganized or edited. Ordinarily, American
participants simply received flat refusals.

   In an effort to resolve this thorny problem,
IREX and the Ministry in 1973 arranged to cross-
reference and forward requests for archives to
the archival authorities at the same time IREX
forwarded nominations to Moscow. They also
reached "an understanding that guarantees of
archival access would accompany each placement
decision." Experience in the following year
demonstrated that this effort produced some
progress, but some scholars who fought vigorously
to obtain the collections were still unsuccessful.
By the spring of 1975 IREX had established direct
contact with the Main Archival Administration;
this may lead to further progress. In June 1975
the Ministry informed IREX that six applications
for archives the following year had been denied,
four were under review, and twenty-seven would be
honored in whole or in part. However, IREX officials were frankly not confident that American
participants in 1975-76 would be significantly
more successful than their predecessors. Moreover,
requests made after participants have arrived and
discovered new sources will no doubt require enormous effort and produce the usual delays and
refusals.

   Using microfilming equipment raises the same
issues, intensified because Americans have become
so accustomed to various systems of reproducing
materials for later study, plus that of discrim-

inatory prices. Soviet reproduction and microfilming equipment is much inferior to ours, and
Soviet libraries have much less equipment than
ours ordinarily have. Although some participants
have succeeded in having quantities of materials
microfilmed, most have encountered difficulties,
delays, and often utter failure. Soviet librarians
and archivists often insist on placing restrictions
upon the amount and quality of material that may
be reproduced. For example, the Director of the
Central State Archive of Ancient Acts has insisted
on reading all pages requested by some participants
before they could be reproduced. Moreover, after
1962 in many cases and after 1964 in all cases but
one, Americans and other foreigners could obtain
microfilmed material only if they paid in foreign
currency or were able to provide microfilm from
their own archives in return. For several years
the rates Americans paid were three times as high
as those listed for Soviet citizens. This dis-
criminatory payment issue was resolved in May 1969,
when the Ministry consented to establish a fund of
150 rubles (approximately $125 at the official
rate of exchange then) for each participant for
microfilming material, in return for the Committee's
agreeing to meet all special research costs of
Soviet participants here.

The Soviet government continues price discrimination against foreign scholars, presumably
because of its great thirst for dollars. Thus,
American summer language teachers in 1967 had to
pay fifty-five rubles for a hotel room for two in
Kiev, almost three times the tariff for Soviet
citizens, and they had to pay for the twenty-four
hours before arrival, while the rooms were being
prepared. Similarly, Western scholars at the
International Conference on Magnetism in Moscow
in August 1973 paid eighteen rubles a day at conference exchange rates for rooms for which Soviet
scientists paid three rubles.[5]

The Soviet participants in general have been
a credit to their society and have raised few

[5]Earl Callen, "Moscow. Notes on a Scientific Conference," The Atlantic, CCXXXIII, Number 5 (May, 1974), 18.

problems. From 1958 through 1969 the average age
in the program for junior scholars was thirty-four,
just a year higher than that in the British Council exchange; the average age of our participants
has been twenty-six. Indeed, between 1967 and
1970 only one Soviet participant in all the Committee and IREX programs was under thirty years
of age.

The Ministry's system for selecting Soviet
participants remains a puzzle, although the
Ministry, rather than the universities, clearly
is in control. Several Soviet participants informed me that they had not applied but were
nominated without their knowledge. Apparently,
after the first year or two, the Ministry requested nominations from faculties in those fields
of research on which the government had chosen to
concentrate and then made the selection decisions.

We do know from conversations with Soviet
university administrators and scholars that the
Ministry did not consult them when our universities invited scholars to serve as visiting
lecturers. Indeed, some Soviet scholars have
informed American friends that the Ministry had
not told them of Committee invitations and had
provided utterly artificial and false reasons why
they could not accept, apparently a common practice
throughout the Soviet system of higher education.
In 1965 the Soviet Academy of Medical Sciences and
the Ministry of Health declined the invitation extended to Zhores Medvedev to the Seventh International Congress on Gerontology in Vienna in 1966
on the grounds of "extreme over-pressure of work."
In 1966, after Medvedev had refused the Ministry
of Health's request that he decline an invitation
to give a prestigious lecture in London, the director of his institute rejected it for him "because of a great press of work." When the London
invitation was renewed through Academician V. A.
Kirillin, the head of the State Committee on
Science and Technology, Kirillin denounced Medvedev
for "intercourse with foreign firms." Kirillin
then went himself to the United Kingdom, where he
received an honorary degree from Oxford and urged
the British government to increase cultural and

scientific links with the Soviet Union. According to Medvedev, only twenty percent of the invitations made to Soviet scholars from abroad reach their institutions. Moreover, of every twenty Soviet applications to attend international congresses, the authorities grant only one or two. Most permissions go to senior scientific administrators, not to creative scholars.[6]

A few Soviet participants have been hacks, rewarded the opportunity for research and travel in the United States for services not related to scholarship. A few had no serious scholarly interests, and two or three clearly were KGB agents who were sent to review and control their fellows and perhaps to undertake other activities as well. Several engaged in activities not tolerated on campuses in any society, but more Americans misbehaved in the Soviet Union. One Soviet scholar, apparently upset by the freedoms he enjoyed and fearful of reports he believed other Soviet scholars were sending home about him, in December 1963 decided to defect, attempted then to commit suicide, and suffered a nervous breakdown before he freely chose in April 1964 to return to the Soviet Union. Two others had some sort of nervous breakdown and returned home early.

Soviet participants have raised some special problems for American universities. Approximately eighty percent of the Soviet nominees are interested in science or technology (only ten percent have been humanists) and require scarce and expensive laboratory space and equipment. Soviet graduate training is in general far more narrow and specialized than ours, so that the interests of our professors and graduate students often are vastly different from those of Soviet participants. This often forced the university to purchase special equipment and materials. In 1965, for example, these costs amounted to $35,000.

In the early years, many Soviet participants had inadequate command of English, and the Ministry

[6]Zhores A. Medvedev, The Medvedev Papers, (London, 1971), 26, 54-69, 114, 130-31.

was unwilling to accept any of our remedial
proposals. Thus, a Committee review of the
Soviet participants in 1962-63 revealed that
only twelve of the thirty-nine had an easy command of English and that more than half had required additional work to enable them to benefit
from their opportunity. This problem later on
became substantially less important, particularly
when the Ministry in 1967 after eight years accepted the Committee's proposal for an intensive
language program for a month before the fall
semester began.

Most of the difficulties involved in negotiating with the Russians derive from the basic
differences between the Soviet and American political systems, their asymmetries in approach and in
goals, and particular Soviet policies and practices
that denied qualified Americans the opportunities
to study in the Soviet Union, shortened their visits
there, and restricted their travel and access to
materials. A good many other difficulties hampered
and annoyed participants on both sides, because
research and instruction are organized in different
ways, ranks and schedules vary, and dedicated
scholars in the two systems simply have different
working habits. In addition, however, some characteristics of Soviet administration significantly
affect relations and negotiations.

Perhaps the most striking features of Soviet
negotiating teams are their remarkable rigidity,
maintenance of accepted patterns, and inability to
reach decisions even on proposals of great benefit
to the Soviet Union. In the annual negotiations
for placement of participants, Soviet officials
have had only a limited capability to move from
their initial positions. Transferring an American
from Moscow to Leningrad even in 1975 is a long
and tortuous process. The Committee proposed a
summer program for language teachers from high
schools, colleges, and universities in 1958. This
was formally included in the agreement signed by
the two governments in November 1959, but it became
a reality because of Ministry delays only in 1963.
Similarly, the proposal that each side establish
funds for the participants' purchase of research

materials and microfilm was made first in 1965
and accepted only in May 1969. NASA made twenty-
seven proposals in the 1960s to the Soviet counterpart organization before any agreements concerning
joint research in space were reached.

The record of our relationships is littered
by Soviet refusals to accept, and in some cases
even to consider, proposals the Committee regarded
as mutually beneficial, but of especial advantage
to the Ministry. For example, it was clear after
the first year that some Americans would prefer one
month rather than a semester or an academic year
and that others would prefer eighteen months.
Similarly, the Soviet participants studying American
agricultural techniques preferred twelve months to
the regular academic year. We therefore proposed
measuring participation in total months, rather
than in academic years, allowing participants to
study for periods ranging from three months to
eighteen months. In fact, the second cultural exchanges agreement, signed on November 21, 1959,
allowed participants to spend from five to fifteen
months in the host country. However, the Ministry
still has not accepted this practice.

Soviet inability to meet agreed deadlines remains another dominant and depressing characteris-
tic. The Committee had anticipated this for the
first year or two, and Munford made six trips to
Moscow between March 1958 and September 1959 to
assist the Ministry to meet target dates. Soviet
performance, however, was wretched in the first
two years and only in recent years has become adequate. Thus, on August 2, 1958, the Committee
received only very scanty data concerning the
junior scholars who were due in this country five
weeks later. The next communication arrived on
November 23, giving seventy-two hours' notice for
the first fifteen participants, who then arrived
on a plane different from that which the Ministry
had indicated. None of the fifteen matched the
descriptions provided earlier. The Ministry requested their visas only on September 19, after
classes had begun. The visas were available at
the American Embassy on October 20, but the Ministry did not collect them until November 3, still

three weeks before the Soviet group left Moscow. Even so, the Ministry blamed the Embassy for the late arrival.

The second year provided some improvement, but not much. The Ministry had agreed to place American nominees by May 15; seven of the thirty-two withdrew on July 10 to accept academic positions or other fellowships because they could wait no longer. Twenty-seven Soviet nominees then arrived in New York on September 29, in most cases two weeks after their classes had begun.

Between 1958 and 1969 the Soviet nominations never arrived on the date that the Ministry had agreed to observe. On occasion they were two or three months late. Only once in eleven years did negotiations for placement begin on schedule. The Ministry was even tardy with its nominations for the summer programs for language teachers. Soviet applications for visas were made ordinarily just a few days before the participant was due in the United States, and most Americans had to wait for their visas until a few days or even hours before they departed from this country.

The program that has suffered most from Soviet tardiness was that for senior scholars, which was begun in 1962. In the first five years of this venture, the Committee nominated eighty-three scholars. The Ministry accepted fewer than half and provided no replies concerning twenty-five. On March 20, 1964, the Committee nominated a number of senior scholars for research. The Soviet reply, due on June 15, 1964, arrived on March 11, 1965, when the nominees had long abandoned their plans for leave from their university functions. Soviet nominations for this program have also been extraordinarily late. For example, the Committee received on February 18, 1965, a set of nominations mailed in Moscow on February 10 for Soviet scholars who wished to spend the second semester in our universities. IREX reported in April 1973 that some Soviet responses to nominations were ten months late.

The experience of other programs has been sub-

stantially similar. For example, the ACLS noted
in 1966 that it responded to Soviet nominations on
the average in two and one-half months, while the
Soviet Academy of Sciences required six and one-
half months. After fifteen years of experience,
the Public Health Service reported that the minimum
period of time for Soviet response to correspondence
was thirty days and that three or four months was
more common. The Deutsche Forschungsgemeinschaft
has reported that the Ministry ordinarily took
twelve months to reply to German nominations.
Similarly, a museum director whom the British
Council invited in 1960 arrived only in 1964. The
Italian Ministry of Foreign Affairs in April 1971
made sixty-four nominations, but not one response
had been received more than a year later.

The Committee abandoned the lecturers' exchange in the 1966 agreement because of the
Ministry's long delays in communication. For
example, on July 17, 1963, the Committee forwarded
eight nominations. It had received no reply on
January 14, 1965--eighteen months later--even
though it had pressed on several occasions.

The incompetence of Ministry officials no
doubt reflects general inefficiency that Soviet
citizens accept uncomplainingly, but it also dis-
closes the status of the Ministry of Higher Education in the Soviet government. The problems our
National Academy of Sciences has encountered in its
exchanges with the Soviet Academy of Sciences are
much like those the Committee and IREX have encountered. However, the Soviet Academy has more
authority, more competent personnel, and fewer
restrictions than the Ministry, and its administrative performance has been significantly more prompt
and efficient.

The Ministry's shabby and crowded quarters on
12 Zhdanov Street in Moscow illustrate the Ministry's
standing, as do the quality of the staff and the
equipment. Only two or three of the Soviet officials
engaged with the Committee's program between 1958
and 1969 had any knowledge of English, and the
office had no translators. After the first year,
the Committee forwarded nomination documents both

in Russian and English, but our correspondence was
generally in English. Ministry officials told us
that they sometimes had to wait six or eight weeks
to locate a translator for an essential letter.

Anyone who has read about Soviet administrative
procedures and about the Russian bureaucracy since
Gogol would have sympathetic understanding for the
men and women in the Ministry, and for those who
had to work with them. The Soviet officials are
badly overworked. They are remarkably ignorant of
Soviet education and its needs, and even more of
American education. Moreover, perhaps like typical
Russian bureaucrats, they are generally apathetic
concerning their functions, which are generally
temporary assignments and not permanent career
interests.[7]

The offices of the Chief of the Foreign Affairs
Administration in the Ministry, responsible for exchanges with all countries, before 1969 had only
two telephones. On one occasion in 1964 neither
telephone worked for several weeks. The office had
so few secretaries that the phones were left un-
attended throughout the entire day when the staff
was engaged in discussions or negotiations with
foreign representatives. The Ministry made no
international telephone calls to the Committee or
IREX until March 4, 1974, perhaps because of budget
constraints, perhaps because of language deficiencies in the Ministry staff. Establishment of direct
communications between IREX and the American Embassy and the Soviet Academy of Sciences as well
via telex has helped enormously, but the problem
does not reside in the instruments of communication.

Ministry officials had little authority on even
routine matters. Party control from an important
level was assured by men such as K. N. Kulikov, who
was identified in his obituary in Izvestiia on
September 27, 1969, as "an official in the apparatus

[7]Not all the inefficiency was in the Ministry. The
British Council learned in 1961 that the Ministry's nominations for that year remained in the State Committee for
Cultural Relations with Foreign Countries for two months
before they were forwarded to London.

of the Central Committee of the Communist Party
of the Soviet Union for fifteen years." Kulikov
rose through the ranks of the Komsomol and the
Party, and he was Chief of the Foreign Affairs
Administration in the Ministry from 1961 until
his death in 1969. He was an intelligent, shrewd
man, but his knowledge of Soviet education was
greatly limited, and his knowledge of education
in the United States was minimal. His role in
negotiations, evidence provided by carbon copies
of letters that were mistakenly forwarded, and
discussions with Ministry officials revealed that
no actions, even of the most rudimentary nature,
could be completed without his approval. In
addition, the Deputy Minister of Higher Education
apparently reviewed and approved all correspondence
with the Committee before it could leave the office. On occasion the Committee received an extra
carbon copy that revealed that a letter had received several approvals after being signed. The
Moscow post office stamp was at least four days
later than the date on which the letter had been
written.

Some of the inefficiency was ludicrous. For
example, the Ministry and the Committee agreed in
March 1961 that the Committee would arrange an intensive language and orientation program at Princeton University for the forty-six Soviet participants
in the program that fall. Previous experience had
already demonstrated that the Committee would need
to nudge the Ministry to ensure prompt arrival of
Soviet participants. Numerous letters and cables
flew from Bloomington to Moscow, and the Committee
late in July asked the American Embassy to prod
the Ministry to request visa applications. The
Embassy received twenty-six applications on August
14, a week before the Soviet participants were due
at Princeton. The Ministry discovered four days
later that it had forgotten to make airplane reservations and that all air lines were solidly booked
because an international biochemistry congress in
Moscow was just ending. After the Committee had
disbanded the faculty and had urged the Soviets not
to dispatch the Soviet participants until September
10, the Ministry on August 23 bundled twenty-three
scholars to the United States, where of course

none of their host universities was prepared to receive them.

The data the Ministry has provided the Committee and IREX concerning Soviet nominations have
always handicapped those eager to place Soviet men
and women in the institutions best suited to serve
them. The Committee sought to assist in every way
it could: it provided forms that indicated the
kinds of information American universities needed
to make sensible decisions; it sent sets of application blanks and catalogs from our major institutions; it even assisted a Ministry official in
visiting twenty-one American institutions and
their graduate admissions offices. However, the
problem persists. Thus, since 1963 the Ministry
has often provided an English translation for each
Soviet application. Unfortunately, the original
often does not correspond to the translation. For
example, an original of one application listed
five publications, but the translation identified
four completely different ones. In both cases the
citations were incomplete and difficult to locate.
IREX has noted some improvement, but not a great
deal.[8]

[8]The British Council, the Deutsche Forschungsgemeinschaft, and other Western organizations that administer
academic exchange programs with the Ministry have had
similar experiences. The Canadian government, informed by
our experiences and those of the University of Toronto,
has sought to escape this problem by incorporating the
following detailed statement in the annex to its December
1973 agreement with the Soviet government: "The data sheets
submitted will include the following information: name of
candidate, place and date of birth, present address, education,
place of work or study, proposed field of study or research,
including a statement on the proposed research topic, list
of publications if applicable, university or institute at which
participant is principally to reside, other institutions,
universities, or organizations he would like to visit, names
of specialists in the receiving country he would like to meet,
foreign language competence (written and spoken), marital
status, whether the participant will be accompanied by de-
pendents, each dependent's name, place, and date of birth if
applicable, and the approximate date of arrival in the
receiving country."

Consequently, in spite of the imaginative
efforts made by the Committee, IREX, and the participating universities, we placed a number of
Soviet students in institutions not competent to
assist them. No one example can provide an accurate
illustration of the problem that Ministry misinformation created, but two illustrations, taken from
1967 and December 1968 will present the flavor. In
the first, none of the four scholars with whom the
Soviet participant wished to work had been at the
institutions listed for more than ten years. One,
the first choice, had left seventeen years earlier.
In the second, the Ministry nominated a Soviet
historian who wished to work at Columbia University
with Professor Henry Steele Commager, who left
Columbia in 1956; at Harvard University with Professor Samuel Eliot Morison, who retired in 1956; and
in the Library of Congress, which he placed in
New York City.

Soviet administrative inefficiency was annoying
and frustrating, but unjustified Soviet newspaper
attacks on American scholars and organizations constituted a more fundamental concern. These attacks,
in which the Ministry of Higher Education played no
role, so far as the Committee could determine, were
directed against more than twenty scholars, Harvard
and Columbia Universities in particular and the
universities en masse, and the Committee and IREX.
They were designed primarily to dissuade Soviet
scholars and intellectuals from close contact with
foreigners. The charges made have usually included
conducting anti-Soviet propaganda or being "ideological saboteurs." They often incorporated as
well that of being in close contact with the Embassy
and even employed by the CIA. They have ordinarily
been directed at younger Americans. The percentage of Jews among those assailed has been
noticeably high, apparently to take advantage of
traditional Russian antisemitism and to relate the
attacks to those on Israel and "Zionism."

I believe that there may have been some substance for some charges made, though not for their
wild and scurrilous nature. For example, one of
the participants denounced for black market activities may have been guilty. Three of the partici-

pants criticized for their publications were
critical of the Soviet Union or of the Ministry
of Higher Education, but in a responsible fashion.
Six participants accused of spreading anti-Soviet
propaganda did make comments critical of the Soviet
system or of Soviet leaders in conversations with
Soviet scholars and graduate students, but again
they were responsible. Two participants accused
of being Zionist agents were Jews, were and are
friendly to Israel, and could, I suppose, be called
Zionists under the loose definition used in the
Soviet Union. So far as I know, the other charges
made had no justification or foundation.

The Soviet press accused three participants in
the program of being spies and made vague charges
that six others were. Three were charged with
seeking to persuade Soviet scholars to defect. The
newspapers provided no evidence to support these
charges, and the Committee found none. Two of the
attacks were particularly irresponsible and in-
decent. Thus, Izvestiia on October 30, 1966, accused Marshall Shulman, then at Harvard University,
of censoring the correspondence of Soviet participants at Harvard and of seeking to persuade a
participant to remain in the United States. He
was completely innocent of the "odious, unfounded,
and unwarranted" charges. On May 7, 1968, Pravda
accused Jeremy Azrael of the University of Chicago
of informing the American Embassy on a fellow
participant in the program, gathering intelligence
information in the Soviet Union, particularly
through interviewing intellectuals for the CIA,
carrying on anti-Soviet propaganda, and collecting
data concerning Soviet participants in the United
States.

The most serious press attack, one that
threatened the continuation of the program, was a
long, rambling assault in Pravda on March 1, 1967,
which skillfully took advantage of the revelations
the American press was then making concerning the
CIA's financing of other private organizations,
such as the National Student Association. The
article reflected considerable knowledge of Committee working methods. For example, the authors
had read some correspondence between the Committee

and its participants and between the Committee and
the universities. They had also acquired personal
information concerning an individual participant,
known only to him and to two members of the Committee staff. This essay praised the Committee for
its positive contribution toward more friendly
relations with the Soviet Union and indicated that
"not all" participants had served the CIA, which
it alleged was trying to prevent or hinder academic
exchange programs. It denounced the Ford and
Rockefeller Foundations, and it accused the CIA of
financing organizations such as the Committee. It
charged that the CIA and the FBI reviewed each
candidate before he went to the Soviet Union and
that two alumni participants who took part in the
language and orientation program were CIA representatives. The article did not accuse me directly
of being a spy, but it declared that I was not "a
pure scholar," perhaps because I have freely revealed that I served in intelligence organizations
during World War II and the Korean War. In short,
by taking advantage of unrelated revelations in the
American press and by skillful use of a handful of
facts, it wove a narrative that suggested through
guilt by association that the Committee, other private organizations, and individual scholars were in
fact engaged in espionage and other covert activities.

The Committee and the universities should perhaps have ignored this article, even though, perhaps
because, it appeared in the official daily organ
of the Soviet Communist Party. However, this false
and irresponsible series of charges led the universities engaged in the Committee's work to consider abandoning the program, as they had before
Professor Frederick Barghoorn was released in 1963.
The Committee, the presidents of the member universities, and other organizations, such as the
ACLS and the National Academy of Sciences, made
very vigorous protests pointing out the falseness
of the charges and the hazards they raised.

It is of course impossible to prove that one
is not a spy or a communist. The Ministry in effect
exonerated the Committee because it continued the
exchange programs. One of its senior officials

even apologized in a discreet way for the attacks.
Ministry officials were especially cordial in the
May 1967 discussions concerning placement of participants for 1967-68. Many Americans demolished
the bases of the charges made against them by re-
turning to the Soviet Union for research. The
falseness of the charges in my case was exposed in
the summer of 1967 when I went to Moscow and traveled through Eastern Europe; again in 1969 when I
visited the Soviet Union and Eastern Europe; and
in three later trips through Eastern Europe, actions I would not have undertaken if I had ever
been a spy and one that the governments of these
countries would not have tolerated if the charges
had had any foundation.

The attack was renewed in the spring of 1970
with the publication in Leningrad of a seventy-
page pamphlet entitled "Scientific Exchange or
Ideological Diversion," praised immediately by Yuri
Zhukov in Leningradskaia Pravda on May 17. In fact,
Zhukov added that an IREX participant that year had
sought to persuade Soviet Jews to leave for the
United States. The essay was especially significant
because it devoted several pages to a critique of
Allen Kassof, executive director of IREX, and it
cited conversations Kassof had had with Soviet
scholars, who either volunteered the information
to the author or whose conversations with foreigners
some Soviet agency recorded and gave to him. It
summarized and was typical of the charges often
made against Western visitors. It lumped American,
Belgian, English, Danish, and Swedish participants,
accusing them of immoral activities, visiting closed
cities, taking unauthorized photographs, serving
as agents for intelligence organizations, recruiting
defectors, and engaging in the black market, anti-
Soviet political propaganda, activities on behalf
of Zionism, and unscholarly criticism of the Soviet
Union. As an elementary review of the "problem of
the contemporary history of ideological struggle,"
it was clearly designed to warn Soviet intellectuals
against contacts with Westerners. Its failure to
include German or French scholars in the attacks,
because the Soviet Union was then wooing the Federal
Republic and France, revealed its political motivation.

Kassof in his 1970 report on continuing problems cited "groundless accusations of wrong-doing by the Soviet press and publications and personal indignities addressed to some of our participants," and he stated that he hoped they would not be renewed. However, Literaturnaia Gazeta on May 5, 1971, charged that three scientists, two on the National Academy of Sciences program and the other a senior scientist on the Committee exchange, had assisted our Embassy's cultural attaché, "actively used by American intelligence," in trying to recruit a Soviet scientist for espionage.

The history of academic exchanges, especially before 1972, is full of incidents involving KGB harassment, seduction, and blackmailing of junior and senior scholars from all countries that have exchange agreements with the Soviet Union. In fact, the reports of Von Herberstein in the sixteenth century, Olearius in the seventeenth century, Custine in the nineteenth century, or accounts written in any age by foreign visitors reveal that such police activities are a constant factor in Russian history. Adam Olearius's statement in 1634 that "the Russians in Moscow greatly distrust foreigners, who are constantly watched by the secret police. Each of their movements is noted and signaled to the central administration," applies still today and will no doubt apply as well in 1984. Indeed, one Soviet scholar remarked, "Poverty may be eternal in your society, but in our country it is 'the secret police we will always have with us'."

Because of the KGB, all American participants have returned home with a deeply increased understanding of the totalitarian aspects of Soviet life. They came to consider the Soviet postal system as the "opened mail" and to realize that any diaries would have official readers. They were never certain who their Soviet friends were and who were, or were forced to become, involuntary informers or agents provocateurs. Some had close friends regretfully discontinue relationships because they were frightened by police interrogation, and others severed ties in order to protect Soviet acquaintances. All learned never to mention one Soviet friend to another. Some were followed frequently,

particularly just before they left the Soviet Union
or during trips outside of Moscow and Leningrad,
although the Soviet shadows involved must have
found the ordinary tour from dormitory room to
cafeteria, library, archive, or theater very dull
indeed. Others had their rooms entered and skillfully searched in their absence. All of them, as
well as their Soviet friends, came to believe that
the rooms in which they lived, which usually were
rooms in which other Americans had lived in previous
years, had listening devices installed in the walls
and that their telephone conversations were monitored. A few even found these devices.

Most participants learned that some officials
in the Ministry of Higher Education and in the
university foreign student offices, generally the
most amiable, attractive, and efficient, were KGB
officers or had responsibilities to the KGB as well
as to the university. All came to appreciate that
all organizations or institutions dealing with
foreigners had "foreign departments" responsible to
the KGB. In addition, a small percentage had direct
and unpleasant experiences with the secret police.
Fortunately, none thus far has learned, as some of
their predecessors did in the late 1930s, that
Soviet authorities had cited entirely professional
and innocent conversations when they arrested and
executed Soviet scholars.[9]

Of the 320 participants in the Committee's
program for junior scholars between 1958 and 1969,
the Soviet government expelled 7 without cause and
without consultation or advance notice to them,
their university, or the Committee. In two of the
seven cases, it provided no information, even in
the form of attacks in the press. In every case
the KGB had kept the Americans under careful surveillance and in most cases had staged incidents.
In one case the KGB cleverly lured an American into
"immoral behavior." In two instances, the expulsions followed bungled and unsuccessful provocation
efforts, in one of which the foreign student offices
of both Moscow State and Leningrad State Universities

[9]Calvin B. Hoover, Memoirs of Capitalism, Communism, and
Nazism (Durham, 1965), 8-9.

played important roles. In others, the Soviets
fabricated or grotesquely twisted "evidence" in
an effort to "justify" the expulsion. Thus, one
was expelled for alleged participation in narcotics
traffic, another for "penetration in areas possessing military objectives" a year earlier, and
the last two for distributing anti-Soviet literature. So far as the Committee could determine,
these individuals were innocent of the charges.
With two exceptions, the Ministry of Higher Education failed even to respond to our complaints
about the injustice and the procedures used.

So far as we can tell, these expulsions were
designed primarily to frighten Soviet citizens from
contact with foreigners, to discourage Americans
from participating, and to demonstrate Soviet
"political" displeasure over particular incidents.
Thus, two expulsions occurred in June 1960 after
the U-2 flight and the break-up of the Paris summit
conference. Another followed the Department of
State's expelling two Soviet participants who had
traveled extensively in the United States without
informing the Department.[10]

Since 1968 the Soviet government has not expelled any participants in the main academic exchange program. However, two participants in the
National Academy of Sciences exchange were expelled
in 1971, one for "collecting slanderous information"
from "Zionists," and the other for "violating the
hospitality of the Soviet Union" by talking with
Academician Andrei Sakharov and by visiting laboratories and lectures at Moscow State University
without requesting permission.

Eighteen other junior scholars left early because they were frightened by the intense interest

[10]The Department of State expelled three Soviet participants for deliberate violation of the Department's travel
regulation. Two Soviet scholars were required to return to
the Soviet Union because they were expelled from their
universities, one for gross misbehavior and the other because
he was not qualified for the course of study he requested
and because he refused to participate in classes and
seminars.

the KGB had demonstrated in them, or after the
American Embassy had urged them to leave because
of the vivid way in which KGB interest had been
expressed. One, for example, received splendid
gifts for members of his family, accepted funds
for travel alone throughout a good part of the
Soviet Union and for a trip abroad, and was offered a Soviet academic position at an attractive
salary. Another was offered a manuscript for
delivery to a publisher abroad, and a third was
offered drawings of a new missile. The KGB heavily
grilled a fourth after his notes of professional
discussions with Soviet scholars in his field had
been stolen; a Soviet officer even used the diary
and displayed detailed knowledge of the scholars
during the interrogation. Another American, after
the university foreign student office had lured
away his fellow students, was "interviewed" while
at work in a Soviet archive and charged by a member
of the KGB as being a spy and a homosexual. He was
assured no charges would be pressed if he would
provide information concerning his fellow students
and Embassy officials. Another, away from his
university on a brief trip, awoke to find three
members of the KGB and a photographer in his room.
They charged him with homosexual activities and
made the customary threats and offers. Another had
the same kind of experience, even more unpleasant
in his case because he had been born in the Soviet
Union and was told that his relatives would suffer
if he did not provide information concerning Embassy
officials. Another was lured by a "friend" into a
restricted area, where he was arrested and urged to
provide information. Another took a drink in a
restaurant with a group of Soviet friends and woke
to discover that he was charged with assaulting a
Soviet policeman. He was informed that the charge
would be dropped if he would provide information
to Soviet officials. One was pressed for information concerning the "progressive left." Finally,
another was skillfully seduced and quizzed concerning the activities and views of the American
participants, his Soviet friends, Soviet faculty
members whom he knew, and Embassy officials.

   Participants in the Committee program were of
course not the only Americans in the Soviet Union

subject to this, because the smaller programs administered by the ACLS, the National Academy of
Sciences, and other institutions endured similar
incidents. IREX has reported no police incidents
since 1969. However, some participants are still
followed and harassed, especially when traveling,
and their Soviet friends are sometimes questioned
and threatened. Both Soviet and Western newspapers
reveal that scholars, businessmen, tourists, and
visitors of all kinds from Western countries still
suffer from such incidents, which apparently are
fewer in number than in recent years.

One can only speculate concerning why particular
individuals fell prey to the KGB, and whether any
have concealed KGB approaches made to them. It is
apparent that the KGB was more likely to select men
and women from the Russian Research Center at Harvard
University and the Russian Institute at Columbia
University, on occasion attacked in the Soviet press
as "spy centers," than graduate students from other
institutions. In general, it obviously chose those
whose knowledge of Russian was particularly fluent
and who were able to make friends most easily.
Those who had a Russian family background, particularly those who were born in the Soviet Union, were
especially likely targets. The number of Jews
selected for attack by the KGB and by the press as
well seems high.[11] It is clear also that several
police interventions were retaliations for the expulsion of Soviet agents (not Soviet students) from
the United States, and a number were directly related to the high degree of tension then current
between the two countries. At least one intervention occurred each year through the 1960s. Slightly
more than half of the known police actions occurred
between 1966 and 1969. 1967 was a particularly
ominous period. Most language teachers that summer
had encounters with the KGB, and known KGB activities were greater than in the previous five years
combined, perhaps because of the situation in
Czechoslovakia, perhaps because of the celebration

[11]Of the seven expelled from the Soviet Union between
1958 and 1969, five were Harvard graduates, one was from
Indiana University, and one was from the University of
Washington. Four were Jews.

of the 1917 Revolution, perhaps because the Soviet
police were then especially annoyed by and active
against native critics, such as Sinyavsky, Daniel,
and Litvinov.

The most important part of the explanation is
the character of the Soviet political system, especially the emphasis on political monopoly, absolute control, and carefully monitored relationships
with other parts of the world. The system rests
not only on Soviet communist suspicion of others,
and of each other, but also on the suspicion that
Custine and others noted earlier. The government
of Brezhnev very much resembles that of Nicholas I
or Pobedonostsev in the suspicion with which it
views other states, other peoples, and its own
people, and in the plot mentality that corrodes its
approach toward everyone, native or foreign, in the
Soviet Union. Indeed, the treatment given Paster-
nak and Sakharov is similar to that given Chaadaiev
in the 1830s and Tolstoy seventy years ago. As one
participant expressed it, "We are propaganda, simply
because of our presence here."

Security police systems in all countries tend
to be more infected with fear and hostility than
other parts of even the most conservative establishment, but the KGB considers even requesting a telephone book espionage. In the "great debate" within
the Soviet ruling group about the advantages and the
hazards of continuing exchange programs, it is likely that many KGB leaders and many of the other most
conservative elements in Soviet society are critical
of exchanges, with the suspicion waxing and waning
as relationships within the Soviet Union and in international politics change and as apparent benefits
and costs rise and fall. This no doubt accounts for
some KGB interventions against our participants and
for the constant vigilance campaigns and the press
attacks upon Soviet intellectuals.

The principal purpose of the KGB actions against
foreign scholars in the Soviet Union is to frighten
Soviet intellectuals and to isolate them as much as
possible from contacts with Westerners. In addition, they are designed to deny access to information, to discourage serious interest in studying

in the Soviet Union, and to encourage caution among foreigners in their actions in the Soviet Union and in their writing. The KGB's efforts clearly have been successful in frightening many specialists from studying there. Some American scholars discourage their graduate students from going to the Soviet Union. One, a forthright activist in the United States, even sought to remove his name from the papers of one of his students before they were forwarded in nomination to the Ministry.

The KGB also operates on the assumption that a little fear is salutary. Occasional frights will, they believe, ensure that all Western participants will be careful in their contacts with Soviet intellectuals, whose continued isolation is their prime target. The KGB may believe that such a campaign will encourage prudent reporting upon return. Thus, even the assumption that rooms are "bugged" or the fact that ordinary conversations on scholarly problems or the exchange of scholarly publications can jeopardize the position and even the life of a Soviet scholar will, they believe, intimidate Americans and therefore assist the KGB in maintaining a kind of intellectual and spiritual apartheid.

In addition, certain special professional KGB interests may have some influence. The secret police, for example, seek to acquire information about officials in the American Embassy, about whom participants constitute a potential source. Some KGB activities may simply constitute practice or serve to maintain professional morale and a proper sense of vigilance among their Gletkins. KGB officials may also believe that one day, after dozens, hundreds, or even thousands of efforts to trap and frighten foreign visitors or scholars, they may find one recruit to the Soviet intelligence apparatus for work in his home country.

CHAPTER SEVEN

Eastern Europe: Another World

With the exceptions of Yugoslavia, Greece, and Albania, and of Romania since 1962, that part of the world now called Eastern Europe has been firmly under the dominance of the Soviet Union and of communist parties and governments loyal to it since the end of World War II. The Soviet army, which had overrun most of the area in the drive that helped end the war, still maintains forces in Poland, the German Democratic Republic, Hungary, and Czechoslovakia. After the war the Soviet Union installed governments that communists by 1950 called People's Democracies and that the rest of the world then called satellites. It made their armies and political police instruments of Soviet will, and it lashed their economies to that of the Soviet Union. When the new regimes possessed what Lenin called the commanding heights in their hands, they set out to destroy rival political groups and institutions, acquired authority over the economies, tightened all controls, and then purged even the communist parties of those whose loyalty to the Soviet Union was not absolute. By 1950 they had begun the attempted transformation of the lives of their peoples in a massive effort to "build the foundations of socialism" on the Soviet model. The peoples of Eastern Europe were so isolated that the outside world could communicate with them only by

radio, which was consistently jammed, and free
floating balloons, launched in Western Germany
and carried by prevailing winds across Eastern
Europe.

Greece and Yugoslavia alone then escaped the
Soviet cordon. Greece was able to maintain its
independence because the Greek people, provided
with economic support and military equipment by
the United States and other Western countries, in
a bitter civil war defeated the Greek communists,
whom the Soviet Union, Yugoslavia, Albania, and
Bulgaria supported. Yugoslavia remained an independent communist state after Stalin ousted it
from the Cominform in 1948 because of Tito's reso-
lute vigor, the united nationalist support of the
Yugoslav peoples, massive economic aid and military
supplies from the Western states, and a kind of
protective umbrella that the United States held
over Yugoslavia.

The new regimes, eager to solidify control over
their populations and determined to destroy all
Western influence, flouted the treaties they had
signed at the end of the war. They harassed Western
missions, arresting, imprisoning, and torturing
their employees. They closed Western information
agencies and restricted and then eliminated all
Western news services. They nationalized Western
properties without compensation. Hungary in February 1950 imprisoned an American businessman,
Robert Vogeler, and the Czechoslovak government
in April 1951 arrested and imprisoned an American
newspaper correspondent, William Oatis, as symbolic
closings of the door to the West. The actions of
the Bulgarian government were so reprehensible that
the United States closed its legation in Sofia from
1950 until March 1960.

After the death of Stalin on March 5, 1953, a
series of changes within the Soviet government and
of Soviet policies toward Eastern Europe gradually
produced a thaw and a relaxation of tensions. Within the Soviet Union the new collective leadership
released many political prisoners, slightly let up
on the severe controls, and talked a good deal about
increasing supplies of consumer goods. In foreign

policy it helped arrange an armistice in the Korean
War and launched a grandiose campaign for "peaceful
coexistence." At the twentieth party congress in
February 1956 it launched a campaign of de-Staliniz-
zation and introduced a series of important ideological changes, which suggested that war was not
inevitable, that socialism could be attained in
some states through peaceful means, and that there
were several roads to socialism besides that of
the Soviets. The new Soviet policies in Eastern
Europe, the expressions of resentment that surfaced
because of the relaxations, and the remarkable
economic, political, and spiritual recovery of the
West European peoples and states together produced
a series of changes within Eastern Europe that ultimately made academic exchanges possible under
arrangements similar to, but superior to, those
established with the Soviet Union.

The New Course designed to make the regimes
more palatable led instead to violent explosions,
first in Eastern Germany in 1953 and then in Poland
and Hungary in 1956. These eruptions were based on
immense and deeply felt dissatisfactions and resentments. They reflected also the erosion of ideology,
the revival of nationalisms, and the growth of anti-
Soviet feeling among the suppressed peoples, even
those groups most favorably treated--the workers,
the intellectuals, and the students, all of whom
were impressed by the vivid contrast between the
promises made and the realities they had to endure.
It is not surprising that the decade of utter isolation had heightened interest in political, economic,
and intellectual ties with Western Europe on the
part of the great majority of the educated, communist and noncommunist alike. Above all, both the
governments and the peoples of these countries had
become convinced that they could obtain economic
benefits from the West with Soviet permission, by
"working between the feet of the Great Powers."
Thus, popular hope to restore the traditional ties
with Western Europe and the efforts of the regimes
to obtain respectability and scientific and technical assistance ran along parallel courses.

The recovery of the peoples and states of
Western Europe from the destructions caused by the

war played a most important role in the revival of
hope, the growth of nationalism, and the explosions
of 1956 and 1968. The vitality of the West European
states and the American guarantee over them sig-
nified the success of the doctrine of containment
so far as Europe itself was concerned. In the
1950s the belief that Eastern Europe might be
liberated by Western arms and the proposal that
Western and Soviet forces should disengage in
central Europe both evaporated. At the same time,
the cataclysmic fear that there was "a finality,
for better or worse about what has happened in
Eastern Europe," also began to fade away as historical perspective overcame the shocks of war and of
the postwar crises. Thus, even after 1956, after
the Berlin Wall was erected in August 1961, and again
after the invasion of Czechoslovakia in 1968, hope
has become stronger that the East European states
will gradually regain more freedoms and rejoin the
European community.

Western leaders and peoples also began to
recognize that immense Soviet power and skillful
control were balanced by the spiritual and intellectual weaknesses of the communist regimes in
Eastern Europe. Western observers came to appreciate the extraordinary vulnerability to ideas that
corrodes the Soviet system, particularly in Eastern
Europe. Then, the chasm between the economies of
Eastern and Western Europe, in spite of the considerable progress made at crushing cost in the East,
persuaded leaders on both sides to accept the advantage of improving relationships. Finally, Western peoples concluded that recognizing contemporary
Soviet control over Eastern Europe did not mean
approving it and that a "vast possibility of peaceful change" existed throughout Eastern Europe, even
under restrictions Moscow dictated.

The 1956 revolt in Poland brought a national
communist leader, Gomulka, from prison to rule, and
he introduced substantial relaxations of controls.
The Soviet government reluctantly accepted the
Gomulka government and its policies, and later it
maneuvered Wladyslaw Gomulka into restoring many
of the earlier constraints. The revolt in Hungary
led to massive and forceful Soviet armed inter-

vention, which crushed the revolution and installed
Janos Kadar as head of a regime thoroughly loyal
to the Soviet Union.

Some Western observers judged that the 1956
revolts marked "the beginning of the end of communism." Others considered them a crushing set-
back to dreams of increased freedoms and of closer
relations with the West. Paradoxically, the revolts
in Eastern Europe and Soviet reactions led not to
the re-establishment of controls as fierce as those
exercised between 1947 and 1953, but to further
relaxation and above all to greater Soviet acceptance of increased contact with the West. The Soviet
government apparently recognized the desperate need
to reduce the magnetic attraction the West exercised
upon Eastern Europe by tolerating some controlled
relationships that would also strengthen the East
European economies. It no doubt also believed that
the Gomulka and Kadar regimes and the demonstration
of Soviet resolution together ensured the Soviet
position, without at the same time multiplying
fears of Soviet expansion in other parts of the
world. Soviet policy also reflected the confidence
and ebullience of Khrushchev, who launched a program
to make the so-called virgin lands agriculturally
important, abolished the machine tractor stations,
and talked of overtaking and surpassing American
production in significant agricultural and industrial fields. The appearance of the first sput-
niks on October 4 and November 3, 1957, helped
increase Soviet self-confidence. This was both
reflected in and mounted because of the vigorous
diplomacy of Khrushchev and Bulganin, the new emphasis upon peaceful coexistence, the temporary
return of Tito to friendly relations with the Soviet
Union, and Khrushchev's visit to the United States
in 1959. In short, after 1956 some West Europeans
and Americans perceived new opportunities to overcome the bafflements the Soviet Union and these
regimes had established and to reopen relationships
with Eastern Europe.

American scholars and academic institutions
gave precedence to Russia and the Soviet Union over
Eastern Europe when establishing priorities in research, instruction, and academic exchanges, as our

government did in defining foreign policy. The
first two important graduate programs, the Russian
Institute at Columbia in 1946 and the Russian Research Center at Harvard in 1947, both concentrated
exclusively upon the Soviet Union. In fact, in
1946 less than five percent as many scholars were
interested in Eastern Europe as in Russia. Moreover, our scholars, and the public in general, have
traditionally neglected Eastern Europe, which they
considered a backward part of the world buffeted
between Russians and Germans, peopled by wild and
unruly groups in constant conflict with each other,
and the immediate cause of both world wars. Scholars interested in Eastern Europe tended to have a
kind of inferiority complex because they attracted
little attention and commanded little influence in
their profession. The enormous expansion of
interest in Russia only increased their feeling of
neglect.

Yet, many of those most responsible for beginning Russian studies, particularly Coolidge at
Harvard, Mosely at Columbia, and Robert J. Kerner
at the University of California in Berkeley, combined a powerful interest in Eastern Europe with
that in Russia. Their activities helped to promote
the study of Eastern Europe. Exile and refugee
scholars, many of supreme quality, such as Oscar
Halecki and Otokar Odložilík, were also important
in expanding this activity. The Soviet role in
that area and the 1956 explosions inevitably increased both scholarly and popular interest, which
always follow the headlines.

Finally, the Inter-University Committee with
its earliest travel grants helped stimulate interest
in Eastern Europe among Russian specialists. The
Committee encouraged these Fellows to travel through
Eastern Europe, preferably on their way home from
the Soviet Union, to obtain greater return from the
immense investment in travel for such a short period,
to acquire insights into the Soviet Union from even
brief comparisons with other countries that communists ruled, and to use Eastern Europe as a kind
of decompression chamber after the plunge into
Soviet reality. Many, of whom I was one, were fascinated by their first experiences in Eastern

Europe, as Coolidge and Mosely had been earlier,
and they later encouraged the expansion of East
European studies and academic exchange programs
with Eastern Europe.

Scholarly relations with Eastern Europe were
opened not by scholars, universities, or governments but by the Rockefeller and Ford Foundations.
These private institutions used their enormously
expanded incomes after World War II in many fruitful
ways. The Rockefeller Foundation concentrated upon
promoting research in biology and agriculture
throughout the world and, briefly, upon expanding
the study of other areas and of international
politics, largely within the United States. The
Ford Foundation emphasized expanding and improving
higher education, with particular stress upon the
study of foreign areas and of international politics.
The foundations' interest in Eastern Europe in the
mid-1950s was a natural and pragmatic expansion of
their domestic and foreign programs. Their senior
officers during the war had become keenly aware of
the tensions and hazards of international politics.
They also realized that the two world wars had had
their origins in a sense in Eastern Europe. Most
of them also accepted the thesis expounded by Walter
Lippmann in 1947 that the world would not enjoy
peace until Soviet armed forces had left Eastern
Europe. The relaxation of tensions after the death
of Stalin and the 1956 eruptions in Poland and
Hungary consequently increased their interest.

Both foundations began their programs with
Poland because the Polish government after 1956 was
eager to increase contact with Western states.
Moreover, after 1953 the flow of tourists, largely
of Americans of Polish descent to Poland, reflected
profound popular interest in both countries. Finally, of course, Polish relationships with the West
had traditionally been stronger than those of any
other East European country.

The Rockefeller Foundation had demonstrated an
interest in Eastern Europe and in Russian and East
European studies already in the 1930s. It helped
establish the Russian Institute at Columbia University in 1946, and it assisted until 1968, when it

ceased supporting international studies. It also
helped establish the Russian Research Center at
Harvard University, and it provided important
grants to institutions abroad, particularly to the
École Pratique des Hautes Études in Paris, St.
Antony's College in Oxford, and a number of universities in Japan.

The Foundation officers were therefore especially impressed and concerned by developments in
Poland in 1956, and they considered establishing a
program that would enable Polish scholars to visit
the West for the first time since before the war.
A number of Foundation officers visited Poland in
February 1957, and the Foundation shortly thereafter provided laboratory equipment and materials
to all Polish universities except the Catholic
University in Lublin. At the same time, it launched
a fellowship program that enabled a number of young
scholars, primarily in scientific and medical fields,
to study in Western Europe and the United States.
More than forty Polish scholars visited this country
in 1957 alone, and the Foundation provided funds for
travel in Western countries for approximately forty
Polish scholars each year from 1957 until 1964. The
Foundation also assisted a few Czechoslovak and
Yugoslav scholars, and it enabled a small number
of American scholars, primarily in medicine, to
consult with colleagues in Poland.

The Ford Foundation played an even more important role. Its International Training and Research
Division, between its establishment in 1951 and
1967 when its functions changed, contributed more
to improving and expanding the study of other areas
of the world than any other American institution.
However, the International Affairs Division, established in 1949 to coordinate Foundation activities
in reducing international tensions, played the
central role in opening scholarly relations with
Eastern Europe. It sought to increase understanding
of the conditions necessary for establishing and
preserving peace, to improve the structures and
procedures of private groups interested in international relations, and to strengthen the United
Nations and its associated agencies, and it inevitably became interested in the Soviet Union and
Eastern Europe.

Until late in the 1960s this venturesome division supported a large number of conferences or forums of important Soviet, East European, American, and other leaders, largely on international politics, but occasionally on scientific relationships, economic growth in less-developed countries, and various approaches toward peace. It was an important financial supporter of the Pugwash and Dartmouth Conferences, and in 1966 it began to support groups interested in establishing cultural relations with the People's Republic of China.

Developments after 1953 and the 1956 explosions therefore excited the officers of the International Affairs Division and the Foundation trustees, who decided in November 1956 to examine ways and means of reopening "channels of communication" with Poland on at least a short-term basis. This announcement stimulated an invitation from the Polish government, and a group of Foundation officers visited Poland in February 1957. In the following month the trustees announced a one-year pilot program of $500,000 "to establish and renew contacts with Western colleagues" and to provide books "for Polish humanists, social scientists, architects, and engineers, in the interest of national security," and "in full knowledge reverses are possible." The Foundation trustees and officers were interested in helping Poland identify and train potential leaders, convinced that first-hand exposure to Western Europe and the United States would have important intellectual and political consequences.

In the first year, 1957, twenty Polish scholars went to the United States and fifteen to Western Europe, while ten American and West European scholars went to Poland, each for an academic year. In addition, twenty nonacademic intellectual and cultural leaders visited the United States and twenty-five Europe for two months. Twenty-five Polish graduate students received aid for study here and twenty in Western Europe, and ten American and West European students studied in Poland, each for an academic year.

After the program had been in operation for two or three years, both Polish and American officials and scholars realized that Polish scholarship

would obtain increased benefits and American funding
would be most effectively used if the fellowships
were concentrated in a select number of fields and
if Polish, American, and West European scholars engaged in joint long-term research projects on large
subjects of common concern. Therefore, joint research in fields such as applied linguistics, educational planning, social and applied psychology,
urban planning, public administration, and business
management gradually became important elements of
the Ford venture.

It is difficult to determine just how many
Polish scholars participated in this twelve-year
Ford program. Some traveled to Western Europe,
some to the United States, and some to both. Some
received more than one grant from the Foundation,
and some combined Foundation awards with aid from
other institutions. Most engaged in research, but
some took part in training workshops or round-table
discussions. Some participated even when the relationship between the Foundation and Poland was
broken because they had received grants before the
disagreement. Moreover, even after the project
was formally ended and the Foundation in 1968
transferred its academic exchange activities to
IREX, until late 1974 it annually brought a handful of intellectuals from Eastern Europe to this
country. However, more than 330 Polish humanists
and social scientists participated between 1957
and 1962, and more than 100 studied in this country
or in Western Europe between 1964 and 1968 on fellowships from the Ford Foundation. Between 1957
and 1966 the International Affairs Division spent
more than $6,000,000 on its programs devoted to
Eastern Europe.

As the Foundation officers had hoped, the
presence of Polish scholars in West European and
American institutions, and the increasing contact
of all kinds that the Foundation encouraged, created
interest in exchanges among other organizations.
Some private foundations, like the Ventnor Foundation, were especially interested in improving
medical facilities. Others, such as the Pulaski
and Kosciuszko Foundations, reflected powerful
interest among Americans of Polish descent who

wished to assist Polish scholars to come to the
United States and to strengthen ties between the
two countries. The Pulaski Foundation in 1964 even
began to bring Polish undergraduates here. The
Brethren Service Commission since 1957 has brought
to this country twenty to thirty Polish farmers
each year to study agriculture, a program it expanded later to Bulgaria. The National Student
Association in 1959 began an exchange of two graduate students each year with the Union of Polish
Students.[1] In the same year, the International Institute of Education in New York established another
program for five students each way.

Finally, our government became increasingly
active, limited only by its financial resources
and by caution lest it jeopardize these successful
private programs. Beginning in 1958 the Department
of State began to bring selected Polish political
leaders to the United States for short tours, a
program that it had begun in other countries in
1948. The Fulbright-Hays program was extended to
Poland in 1959, when it brought ten Polish scholars
here for research, and later to other East European
countries. By 1970 as many as forty-three Polish
scholars were studying in the United States annually on funds from the Department of State, the
Department of Agriculture, and the Public Health
Service. In another program of enormous benefit,
the Department of State extended the Information
Media Guarantee Program to Poland, until 1967 providing more than a million dollars each year to
assist in the purchase of American publications and
films, which are vitally necessary for libraries
and basic intellectual relationships. In October
1972 the Polish and American governments signed an
agreement on cooperation in science and technology
that provided for joint research and shared funding
in a large number of fields, from architecture to

[1]As mentioned earlier, this student exchange, founded
on idealism, hope, and innocence but desperate for funds after
the first year or two, sometime in the early 1960s began to
accept financial support from the CIA. When this became public knowledge in the winter of 1967, the embarrassed association quickly withdrew the sole participant then in Poland and
ended its program.

chemistry, mining, and pollution control. This was renewed and expanded in October 1974.

As a result, scholarly exchanges between Poland and the United States grew rapidly. They doubled from 1957 to 1958. Between 1956 and 1960, more than one thousand Polish scholars came to this country. On occasion in the 1960s, more than three hundred Polish scholars were here on long-term research grants, in most cases from universities, that used private foundation or National Science Foundation funds.

The success of these ventures and the evidence of their immediate value to Poland encouraged other East European governments to invite the Ford Foundation to establish similar arrangements. Programs of approximately the same size (twenty-five scholars and five cultural leaders each year) were established with Yugoslavia in 1959, with Hungary in 1962, and with Romania in 1965, and smaller ones with Czechoslovakia and Bulgaria in 1968. The program with Yugoslavia became the Foundation's largest in Eastern Europe. Moreover, just as the Foundation program with Poland led many universities, other institutions, and the government to sponsor study opportunities for Polish scholars, so these persuaded other institutions and the Department of State to begin programs in the other countries. In 1970, 154 Romanian scholars were engaged in research in the United States, a great number of them on grants from the Department of State, a few on the IREX exchange program, and the remainder aided by universities and other foundations. Thirty-five Americans were in Romania at the same time, including professors teaching language and literature in three Romanian universities.

These efforts all benefited substantially in organization and administration from experience in Poland. In 1962, for example, all Yugoslav participants were in economics, sociology, and law. The Czechoslovak program established in 1968 concentrated upon business management and public administration. In all these countries, particularly Yugoslavia and Hungary, Foundation officials and consultants and their counterparts in Eastern Europe

agreed that the programs would be particularly
fruitful if the East European scholars would review
their needs, draft proposals to help meet those
shortcomings, invite a group of American specialists
in those fields to visit, meet scholars, and review
proposals, and then discuss with the Foundation a
program that would help efficiently meet national
requirements. Consequently, cooperative ventures
increased in number and importance, and efficiency
and good will both increased.

These experiences in the 1960s led to other
impressive approaches, particularly conferences in
Eastern Europe bringing together specialists from
the United States, Eastern and Western Europe, and
the Soviet Union on subjects of mutual interest.
The best example of this was a conference held at
Lake Balaton in Hungary in 1968, after two years
of planning, under the direction of Earl Heady of
Iowa State University. Financed by the Ford Foundation and by the governments of Hungary, Czechoslovakia, and Romania, this conference attracted
about one hundred agricultural specialists for a
two-week period to discuss economic decision-making
and planning models at farm, regional, and national
levels. Approximately one-half of the participants
came from the United States and Western Europe, with
the other half from Eastern Europe and the Soviet
Union. The invasion of Czechoslovakia on August
20, 1968, discouraged similar meetings, but IREX
was able to arrange others in the 1970s.

After the exchanges with the Soviet Union had
survived three years, the universities that participated in the Committee at their annual policy
meeting in November 1961 decided to expand the
academic exchange program to include Eastern Europe.
The Committee decided to concentrate its efforts on
Czechoslovakia, Hungary, and Bulgaria. It eliminated Poland and Yugoslavia because of the relative
ease with which Americans were able to study in
these countries and of Polish and Yugoslav scholars
to come to the United States, particularly under
Ford Foundation auspices. It dropped Romania from
consideration because the Department of State and
the Romanian Ministry of Foreign Affairs in December
1960 had established a cultural, technical, and

educational exchange program; this provided for an
exchange of from three to six scholars each year.
It did not consider Greece because it was a friendly and democratic state, and Greek and American
scholars could easily arrange to study in the other
country. In addition, the Ford Foundation's Foreign
Area Fellowship Program in its definition of foreign
areas in the early 1950s had placed Greece in the
Middle East, rather than in Eastern Europe. The
Foundation's and then the federal government's fellowship programs thus omitted Greece from East
European grant programs, while at the same time,
for other reasons, they excluded it from Middle
Eastern programs as well. This definition has had
an important influence on our study of Greece, because university programs devoted to Eastern Europe
and to the Middle East both neglect Greece.

Albania was omitted because so little interest
appeared. East Germany was rejected because of the
erection of the Berlin Wall in August 1961. Moreover, our government did not recognize East Germany,
and few scholars were willing to venture into a
country where they would receive no diplomatic protection. However, I conducted informal discussions
with East German scholars at international conferences in 1960 and 1965. IREX resumed these talks
in October 1972 and included funds for East Germany
in its 1973-74 budget. The government of the German
Democratic Republic chose to delay formal discussion
of an exchange program until the United States and
other governments had recognized it. Most observers
thought that East Germany would insist that any
academic exchange be part of a cultural affairs
agreement between the two governments, but in
February and March 1975 it negotiated a two-year
program with IREX to begin in the fall of 1975 for
a total of twenty months each way each year.

In preparing its proposals for Eastern Europe,
the Committee naturally benefited from experience
with the Soviet Union. Consequently, it prepared
draft proposals designed to resolve in advance the
problems that plagued its programs with the Soviet
Ministry of Higher Education. Thus, the drafts
specified that all institutions of higher learning
should be included and that spouses and children

could accompany participants. They did not distinguish between senior and junior scholars. The
proposals were modest, from two to five scholars
during each of the first two years. The accompanying letters described the Committee's experience
in administering programs with the Soviet Union,
thus reassuring these governments that the Committee and its work were respectable. They indicated
that Committee representatives would like to travel
through these countries and visit a variety of
institutions on their way home from a visit to the
Soviet Union in June 1962.

Each of the three countries agreed to an exchange of three junior and senior scholars each
year, beginning in September 1963. The programs
expanded gradually but impressively from this small
base, except for cautious and reserved Bulgaria,
which even refused to accept books offered by the
British Council. The Bulgarian exchange rose from
three in 1963-64 to five for a total of fifty
months per year for 1966-67. After Pravda on
March 1, 1967, alleged that the Committee was an
instrument of the CIA, the Bulgarian government
reduced the program to fifteen months, demonstrating
that it did not consider the charges true but re-
proving the Committee for being subject to Soviet
criticism. The figure rose to twenty-three months
in May 1970 and to twenty-eight in 1974-75. These
numbers seem adequate for both sides.

The Hungarian exchange also progressed slowly
because the Ford Foundation had established its
program for scholars from Hungary in 1962. Thus,
it grew from three scholars in 1963-64 to eight
for a total of thirty-six months each year for the
period from 1965 through 1968. The Hungarian
government ended the exchange in June 1968 after
one year's notice, because its chargé d'affaires in
Washington, Janos Radvanyi, had defected to the
United States. However, even after "these un-
friendly events," the Hungarians allowed two
American participants to extend their terms of
study. The program was resumed at a level of fifty
months per year in January 1969 and was raised to
seventy for 1974-75. A good number of Hungarian
scholars (eighty-eight in 1970) studied in the

United States throughout all of these years under other arrangements.

The exchange with Czechoslovakia, timorous in 1962 and 1963, grew rapidly and was most satisfying and promising until the 1968 invasion. It expanded from three in 1963-64 to four the following year, nine in 1966-67, and eleven for 1968-69. The Czechoslovak government in December 1964 even offered three bonus fellowships in organic chemistry and forestry. In 1964 the Czechoslovak Ministry of Education accepted two additional two-year fellowships that the Committee, with Department of State funds, offered for promising young scholars in American studies. Interest in programs with Czechoslovakia was so high that a number of universities established direct relationships with Czechoslovak institutions. Czechoslovakia in 1968 accounted for one-half of all long-term visitors from all of Eastern Europe in the United States. Indeed, the Czechoslovaks by August 1968 had already used their quota for 1969-70 as well. Committee and IREX officials were in London on their way to Czechoslovakia in particular and to the other East European countries on August 20, 1968, prepared to expand the exchange programs significantly. The program negotiated in January 1969 reduced the number to fifty months per year, where it remains in 1974-75. However, IREX has placed Czechoslovak scholars above this annual base, as did the Committee.

The enormous increase in interest among Czechoslovaks was reflected in the number of Czechoslovak scholars in this country, which rose from 83 in 1965 to 208 in 1967, 422 in 1968, and 405 in 1969, almost all of whom were sponsored and supported by universities and other private institutions. In the fall of 1969 the Ministry of Foreign Affairs assumed responsibility for all educational, scientific, and cultural contacts, and imposed severe restrictions on travel abroad. The figure then dropped dramatically to 101 in 1970.

The Committee's establishment of programs with these three governments encouraged the National Academy of Sciences to complete agreements in 1966

with Czechoslovakia, Hungary, Romania, and Yugoslavia for exchanges of 40 months per year for each
country, except Yugoslavia, which agreed to only
16. These exchanges remained small, although they
grew to a total of 228 months for 1972-73, largely
because scientists from these countries found it
relatively easy to come to the United States under
other auspices and because few of our scientists
were interested or had the language qualifications
necessary for studying in Eastern Europe. Moreover,
the average length of study for our scientists was
short; in 1972-73, ninety-two American scientists
spent an average of 2-1/2 months in Eastern Europe.
In 1968, fewer than ten percent of the East European
scholars in the United States were participants in
an official exchange program, and the percentage
of American scholars in Eastern Europe under formal
auspices was even smaller.

The changes within Eastern Europe in the 1960s
led to proposals for revised and expanded programs.
Thus, in 1967 when the Ford Foundation reviewed its
international activities, it suggested exchanges of
teachers of languages and literature between universities in Eastern Europe and the United States;
cooperation in establishing and strengthening
American studies centers and East European studies
centers; and joint research projects on issues such
as urban planning and pollution. Obtaining published materials quickly and easily was (and remains) a concern for scholars on both sides. Therefore, particularly in Prague and in Warsaw, I
proposed that a private American university establish a university bookstore on the property of the
Academy of Sciences, in a kind of sanctuary, in
which any Czechoslovak or Polish citizen could buy
with local currency any American book (no newspapers
or periodicals, at least at first) he wished. The
Foundation was to provide a small grant to help
establish the bookstore, which would also have served
as a central purchasing agent for all university and
other libraries interested in purchasing books,
journals, and newspapers from Poland and Czechoslovakia. The dollars that our universities would
have spent for Polish and Czechoslovak publications
would have been pooled to purchase the American
books sought by Poles and Czechoslovaks, and the

local currencies accumulated in Warsaw and Prague
would have been used to pay for Polish and Czechoslovak publications for our libraries. Any surplus
of Polish or Czechoslovak currencies would have been
used to purchase copies of older publications available in Eastern Europe but not in the United States,
or for microfilming newspapers and journals.
Czechoslovak and Polish officials were deeply interested, but they did not accept the proposal, in
part because of the opposition of their national
book monopolies, but particularly because their
governments would have had to surrender their censorship controls, which remain essential to these
regimes.

IREX devoted the early 1970s to converting the
Ford Foundation programs for Poland, Romania, and
Yugoslavia into genuine exchanges at substantially
the level the Foundation had supported from these
countries to the United States. Yugoslavia raised
difficulties because Tito's government became increasingly repressive concerning relations with
Western states, delaying responses to IREX nominations, generally rejecting those with Slavic names,
and in effect denying the field work essential for
anthropologists and sociologists. Moreover, IREX
in its first agreement in 1968 had recognized Yugoslav financial problems and generously undertook
to support both Yugoslavs in the United States and
Americans in Yugoslavia, as well as to pay for all
travel. Eight months of determined negotiations
with the Yugoslav Federal Administration for International Scientific, Educational, Cultural, and
Technical Cooperation were required before agreement
was finally reached on July 18, 1974, to move toward
a reciprocally financed program by 1975-76. With
this agreement, IREX's exchanges with the six
countries of Eastern Europe amounted to a total of
368 months annually.

IREX has also been able to arrange or support
a series of joint and international conferences that
offer great promise for expanding relationships.
Thus, in 1972 it sponsored a conference in Sterling
Forest, New York, on Romanian-American cooperation
in the social sciences. This led to a joint seminar
on economic relations in Bucharest in May 1974.

IREX supported an international conference on Bulgarian studies at Madison, Wisconsin, in May 1973 and one of Romanian and American historians in Romania in 1974. It helped organize four Polish-American conferences in Poland in the summer of 1974, one of jurists, one of historians, one on the application of computers in the social sciences, and one on public policies in industrially developed countries.

The Department of State has made even more impressive progress with its programs than has IREX. The 1972 scientific and technical agreement with Poland was followed by a similar one with Hungary and a larger accord with Romania in December 1974. Extension of the Fulbright-Hays program to some countries in Eastern Europe brought substantial advancement. Thus, in 1973-74, at a time when five Soviet scholars were scheduled to come to the United States for one semester on this program, eighteen Poles, forty-four Romanians, and thirty Yugoslavs studied or taught here.

Analyzing the differences between the American and West European exchange programs with Eastern Europe and between the American programs with Eastern Europe and the Soviet Union illuminates the particular role the East European states play in East-West relations and the dilemmas closer relations raise for their governments and for the Soviet Union. Briefly, the West European ventures were later, in general, than the American. They almost inevitably became larger than ours, in part because the distances are not so great and travel costs are minimal. Thus, the West European governments find it easy to arrange summer school sessions, short-term visits of scholars and outstanding intellectuals, colloquia and conferences, exchanges of groups of specialists and delegations, and exhibits. The West European exchanges are also far more political, perhaps because in every case a government ministry or agency administers them, and also because scholarly interest in Eastern Europe is not high, except in the Federal Republic of Germany, which did not establish formal exchange programs with any East European states until 1970. By 1975 all Western states except Spain and Portugal had agreements and

active programs, in every case imbedded in inclusive
cultural exchange agreements between two governments. These exacting agreements closely resemble
each other, to the point that some of the smaller
ones, such as those of Denmark and Norway with Bulgaria, faithfully follow the model of the more substantial efforts. However, even these tiny agreements reflect the powerful desire of both sides to
maintain and increase relationships.

The programs the British Council administers
are probably the largest and most effective of any
with East European countries. They also constitute
a striking comparison with those of the Committee
and IREX. The British Council had cultural centers
in most East European countries before World War II
and re-established them after the war. In fact, it
had twenty-six representatives in Prague, Brno, and
Bratislava in 1947 and nine in Hungary in 1948.
These centers remained open in Poland and Yugoslavia but were closed in Bulgaria, Czechoslovakia,
Hungary, and Romania in 1949 and 1950. Consequently, the British Council did not need to re-establish
relationships with Poland and Yugoslavia. After
three years of talks, a representative of the
British Council visited the other four countries
in April 1962, exchanging letters that established
cultural exchange programs, including scholars and
teachers.

The basic interest of the British Council, like
that of the European governments, was to establish
a foundation on which it could project a favorable
image into Eastern Europe, increase political influence, and expand opportunities for trade. The
British in this part of the world, as in other areas,
have emphasized improved and expanded English
language teaching and the establishment of centers
and libraries. For example, already in the 1950s
the British Council maintained libraries in Warsaw,
Krakow, Belgrade, and Zagreb. In each of its four
new programs, the British have presented books to
important libraries. Thus, the Council persuaded
the Czechoslovak State Library in Prague to establish a special section for books in English. It
presented more than five thousand volumes to this
section in 1966, and the library had eight thousand

English volumes when the Soviet armies invaded in
1968. The interest in learning English and the
success of the British Council in satisfying this
demand were so great that the Council was providing
language teachers in Budapest as early as the summer
of 1963. Six teachers of English were engaged in
instruction in Czechoslovakia in 1966. In that
year, 260 Polish teachers of English spent short
periods of study in the United Kingdom. Even in
1969, Czechoslovakia began an exchange of secondary
school language teachers.

Until the mid-1960s British scholars demonstrated little interest in spending a semester or an
academic year in Eastern Europe because of declining
interest in this area in British universities after
World War II. For example, the School of Slavonic
and East European Studies at the University of
London, the largest institute of its kind in the
United Kingdom, graduated only one Ph.D. dealing
with Czechoslovakia between 1947 and 1962. In
1962-63 the British Council obtained no applications
from scholars who wished to spend a year in Bulgaria
or in Romania.

Interest increased dramatically in the late
1960s, largely because the University Grants Committee increased funds for East European studies
and because language instruction for undergraduates
expanded rapidly in the provincial universities.
This led to a number of direct exchange programs
between British and East European universities,
such as that between Charles University in Prague
and the University of London in 1966 for the exchange of language teachers, and agreements in the
following year between three provincial universities
and Sofia. By 1971 British universities had agreements for exchanges of lecturers with universities
in four other countries in Eastern Europe. By
1970 a number of institutions were sending undergraduates to Czechoslovakia and Bulgaria to improve
their Russian and were exchanging other undergraduates with institutions throughout Eastern Europe.
For example, the University of Sussex began to send
four to six undergraduates to Charles University to
study Russian and to accept six Czechoslovak students interested in improving their knowledge of

English. Leeds University has a similar program
with Brno, and Bradford with Prešov in Slovakia;
the Bradford curriculum requires its Russian language
majors to spend five months in Prešov, which also
provides three Russian language instructors for
Bradford. Sheffield and Olomouc, Glasgow and
Charles University, and Bradford and Skoplje constitute other such matches.

The programs administered by the French and
Italian Ministries of Foreign Affairs are very much
like those of the British Council. Italy completed
its first cultural exchange agreement with Poland
in 1961, and followed with Bulgaria in 1962 and
Romania in 1963. By 1971 Italy had established
agreements and even mixed commissions to administer
exchanges with all the East European states, including Albania. In that year, Italy had exchanges
of chairs or professorships with Hungary, Poland,
Romania, and Bulgaria. In 1972 fourteen professors
from Eastern Europe taught in Italian universities,
and a similar number of Italians were teaching in
Eastern Europe. In that same year, Italy provided
more than eight hundred months of fellowships for
East European scholars (considerably more than
double the IREX programs) and could send Italians
who wished to study in Eastern Europe for almost
eight hundred months.

The German government and German organizations
did not begin scholarly programs with Eastern Europe
until 1965, when the Deutsche Austauschdienst (DAAD)
began to assist both young and senior scholars from
Bulgaria, Poland, and Czechoslovakia to study in
Germany. In 1965 it made awards to 75 Czechoslovak
scholars for study in Germany, and more than a third
of all DAAD fellowships went to East European scholars that year. In 1967, 178 scholars from Czechoslovakia, 15 from Yugoslavia, 36 from Hungary, and
35 from Poland were studying there. The Humboldt
Foundation awards for 1969 included 62 senior scholars from Czechoslovakia, the largest number from
any country in the world, as well as a total of 36
from Romania, Bulgaria, Yugoslavia, and Hungary.
In that year, one-fifth of all the prestigious
Humboldt fellowships awarded to foreigners went to
East Europeans. In short, the traditional ties

between Eastern and Western European universities
and other institutions of higher learning were
being re-established by the time the Soviet armies
invaded Czechoslovakia in 1968, and those ties
revived and even increased in all countries except
Czechoslovakia after that event.

In some ways American exchanges with East
European countries are similar to those with the
Soviet Union. In all instances, American organizations negotiate with a communist government that
has full control over its end of the exchange process. These governments are interested largely in
improving and increasing their scientific, technical,
and management capacities, and the great majority
of the East European scholars who come to the United
States and Western Europe are in some field or
other of science and technology.

East European nomination of scholars in fields
sensitive for military reasons occurred only in the
first two years. For example, the Czechoslovak
Ministry of Education for 1963-64 nominated three
scholars and three alternates. Five of these
nominees were in sensitive military fields, and
the sixth was an officer in the security police.
Three of the four Hungarians nominated the first
year were also in sensitive fields.

The political controls and restrictions exercised by the East European governments resemble
those of the Soviet Union, but they are much more
relaxed. Americans in these countries have to assume that their mail will be censored. Surveillance
has occurred occasionally or spasmodically, and the
security police have sometimes acted as irresponsibly
as in the Soviet Union. Thus, the Czechoslovak police in 1964 sought to frighten the wife of an
American scholar into becoming an informer. In
November 1973 Hungary summarily expelled an American
scholar, without making any charges or providing any
justification. When IREX immediately postponed
further movement of American and Hungarian scholars,
suspended exchanges scheduled for 1974-75, and insisted upon the scholar's re-admission, the Hungarian
Institute for Cultural Relations after four months
allowed the scholar to return on a tourist visa.

However, some Hungarians, presumably policemen, then
harassed the American, who was also exposed to treatment he considered undignified when he left. IREX
then reduced the 1974-75 program to its formal
quota, postponed indefinitely negotiations for joint
research projects, and suspended its sponsorship of
a Hungarian-American conference on comparative law.

Far more East European scholars almost inevitably seek to study in the United States than
American scholars in Eastern Europe, even though
the East European governments have in general been
eager to expand the exchange on a reciprocal basis
and have rarely rejected our nominees.[2] A high
proportion of young Americans qualified for study
in Eastern Europe has applied for research there,
but of course the basic number remains small, even
though growing. The Committee, the National Academy
of Sciences, the Department of State, IREX, and
other organizations have been imaginative and energetic in stimulating increased interest in all
fields of study, such as geology, linguistics,
mathematics, and music, but the number of those
interested is not large.

Thus, only 20 applied for Czechoslovakia,
Hungary, and Bulgaria in the first year, 1963-64,
and only 36 in 1967-68. The largest number of
applicants for these three countries together in
any one year was 43. The Committee in no year
received more than 8 applications for study in Bulgaria. In the exchange program with Romania that
the Department of State administered, the Department could find no qualified candidates in the third
year. In the fall of 1967, 561 scholars from Eastern Europe were in the United States and only 94
Americans were in Eastern Europe. In 1968-69, when
422 Czechoslovak scholars were here, only 17 Americans were in Czechoslovakia. The following year,
the figures were 101 and 15, still a great disparity.
In 1969-70 IREX placed 63 East European scholars in
this country, while sending only 20 there. Two

[2]This has also been the case in Western Europe. Over
the years, the number of East European scholars who have come
to the United Kingdom has been about twice as great as that of
British going to Eastern Europe.

years later IREX noted that East Europeans had
spent 442 months in the United States, while our
scholars spent only 257 there. The Department of
State statistics for exchanges of all kinds show
that 1,426 East Europeans had come to this country
and that only 288 Americans had gone there in 1970.
Consequently, the contrast between the flood of
East Europeans eager to come here and the number
of Americans qualified and interested to study there
constitutes a problem for those who seek an exchange
that approaches some balance, if only for financial
reasons.

IREX therefore has established a number of
awards to encourage scholars to plan research in
Eastern Europe, to enable institutions to engage
in cooperative research projects with East European
institutions, and to assist graduate students in
the social sciences in particular to acquire language and area training so that they might qualify
to study in Eastern Europe. In 1974 IREX announced
it would consider applications from those who did
not know Hungarian, "if their research topics do
not require a command of the language," and that
it would accept applications for two-year awards,
the first year to be devoted to intensive study of
Hungarian in Budapest. It also encouraged direct
exchanges between individuals and institutions
through planning grants. Still, in spite of these
imaginative approaches, the IREX agreements with
Bulgaria, Czechoslovakia, Hungary, Poland, Romania,
and Yugoslavia for 1974-75 totaled only 368 months
each way. However, because IREX occasionally accepts and places more scholars from Eastern Europe
than the formal agreement provides, it budgeted
for 545 months for 1974-75.

The differences among Bulgaria, Czechoslovakia,
Hungary, Poland, and Romania serve to demonstrate
the acute variety that exists within Eastern Europe,
which President Johnson recognized in his February
1964 proposal for "treating different East European
countries differently." Even the organizations
that administer the exchange program differ from
country to country. For example, the Czech and
Slovak Ministries of Education direct their programs,
the Institute for Cultural Relations with Foreign

Peoples the Hungarian, and the Bulgarian Academy of
Sciences the Bulgarian.

The exchange programs with Eastern Europe differ in many ways from those with the Soviet Union.
The Committee and IREX have always negotiated their
own agreements, independent of the Department of
State, and negotiation has been always much simpler
and easier than with the Soviet Union. The original
agreement with each East European country was concluded in just a few hours, and the Committee arranged renewals sometimes by correspondence.
Placement has not constituted a problem. Neither
the Committee nor IREX succeeded in persuading the
Soviet Ministry of Higher Education to shift the
system of counting participants from a semester or
academic-year basis to a man-month basis, which
would have allowed both sides flexibility and would
have increased the number involved. After the first
two years, the East European organizations quickly
agreed to transfer the measurement system to man-
month counting. The efficiency of communications
and of administration is notably higher in Eastern
Europe and generally is like that among West European states. Indeed, by 1975 IREX had telex communications with every capital in Eastern Europe
except Prague (and Tirana), and this shortcoming
was repaired to some degree by telex communications
with Bratislava.

The East European countries provide much more
data concerning their participants than does the
Soviet Union, and they send a smaller percentage
of party hacks. Thus, even in the first year, the
Bulgarian Academy of Sciences provided the home
addresses of its nominees, and the Hungarian Institute for Cultural Relations enclosed diplomas and
lists of its nominees' publications. East European
candidates generally are far better informed concerning American scholarship than are their Soviet
counterparts, and their command of English is significantly superior. The East European states also
send to this country a much higher percentage of
scholars in the humanities than does the Soviet
Union. In 1972-73, for example, four of the sixteen
Hungarian scholars on the IREX program were historians, as were two of the thirteen Romanians. In

1973 six Bulgarian philosophers were engaged in
research on our campuses.

The East European states have been remarkably
permissive in admitting Americans for study, except for the decision of the Czechoslovak Ministry
of Education to deny admission to an American scholar in 1963-64 because the Department of State had
denied admission to Czechoslovak scholars in sensitive fields and to retaliate for a group of
Czechoslovak denials in 1972-73. Moreover, most
American candidates have been interested in twentieth-century history, political science, and
literature, sensitive subjects in countries communists rule. Bulgaria in 1966, after some discussion, admitted an American and allowed him access
to archives for study of the Jews in Bulgaria during
World War II. In 1969-70 the Czechoslovak Ministry
of Education admitted scholars interested in the
nationality problem in Sub-Carpathian Ruthenia
between 1918 and 1939 and Czechoslovak-Yugoslav
relations over the same period. The Czechoslovaks
in 1973-74 even admitted an American interested in
Thomas Masaryk.

Above all, Eastern Europe remains more open
and free. All institutions of higher learning are
accessible to our scholars, regardless of their
age or experience. No city in any of these countries is closed, and travel and field studies are
easy. Americans are not only able to travel
throughout these countries, but they have also
found it simple to enter and leave, obtaining visa
renewals with no difficulty. In fact, one scholar
left Hungary on six different occasions during his
academic year there. Wives and children have been
accepted from the beginning. Moreover, two of the
first Hungarian participants brought their wives,
an achievement that only one senior scholar from
the Soviet Academy of Sciences managed before 1972.

Archives and libraries are open to all Western
participants, and field work raises no problems,
except occasionally in Czechoslovakia since 1969.
Thus, in 1967-68 young scholars spent the academic
year working in the Archives of the Institute of
the History of Socialism, formally of the History

of the Czechoslovak Communist Party, an archive similar to one in the Soviet Union denied to even senior Soviet scholars. As early as 1965 an American scholar was able to use a questionnaire and a poll in research on Czechoslovak journalism. In 1972-73 another was able to interview a significant number of Romanian factory managers in his study of the social impact of technological change.

Poland is so relaxed and open that a number of American universities have established their own exchange programs with Polish institutions. Stanford University and the University of Warsaw in 1964 began an exchange of graduate students that soon led to a substantial Stanford undergraduate program there as well, and Kansas University in 1970 established a short-lived program for fourteen students with the University of Poznan. Indiana University in 1967 established an exciting exchange program with the Institute of History of the Czechoslovak Academy of Sciences.   Each year the Institute sent four thousand books, about the number of volumes published annually in Czechoslovakia that would be of interest to the Indiana University Library. Indiana in return gave the Institute a copy of each book reviewed by the Journal of American History in the field of American history, about five hundred books each year. In addition, it provided two senior fellowships in American studies, including round-trip travel from London. From the beginning, most of the Czechoslovaks brought their wives and families. The Czechoslovak government ended this program in 1970.

In 1974 the University of Florida began to send up to thirty-five students to the University of Poznan for summer study. Romania in 1969 began to send undergraduates to the United States, and in 1971 it sent eight to the United Kingdom, at Romanian expense. After IREX established special grants to encourage "collaborative projects" between American and Soviet and American and East European institutions, sixteen of the nineteen awards for 1972-73 involved projects with Eastern Europe and only three with the Soviet Union.

The experiences of West European organizations
have been similar to ours. Perhaps the best illustration of the East European approach is the system
that the British Council and the Polish Ministry of
Higher Education have used since 1968 for selecting
Polish scholars for twenty-three British Council
fellowships. The Poles nominate forty scholars,
the British Council rates them in priority, and
the Polish Ministry then nominates the top twenty-
three on the British list. The Polish Cultural
Institute in London chooses the British participants
in this program, and a British Council representative participates in the selection process. Similarly, a joint Yugoslav-British board awards fellowships from the Yugoslav government to young
British scholars.

Finally, the countries of Eastern Europe have
been far more receptive to exchange classroom
teachers than has the Soviet Union. The Committee
and American universities as early as 1958 sought
arrangements under which Americans might teach
American literature and English in Soviet institutions, and Soviet scholars might teach Russian language, literature, and history here. The Soviet
Ministry of Higher Education refused even to consider exchanges of teachers until 1972, when the
Soviet government at last agreed to include an exchange of eight instructors in various fields
beginning in the spring of 1974.

Eastern Europe is substantially different.
Since 1955, hundreds of East European scholars have
taught in American universities. Indiana University
in the 1960s appointed Czechoslovak scholars as
visiting professors to teach music, folklore, economics, and theatre. In some years, more than
thirty Polish scholars were visiting professors
in different American universities. As early as
1965, American professors were teaching English and
literature in Polish universities, with funds provided jointly by the Polish universities and by the
Department of State. At the same time, two Americans began to teach English in Czechoslovakia and
one in Bulgaria. The Fulbright-Hays program for
lecturers began to operate in Yugoslavia in 1964 and
elsewhere in Eastern Europe in 1966-67 (seven years

earlier than in the Soviet Union), with one American in Bulgaria, three in Poland, from four to six
in Romania, and thirteen in Yugoslavia. In 1975,
at Polish initiative, several American Midwestern
universities began assisting the University of
Warsaw to establish an American Studies Center, with
a strong library and courses in English given by
American professors on history, literature, economics, art, and such subjects.

The total population of Bulgaria, Czechoslovakia, Hungary, Poland, and Romania is approximately
one-third that of the Soviet Union, and the addition
of Yugoslavia to that group brings the total up to
less than half that of their large eastern neighbor.
However, throughout the 1960s and thus far in the
1970s, the number of scholars from these six countries in the United States and of American scholars
in these six countries in every year has exceeded
those figures for the total Soviet-American exchange.
The growth of exchange programs throughout these
years and the improvements in exchange conditions
were both much more rapid and easier than with
the Soviet Union. In fact, the number of East
Europeans in the IREX exchange increased forty percent in 1972 over 1971. As a British Council representative remarked, "In a word, the East Europeans
are more like other Europeans."

CHAPTER EIGHT

Conclusions and Reflections

Many of us today fail to appreciate the character of the barriers that separate those parts of
the world which communists rule from the United
States and Western Europe, even after the changes
that have occurred in recent years. Even during
the tense 1930s, when the Nazis had begun to inflict their barbarities on some elements of the
German population and to threaten Germany's neigh-
bors, thousands of citizens from other countries
freely traveled through and lived in Germany, as
Germans did in other countries, except the Soviet
Union. Publications and broadcasts crossed boundaries as freely as peoples did. Trade flourished.
Similarly, we forget that more Poles lived and
studied in Western Europe in the sixteenth century
than do today, even though that earlier period endured religious wars, conflicts within and among
petty and large states, and ineffective transportation. The thawing of Soviet policies toward the
West in recent years is therefore just a small step
in the direction of relationships that in earlier
years were traditional between peoples of states on
the verge of war.

Some Soviet and American political institutions
look alike on the surface, but the distinctions are
deep and fundamental. Indeed, Soviet efforts to

adopt Western forms and even to use the same vocab-
ulary to describe their institutions show the attractive power our institutions and values have and
the Soviet need to mask the vast dissimilarities.

The tensions that dominate Soviet-American
relations, and that make formal academic exchange
programs necessary and difficult, depend in part
upon the clashes between two dissimilar political
and economic systems. However, they also reflect
the conflict between two rival ideologies, the
impact history and suspicion have had upon each
society and upon their relationships, and the frank
collision of competing national interests throughout the world. The sharpness of the disagreements
derives in good part from the peculiarities and
asymmetries of the relationship. The two states
have different goals and styles. Our approach is
open, relaxed, and flexible, while the Soviet system
emphasizes secrecy and unity. Both approaches are
so fundamental to their societies that neither can
abandon or significantly modify its principles
without undermining its system. Specifically, the
Soviet Union cannot afford freedom, just as we
cannot abandon it without betraying our most basic
values. The Soviet Union cannot grant Western
scholars, or Western businessmen, the freedoms
essential to Western society and to any economic
and cultural relationship without undermining the
Soviet system, while we face a dilemma just as
crucial.

As this volume shows, Soviet officials hold
their positions firmly, and they are tough and
skilled in their advocacy of Soviet interests. The
constant struggle reflects not only the nature of
the competing positions and of Soviet tactics, but
also the adversary relationship that prevails between the two states. Both in economic and cultural relations, where maximum mutual benefit
demands cooperation, the competitive adversary
spirit transfers the relationship from a relaxed
and friendly one to shrewd, determined bargaining,
to some degree poisons the atmosphere, and prevents
the two parties from moving together toward a cooperative and even interdependent stage.

Between 1958 and 1975 several academic exchange programs carried out as parts of the official
exchanges agreements signed biennially by the two
governments enabled somewhat more than a thousand
American scholars to spend from two months to two
academic years in the Soviet Union. The principal
program enabled approximately 650 graduate students
and young scholars to spend an academic year, generally in either Moscow State University or Leningrad State University; the other programs have allowed more than two hundred teachers of Russian to
spend a summer in a special program at Moscow State
University and approximately three hundred senior
scholars to enjoy one or several months of research
and meeting colleagues, generally in the Soviet
Union's two major cities. Soviet scholars in approximately equal numbers have enjoyed similar
opportunities in universities throughout the United
States. During the period between 1958 and 1975
our government, foundations, and universities together spent less than $50,000,000 to support aca-
demic exchange programs with the Soviet Union and
Eastern Europe, only a fraction of the annual budget
of a major state university in the 1970s or of the
cost of the Apollo-Soiuz joint manned space laboratory in July 1975.

Perhaps as many as 3,000 graduate students and
scholars from all Western countries together spent
a few months or an academic year in study and research in the Soviet Union from 1958 through 1975,
and approximately the same number of Soviets have
studied in the West. In contrast, in 1974-75 alone,
somewhat more than 150,000 foreign students and
scholars studied in the United States. In the same
year, about 25,000 foreigners, of whom only about
200 were from Western countries, studied in the
Soviet Union. In most years from 1958 through 1975,
more students from Iceland than from the Soviet
Union have studied here. In 1972-73 alone, more
than 3,600 British students and approximately 2,000
each from France, the Federal Republic of Germany,
and Greece have attended our universities.

Throughout these seventeen years, less than
twenty Americans have taught for even a semester

in the Soviet Union. Probably no more than two
hundred, and certainly less than three hundred
scholars from Western countries have taught in
Soviet institutions for a semester or a year
throughout this period. About ninety percent of
these men and women were language teachers, and
more than half came from France. In 1974-75 one
large American state university, Indiana University,
had approximately four hundred citizens of countries
other than the United States as members of its
faculty.[1]

Throughout the period since 1958 the United
States, its universities, and its learned societies
have made little progress in expanding the volume
of academic exchanges. Indeed, the 1963-64 peak
for the most important part of the program, that
for young scholars, was reached again only in 1974-
75 and exceeded only in 1975-76. The target the
Committee set in 1964 for the period 1965-70 was
twice as high as the actual figure realized. The
apparent increase in numbers since 1971 is due almost entirely to special short exploratory trips,
subsidized largely by IREX and the National Academy
of Sciences, in hopes that this will lead to important meetings or to joint research projects.
The highly publicized May 1972 agreement for cooperation in science and technology has led to a
large number of brief meetings of working groups
of scientists in a dozen fields (about 150 participated in 1973 alone), but three years later only
one American scientist had begun research in the
Soviet Union under this program.

Moreover, the pattern of the academic exchange
programs has remained substantially unchanged, and
progress has been slow and grudging. Indeed, the
Nixon-Brezhnev agreement in Washington in 1973 froze
the framework through 1979. Basically, academic exchanges are governed by a larger exchanges agreement

[1]Reference to the comparative magnitude of Western
trade with states that communists rule may help keep this
perspective. In 1973 West Germany, the Soviet Union's most
important trade partner, had more trade with tiny Luxemburg
than with the Soviet Union, and its exports to Sweden equaled
those to the entire Soviet bloc.

concluded by the governments. They remain a primitive form of barter or horse-trading, an artificial and unnatural arrangement with a quota system and a restrictive spirit, with access to a laboratory balanced against access to a library, and reciprocity, not equity or mutual advantage, being the guiding factor. The basic restrictions remain, and most changes have been minor and cosmetic. Constant pressure from the Committee and IREX, with vigorous support from the Department of State, and some thawing of the Soviet system have reduced the number of Soviet rejections of qualified candidates. In 1974-75 and 1975-76, the Ministry of Higher Education accepted all IREX nominations in the principal program, as it had in 1962-63, although it did not then place them in Soviet institutions when the academic years began. The Soviets now grant admission to spouses of participants and even to couples with their children. Most of our scholars are still assigned to Moscow and Leningrad, but since 1967 a handful have been sprinkled among other cities, espècially in European Russia, and restrictions on access to archives and on travel have loosened somewhat.[2] In recent years the KGB has been less evident and less barbarous than formerly, though it no doubt observes our participants and their Soviet associates with its traditional care. The Soviet government remains sensitive to research subjects on contemporary politics and foreign policy, but in 1973-74 and 1974-75 it allowed some research on contemporary social problems. Soviet officials in general are more relaxed and flexible in negotiation than earlier. Other Western states have progressed, too, especially France and the United Kingdom. In short, the situation has improved over 1958-59. Above all, one must remember that no American studied in Soviet universities between 1936 and 1958 and that the Soviet decision to send some of their elite to their central rival and to accept Americans in their dormitories touches a most critical Soviet nerve.

However, we have made little progress toward

[2]In 1975-76 the Soviet Ministry placed only three of the fifty-two American junior scholars outside of Moscow and Leningrad.

free interchange of information and ideas. Some
Soviet attitudes and practices have appeared to
change, but the Soviet Union has not shifted its
basic policies. We are still far from the circumstances in which Coolidge, Kerner, and George R.
Noyes worked in relative freedom under the tsars
or in which the Moselys, Robinsons, and Simmonses
lived and worked in the Soviet Union between 1924
and 1936. The Soviet government remains adamantly
opposed to relaxing controls over the movement of
people or ideas, as the two years of negotiations
over the European security agreement and Soviet
actions since the Helsinki agreement was signed
have both demonstrated. Most of the issues that
divide us have therefore remained impervious to
even the most skilled and adroit diplomacy. As
the report of IREX for 1972-73 indicated, "Detente
has not solved any fundamental problems of scholarly
contact with the Soviet Union."

The changes in the program with Eastern Europe
have been far more fundamental and substantial, and
the size and character of the gap in policy and
performance in these exchanges, compared with those
with the Soviet Union, have grown gradually even in
those years in which Soviet policy has relaxed.
Finally, of course, the entire relationship remains
utterly subject to Soviet government control, and
no one can be certain concerning the permanence of
any Soviet policy toward the outer world.

Thus, the academic exchange program has been a
relatively constant and stable element in Soviet-
American relations since 1958. It began and sustained itself through a time of immense ferment and
change within American higher education. It has
been important as a symbol. It has served as a
link between two contentious states at delicate
times, when failure, cancellation, or a breach of
one kind or other might have intensified a crisis.
It has helped bring about other changes, and it has
made prospects for continued peace a little brighter.
But the progress has been slight and painful, when
one considers the imagination, energy, and resolution expended.

In 1955 only a dozen American scholars had

lived and studied in the Soviet Union. Now we
have a relatively large cadre of specialists who
have had that experience. In fact, the academic
exchange program is far less essential for Russian studies than it was two decades ago. Many
scholars became interested in Russian affairs because the Committee helped open the door to the
Soviet Union, and a direct relationship exists
between access to Soviet society, limited as it
is, and the great boom in Russian studies in the
1960s. About eighty percent of those who have
participated in the academic exchange program
have been specialists in one field or another of
Russian studies, generally history, literature,
or political science, in that order. These men
and women in particular have benefited greatly
from the increased knowledge and understanding of
the Soviet Union they acquired from living in
Soviet cities and working in Soviet libraries and
archives, a benefit that they have made national
and even international through their teaching and
publications. Their opportunities have also
helped make their views of Soviet life and policy
less abstract and doctrinaire, and more realistic
and humanistic than they would have been. One
of the principal consequences of these exchange
programs has been the humanizing of Western observers, who had been paralyzed by great slogans
and written generalities. These programs have
deepened our knowledge of ourselves and helped
to carry on the intellectual modernization of
the American university by encouraging systematic
study of other cultures. Our participants' independent judgments help supplement and challenge
the views of government officials on issues of
national concern. Finally, their qualities and
their achievements have helped give Russian and
East European studies a responsible national base.

Our Russian specialists have enjoyed many
common experiences, but they emerged with many
different interpretations of Soviet reality.
Generally, they returned from the Soviet Union
more critical of the Soviet system than when
they arrived. These attitudes may be among the
more important consequences of the academic
exchange program, and they will help shape

our image of the Soviet Union for many years ahead.[3]

American participants in other fields of study, especially mathematics and basic physics, have also benefited, sometimes significantly. In the field of medicine, we have learned from Soviet research on hypertension, immunology, and blood diseases, and from study of Soviet systems of medical education and of providing public health service. Our scientists have also acquired a realistic appraisal of Soviet science, its strengths, weaknesses, organization, and needs, especially in physics, engineering, and the life sciences. The concrete evidence reflected by articles in scientific journals is much less important than the invisible but often priceless leaps in information and insight that occur when scholars come together to engage in research.

American scholars, who have benefited so much from the work of others with longer scholarly traditions than ours, have also appreciated the opportunity to join the international community of scholars and work with some who enjoy less freedom and, usually, less adequate research facilities than we do. We have learned, again, that no one has a monopoly on truth and that there is a difference between the contemporary political condition and the eternal human condition. We already have impressive evidence that our research on things Russian, which benefits from some access to materials in the Soviet Union, helps sustain and enliven Soviet scholarship, which in the humanities and social sciences in particular suffers from restraints with which American scholars have never been afflicted.

Those Americans who have studied in Eastern Europe have in addition been impressed by the faith, determination, and skill with which most East European peoples have sought to defend their national traditions and to regain their freedoms.

[3]Mr. David Bonavia's comment that correspondents arrive in Moscow green, that those who leave after a short time come out white with anger and fear, and that none come out "red" applies to most participants.

The growing national appreciation of the simple truth that the countries of Eastern Europe differ from each other and are vastly different from the Soviet Union may be one of the most important consequences of our increasing understanding of Russia and Eastern Europe. Scholarly studies of Eastern Europe also demonstrate the dynamism of national communism there. They have thus increased our insight into the minority problems facing the Soviet Union and the pressures that have riven the international communist movement.

The academic exchange programs have produced a number of other important side effects. They have, for example, increased the emphasis upon effective teaching of Russian. They have persuaded scholars and universities to cooperate in national programs at a time when they were competing for prestige, funds, and students. They have served as effective barometers of larger Soviet policies, particularly during periods when Western officials have had difficulty fathoming Soviet intentions.

Moreover, free cooperation between our scholars and our government has improved as our participants have increased their knowledge of the realities of Soviet life and of international politics. Few American specialists on Russia and Eastern Europe have written extensively about Soviet foreign policy or Soviet-American relations, but the books and articles published generally reflect balance and objectivity. No specialist on the Soviet Union has joined the currently popular revisionist school, whose members have little knowledge of the Soviet system, have not lived or worked there, cannot read Russian, and usually fail to analyze even the Soviet materials that are available in Western languages, but who assign the bulk, if not all, of the responsibility for the cold war to the United States.

The national interest, of course, is quite separate from that of our scholars, as it is from that of businessmen eager to profit from opportu-

nities for trade.[4] Western governments and peoples
have supported academic exchanges, not only because
they increase knowledge and understanding, but also
because they enlarge Soviet participation in world
affairs and open chinks in the wall around the
Soviet Union. They see the increasing flow of
people and information as a liberating force that
may lead to a mellowing and moderating of Soviet
policy. In addition, these programs, and their
survival already for almost two decades, give us
more leverage in negotiating with the Soviet Union
than we had, for example, in 1955.

Academic exchanges, and other exchanges as
well, increase and improve the Soviet elites'
knowledge of the American people, thus beginning
to reduce some of the misapprehensions caused in
part by Soviet philosophy, propaganda, and way of
looking at the world and in part by simple lack
of information. The Institute of the USA, the
most important Soviet research organization for
studying the United States, was founded only in
1968. Even in December 1971, when the Institute
of History of the Soviet Academy of Sciences organized the first conference of Soviet specialists
on American history, it brought together only 130
men and women from throughout the Soviet Union.
Moreover, many in that group were propagandists,
not scholars. As early as July 1964, after the
academic exchange program had been in operation
for only six years, seven Soviet alumni were serving
in the United States in the Soviet Embassy in
Washington, at the Soviet mission to the United
Nations, or as representatives of the Soviet mass
media. Presumably, they were able to serve their
country better because of the semesters they had
spent in our universities. At the same time, we
gain from having knowledgeable observers report
about us.

The very existence of the exchange programs

[4]Some argue that the notion of gain or loss for academic or scientific exchanges is inappropriate; the programs
represent joint ventures of mutual benefit above and beyond
politics. (See Oliver Korshin, "U.S.-U.S.S.R. Medicooperation," Exchange, IX, No. 4 [Spring, 1974], 29-32.)

and of the more relaxed Soviet-American relationship that they reflect, the increased trickle of
information the Soviet government tolerates, and
the subtle Western pressure to relax Soviet controls encourage dissidence and dissent among intellectuals, ethnic and religious minorities, and
all those who simply want more freedoms. Even the
great majority of utterly loyal Soviet citizens
have been influenced by the observations and attitudes of their colleagues who have traveled abroad
or worked closely with foreign scholars. Thus,
every Soviet scholar abroad and every American and
other foreign scholar in the Soviet Union help
break down the wall which has isolated that country
from the rest of the world.

Soviet rulers have paid especial attention to
these programs and to East-West trade and constantly
measure their advantages and hazards. They have
naturally emphasized research in the scientific and
technical fields central to continued Soviet progress. The scientists and engineers who have benefited from the various exchange programs and from
increased access to professional literature are
among those most critical of the Soviet system, particularly of the restraints it places upon travel
and access to information. They therefore constitute a modest pressure upon Soviet policies. More
important, they have introduced critical information and attitudes directly into the research areas
crucial to the Soviet government and into the higher
reaches of the Soviet system.

The evident brooding sense of dissatisfaction
among some of those most central to their country's
continued intellectual, scientific, technical, and
economic progress already constitutes a serious
problem for the leadership. It will almost certainly grow if contact with the West deepens, and
it may increase even more vigorously should it be
restricted. In this sense, Louis XIV's dictum that
states touch only at the top remains true, and
Western influence flows into the Soviet Union
through the new elites.

However, we pay a price for these benefits.
For those who go to the Soviet Union, the most

annoying costs are the monumental inefficiencies
of the Soviet system, which they cheerfully accept,
and the indecencies and indignities to which many
are subjected and which they bitterly resent. During
the past five years some basic improvements have
occurred, but most changes have been cosmetic.
Glaring inequities still abound; Columbia University
has assisted dozens of Soviet scholars and artists,
but Vitali Rubin, a Soviet specialist in classical
Chinese philosophy, cannot obtain a visa to begin
his appointment at Columbia. Similarly, we gave
Soviet television crews full access to our facilities, while the Soviet government did not allow
American crews to film the launching of the Soviet
spacecraft in the Apollo-Soiuz exercise in July 1975.

Most Americans engaged in any of the cultural
exchange programs are especially concerned because
they occur under an official intergovernmental
agreement. Our scholars, cultural leaders, and
officials were all reluctant in 1958 to accept the
exchanges agreement because we sought free trade in
men and ideas, not a primitive barter, or even
reciprocal trade, in which bureaucrats count scientists and athletes as carefully as bales of cotton.
We still seek arrangements in which scholars may
travel and study freely in the Soviet Union, and
we remain eager to ensure similar opportunities for
Soviets. However, the Soviet government would open
its frontiers and some of its cities, universities,
laboratories, and archives only if the United States
accepted an official agreement. The agreements
themselves, which explicitly define and limit the
opportunities for study and ensure Soviet control
over a substantial part of the activities, therefore constitute a major penalty for us.

Any Western government inevitably becomes involved in important relationships involving the
Soviet Union because of the nature of the Soviet
system. Our government, like others, has been
directly engaged in the cultural relations process
since negotiations began in the fall of 1957, but
it has encouraged institutions such as universities
and private foundations to assume administrative
responsibilities. Direct exchanges between universities failed utterly in the first few years,

but the universities retained until 1969 full control over the most important academic exchanges
under their chosen instrument, the Inter-University
Committee. However, under IREX, university interest and authority have slowly declined and the
central authority of IREX has enlarged. Thus, the
history of Russian studies and of academic exchanges both illustrate how a few gifted and dedicated individuals launched functions over which
individual universities, then a group of universities, a corporation drifting away from university
influence, and finally the government have gradually
increased their influence and control.

The government's role has grown in the last
decade in particular and threatens to become overwhelming, making Washington a kind of St. Peters-
burg-on-the-Potomac. Foundation support will continue to decline, even as prices rise. The
government thus looms as the main, almost the lone,
financial supporter, which will of course increase
its authority. The Department of State's contribution to the IREX budget for 1976-77 may account
for more than half of the total (it was somewhat
less than one-third in 1974-75). When the Department and the National Endowment for the Humanities
contribute the great bulk of IREX's financial support, as well as all those of the National Academy
of Sciences, the Public Health Service, and other
organizations engaged in exchanges of scholars,
exchanges will in effect become a government subsidiary and instrument.

Ironically, the ideas concerning joint research
on common problems that the Committee proposed in
1964 and that were discussed in the Soviet Union
and Eastern Europe in the following three years were
accepted by the Soviet government in the 1970s under
conditions that increased our government's authority
over exchanges and higher education. These agreements on weather, environmental protection, medicine,
science and technology, agriculture, transport, and
oceanography promise benefits to both countries and
progress toward peaceful relations. At the same
time, they also buttress federal influence. Moreover, the dangers are increased by the 1975 Helsinki
agreement, even though the Western states fought to

draft a document which would increase the free flow
of men and information. First, the signatory governments in effect gave a kind of formal approval
to the principle that cultural relations shall be
the responsibility of governments. Second, the
effort to monitor the flow of ideas and people will
only increase the role of government. Indeed, as
President Kingman Brewster of Yale University recently noted, our scholars and universities must
now devote increasing energies to defending their
independence from the expanding powers of their
own benevolent government.

However, the greatest cost we pay in accepting
controlled cultural exchanges with the Soviet Union
is granting respectability and dignity, parity and
legitimacy to a government that denies the freedoms
essential to civilized life. Sending novelists to
a country, or accepting chemists from one in which
historians are imprisoned for seeking objectivity
and in which scientists of independent mind are
hounded from their positions, is a high price, one
that may lead into further moral demobilization and
intellectual corruption. We have become so accustomed to exchanges agreements with the Soviet Union
and the states of Eastern Europe that the restrictions which used to chafe are now quietly accepted.
We are often far more critical of similar restrictions when exercised by other states than we are
of those that communists rule.

Those who support cultural exchanges with the
Soviet Union, whether or not they are aware of the
moral issues raised, point out that we have no
choice, that the Soviet Union exists in an ever-
smaller universe, that the United States itself is
a flawed society in an imperfect world, and that we
must use the instruments available to advance learning and at the same time to press for free movement
of men and ideas. In short, academic exchanges with
the Soviet Union as presently organized are unsatisfactory, but the most satisfactory we can hope to
obtain in current circumstances.

Men such as Sakharov and Solzhenitsyn illustrate with blinding clarity the dilemma that academic relationships with the Soviet Union pose.

They agree that the United States should negotiate
with the Soviet Union in order to reduce the likelihood of war. However, they and their counterparts in Eastern Europe condemn us for weakness
and irresolution and for failing to use our influence, or for wielding it ineffectively, to advance
the rights of the Soviet and East European peoples
and therefore the prospects for genuine peace. They
urge that we not grant legitimacy and respectability
and, above all, not provide scientific and technological assistance to a government that denies its
citizens rights to which they are entitled under
their own constitution.

The Soviet Union and the countries of Eastern
Europe naturally would not allow or encourage academic exchanges unless they believed their benefits
were considerable, and more than ours. Thus, the
Soviet leaders clearly believe that the exchanges
operate to their advantage, just as we believe they
do to ours. In fact, advantages from exchanges must
be considered mutual if they are to survive and
thrive.

Soviet advantages and disadvantages from academic exchanges are in many ways the obverse of
ours. Soviet scholars, of course, have many of
the same interests as Americans. In particular,
they welcome opportunities to go "out," to share
information and insights with fellow specialists,
to acquire a new perspective, and to obtain recog-
nition from the international community of scholars.
However, most have no influence, although senior
scientists, or scientific administrators, may have
some input into central decisions concerning contact
with the outside world.

For Soviet leaders, the main advantages are
clear. They appreciate the respectability and
prestige the exchanges bring and the impressions
that their artists, dancers, and eminent scientists
create. As Zhores Medvedev has revealed in detail,
they also use travel abroad as a patronage instrument, denying those of independent or unorthodox
mind the opportunity and awarding a bonus to those
who faithfully endorse every government action.
They exercise some influence over American

scholarship by denying admission to qualified
scholars with legitimate subjects. Many discouraged
from studying twentieth-century history, the Soviet
economy, or Russian foreign policy thus turn to
subjects more comfortable for the Soviet system, or
even abandon Soviet studies. Some timid intellectuals refrain from protests against Soviet treatment of dissidents and from participating in conferences in which subjects distasteful to the Soviet
government might be discussed. Some may even censor
themselves.

The Soviet Union utilizes cultural exchanges to
narrow the considerable gap between Soviet and
Western science and technology by obtaining access
to the equipment, techniques, and discoveries of
our campuses and laboratories, just as it uses trade
to obtain industrial data and to inject Western
technology into critical parts of the Soviet economy.
Thus, the Soviet Union has obtained significant
increments to its scientific and technical knowledge,
from basic information concerning polio vaccines and
training in econometrics and new systems of business
management to the latest work in electronics, oil
drilling, and biochemistry. In 1969-70 all twenty-
nine Soviet participants in the main academic program were scientists. In 1971-72 thirty-one of
thirty-four were scientists or engineers. In 1973
eight Soviet nominees were computer specialists.
The same proportions prevail in exchange programs
with other Western countries. In 1970, for example,
ninety percent of the Soviet scholars in the German
program were scientists. All thirteen agreements
for cooperative research the Soviet Union has so
eagerly signed in the 1970s involve science and
technology, and American scientists agree that the
Soviet Union learns far more than the United States
does from them.

Finally, the Soviet government seeks to create
the impression that the Soviet Union is not a threat,
that the basic issues which divide the Soviet Union
and the West have been resolved, and that the world
has returned to some kind of placid normalcy in
which Western efforts to maintain military strength
and coordination are unnecessary. They have
achieved considerable success with this policy,

which has contributed to the gradual decline of
Western resolution and unity.

The Soviet price from these programs is in
many ways the American benefit, because the programs
provide dissonant information, stimulate dissidence,
and open up some of the higher levels of Soviet
society to Western ideas. "Cooperating with capitalism" exposes the Soviet government to criticism from
the People's Republic of China and from fervent old-
line communists and radical revolutionaries everywhere, while at the same time it increases hope
among the critics and restless millions. Occasional
defectors are an embarrassment. Moreover, the
Soviet system and the means its leaders use to restrict the costs inflict further damage. The secrecy and the restrictions it imposes upon those
foreigners whom it admits on a carefully controlled
basis create resentment and hostility among many
visitors and a sense of shame among informed Soviet
citizens, as the policies of Nicholas I and Alexander III did in the nineteenth century. Soviet
policies in the established restrictive pattern are
often the most powerful enemies of the system. Thus,
the Soviet blackout of American TV reports from
Moscow early in the summer of 1974 on Sakharov and
the Jewish dissenters was a colossal blunder because
it undermined the massive effort to portray the
system as liberal and open.

However, the main price, and a fearfully high
one, is the infectious spread of Western ideas from
the contacts the exchanges allow. Soviet rulers
claim the enthusiastic support of their peoples,
but at the same time they deeply fear their exposure
to outside influences. Travel, art forms, hybrid
corn and Holsteins, the presence of Soviets in
American dormitories, exhibits of kitchen equipment,
cooperation in cancer research, study of computer
technology, and the adoption of our business management techniques--all affect the Soviet intellectual
elite, as Pepsi Cola, jazz, mini-skirts, jeans, and
grain do at other levels. Any Soviet citizens who
remember Khrushchev's boasts in the early 1960s
about surpassing the United States in important
fields of production must wonder what has happened.
Even the most obtuse Soviet citizen must suspect

from the flow of Western science and technology
that the West retains its cultural leadership.
Imagine the effect here if we were drinking kvas
and importing Soviet equipment to exploit our oil
and gas resources!

The Muscovite rulers clearly appreciate the
price they pay to satisfy their desperate needs and
to obtain the envisaged political advantages. They
apparently believe that the most grave internal
threat is from those most highly educated. The
government of Brezhnev very much resembles that of
Nicholas I, which also sent students abroad, in
its "plot mentality" and in the suspicion with
which it views its own peoples. This ideological
sensitivity is reflected in constant vigilance
campaigns and the refrain that there can be no
peaceful coexistence in ideology. However, the
more they borrow abroad, the more they open the new
Soviet elite to ideas that they consider dangerous.
They have learned that the Soviet Union cannot be
open technologically and closed culturally, and
that any relaxation, even to obtain great benefits,
simultaneously raises great hazards. The Soviet
position at the Conference on European Security and
Cooperation in Geneva reflected this reinforced
fear of "the free exchange of people and ideas."
Soviet insistence that the Conference ensure "respect for the principles of sovereignty and non-
intervention" and "strict observance of the laws,
customs, and traditions of each other" represents
a position already enshrined in the exchanges agreements. The Soviet Union wishes to participate in
cultural exchanges and to increase trade, but on
the condition that it maintain censorship and other
forms of control. It seeks "a fire that will not
burn."

The Soviet Union lives in one world and now
seeks to join the world, but it relentlessly rejects
"ideological coexistence." It demands that its
dogmas be unchallenged with especial insistence
because the Soviet Union in the 1970s has no new
ideas to sell and is stagnant and vulnerable. Fifty
years ago Soviet economic plans and exciting cultural life offered many attractions to the outer
world. Today, the Soviet Union possesses enormous

military power, but it is a society based on faith
and dogma. It has little intellectual vitality in
an age when ideas are, as ever, important. As Sir
Isaiah Berlin noted two decades ago, there is a
"silence in Russian culture."

Thus, the very nature of the exchange program
places the Soviet government on the horns of a
fearful and eternal dilemma. To obtain benefits
that it thinks important, even crucial, it must
risk contamination of its intellectual elite and
of its ideological foundations. To allow ballet
troupes to dazzle crowds abroad, it must accept
the likelihood that some of its best dancers will
defect, no matter how precise the controls. To
obtain scientific, technical, and military information and some political advantages, it must expose
itself to criticism and at the same time tolerate
gentle pressure for similar policies from East
European governments, which are much more interested
than the Soviet Union in freer relationships with
the West. In summary, just as the Department of
State and the universities ever ponder the wisdom
of enduring the inequalities and hazards Soviet
practices create, and the threat to our principles
these relationships pose, so the Soviet rulers constantly discuss the balance between the advantages
they acquire and the "infections" that constitute
the price. They cannot afford freedom, and they
therefore seek a series of reciprocal trade agreements in which they barter opportunities for research useful to us for information useful to them.

Eastern Europe is a part of the Soviet empire,
but yet another world. The dilemma for the East
European governments is even more acute than that
of the Soviet government, as is their need for
access to Western science, technology, and intellectual sustenance. The magnetic and contagious
attraction that the West has for long exercised on
Eastern Europe, intensified by events since 1945,
has been boosted by the various exchanges, the
greatly increased economic ties, and the tantalizing
opportunities to taste the previously forbidden
fruits. These erode the economic, ideological, and
political bases of the governments and weaken ties
with Moscow in the same kind of "unbinding" that

the Russian empire witnessed a century ago.   They
promote pragmatic and more traditional attitudes and
tend to make the communist leaders ever more nation-
alistic.   They also bring closer together the peoples
and their governments--the peoples eager to "rejoin
Europe" and to enjoy the benefits of this century's
advances, and the governments eager to acquire
Western information to modernize their economies.

However, the East European governments cannot
import knowledge from our universities, laboratories,
factories, and farms without importing the ideas and
values at the heart of Western institutions.   These
constitute a continuing source of infection among a
people already vulnerable.   The Soviet rulers have
long considered Eastern Europe a barrier against the
West.   In present circumstances, it has become a
carrier from the West, raising specters of 1956 and
1968 but under more subtle and dangerous circumstances.   It is a section of the Soviet empire not
yet digested, and perhaps indigestible.   In a sense,
the 1956 and 1968 efforts to press dramatically
toward greater freedom or toward "socialism with a
human face" were all successes in the long run, although they were apparent immediate failures.   The
level of information throughout Eastern Europe has
risen substantially.   In spite of all the restrictions, in Czechoslovakia and Romania in particular,
the overall picture is brighter than in 1955.

A shrewd British observer has pointed out that
one can reach the Soviet Union only over a wall and
across a moat, while entrance to (and exit from)
resilient Eastern Europe is simpler, through a
crisscross of turnstiles, which Eastern and Western
Europeans are now mastering.   Moreover, because it
stands at the crossroads of European civilization,
Eastern Europe will remain an especially critical
area and a most likely cause of future tensions
between the Soviet Union and the West.   If the
peoples of Eastern Europe succeed in inching their
way to increased liberties and to greater independence from Soviet rule, the Soviet Union will be
directly affected and the future of Western Europe,
and of the world, will become significantly brighter
and freer.

Academic exchanges, and cultural relations as a whole, have survived all the crises the stormy period since 1958 has produced. Soviet practices have improved somewhat over the years, particularly since 1969, in part because the Soviet government has begun to feel more comfortable with programs that produce substantial benefits, even though they raise great hazards. They also reflect worsening Soviet-Chinese relations; the increasing Soviet need for access to American grain, science, and technology; the decreasing Western fear of communism and of Soviet expansion; the decision of Western and Soviet leaders to turn toward Ostpolitik and Westpolitik, respectively; and the turn from confrontation to negotiation.

This momentum remains subject to lurches of one kind or another. A change in leadership and policy in the Soviet Union or another explosion in the Middle East could destroy the carefully constructed structures and patterns and return us to the stark days of critical confrontations. However, a Soviet return to utter isolation from the West seems most unlikely. Indeed, if these delicate and complicated programs should thrive, they might help produce even more fruitful relationships, not only mitigating conflict but directing some of the ambitions of both countries toward international cooperation in fields such as agricultural production and health care.

Those especially interested in cultural relations in general and academic relations in particular often overestimate their significance. They do in fact play a modest role, and the numbers of people involved will remain small.[5] The importance of academic exchanges, and that of the larger grouping--cultural, economic, scientific, and technological relations--is likely to increase both in an era of negotiation as well as confrontation, but economic and military power, vitality and stability,

[5]According to the Department of State, 13,768 Soviet citizens and 17,071 Americans participated in the various programs under the official cultural exchanges agreements during their first fifteen years, from 1958 through 1973.

resolution, and skill in diplomacy will remain more important in world politics than any mustard seed. Cultural relations, even when skillfully used, can only supplement.

The major issues, the petty wrangles, and the contemporary dilemmas of exchanges between the United States and the Soviet Union are deeply rooted in well-established traditions, which help provide useful historical perspective. The exchange programs also reflect the historical relationship between Russia and the West, one that derives from Byzantium. The policies of Peter, Catherine, and Stalin, who sought to transform Russia and to borrow from the West without being "corrupted" in any way, help illuminate contemporary issues. The political and cultural fascination that the West has exercised on Russia as a European borderland state reflects the attractive power of Western culture, which has been active, positive, and infectious throughout the last several centuries, and never more than today. However, we have reason for caution concerning the supposed impact of Western ideas upon Russia, which has demonstrated a striking capacity to absorb scientific and technical data without substantial effect upon its political system or values. The great English scholar, B. H. Sumner, noted that Peter the Great more than 250 years ago saw the West as the "home of shipbuilding and navigation, the reservoir of naval, engineering, and gunnery skill, the possible supplier of loans, and the hoped-for ally in a great combination against the Ottoman empire." Peter returned to Moscow impressed by "what wealth, trade, manufacturers, and knowledge meant to a country in terms of power and prosperity," but "he did not explore the springs and motive forces of this western achievement; he did not seek to understand the workings of financial, political, or administrative institutions; and he had little or no conception of the slow and varied stages by which England and Holland had grown to be what they were."[6] Peter simply recognized new sources of power and borrowed as rapidly as possible in order to transform Russia.

[6]Benedict H. Sumner, Peter the Great and the Emergence of Russia (New York, 1951), 34, 41.

The external threats that the Soviet rulers perceive today differ in location and character from those Peter saw. They, like Peter, seek to absorb the new elements of power in order to strengthen the state and to make life more palatable. Historians continue to debate to what degree Peter, the first Russian Westerner, successfully resisted Western cultural inroads. However, all agree that the political system has remained absolute in spite of all the contact with the more liberal West.

The United States should promote cultural exchange programs because of the nature of the crisis and because open and peaceful relations are fundamental to our system. Moreover, freedom is our main strength and our best instrument, and we should make full use of it in a contest with a system that is extraordinarily rigid and suffers from conservative leadership. Western Europe and the United States now constitute the intellectual center of the world, in art and architecture, in music and literature, in philosophy (including Marxism), and in all the sciences. We should utilize this remarkable intellectual and cultural vitality. We should rejoice that the contest between the Soviet Union and the West has shifted to include a competition in ideas on a peaceful field, with intellectual weapons--a contest for which we are particularly well equipped and one from which all peoples, though not the Soviet system, will benefit.

However, we must remember that science, art, learning, and our economy are all parts of our total culture and essential elements in our negotiating position with the Soviet Union. We should both defend the freedom essential to our culture and use its products to advance our interests and those of better relations. In particular, we should grant the Soviet Union access to our advanced technology only as it moves toward free movement and equal rights of interpenetration. The United States and its allies should therefore continue to press for free movement throughout Europe. Soviet jamming of radio broadcasts must end. Journalists must be guaranteed the right to function and report freely. We should not be satisfied with vague agreements about reuniting families, but we should insist upon

the free flow of publications and the right of
people to travel. In short, we should use keen
Soviet interest in our technology to obtain the
freedoms essential for the survival of a free Europe
and a peaceful world--or deserve the popular disil-
lusion and the Soviet contempt that failure would
produce. At the same time, we must appreciate that
this approach carries a price and creates a dilemma
because it increases our government's authority
over cultural and other activities. It thereby
places cultural relations, and trade as well, on
the chess board of issues concerning which both
governments negotiate, and it reduces our own
freedoms.

The success with which the West has protected
Soviet dissidents illustrates the Soviet dilemma
and the significant way in which we can marshal our
resources to advance human rights and international
security. The presence of 240 foreign correspondents in Moscow, the skill with which these men and
women and the Soviet dissidents have kept in touch
with each other, the diffusion of information about
the dissidents throughout the world, and broad-
casting back into the Soviet Union information
about them and their views have restricted Soviet
action against them and protected them. Thus, the
Soviet decision to expel, rather than to imprison,
Solzhenitsyn in February 1974 reflected in part his
courage and in part the pressure exerted by the information made available to the world and then to
the Soviet public at a time when the Soviet government was desperate for Western scientific and
technical aid.

Similarly, the warning that the National Academy of Sciences issued in September 1973 served
to safeguard Andrei D. Sakharov, to define the price
of more open relationships with the West, and to
demonstrate that we are determined that the Soviet
Union modify its policies if it is to obtain the
benefits of cultural and economic cooperation.
Sakharov was in serious danger until President
Philip Handler of the National Academy informed the
Soviet Academy that depriving Sakharov of his rights
would end Soviet-American scientific cooperation.
The Soviet government then chose to continue to
tolerate Sakharov and his activities.

If we defend our principles shrewdly and resolutely in this unending struggle, the Soviet government will twist in constant debate over a painful dilemma. It will be forced to choose between reducing sharply or even ending intellectual and economic relations with the West, trying to combine more open relations with the West with ever tighter controls over its own peoples, or adopting a far more flexible and relaxed policy toward control over the Soviet population, one that would almost certainly undermine the system. Consequently, academic relations raise fundamental questions for any totalitarian government.

The very questions raised by this aspect of Soviet-American relations explain why academic exchanges are both sensitive and important to the improvement of relations between the Soviet Union and the United States. These exchanges are less crucial than discussions concerning limitations of nuclear weapons and those concerning the reduction of military forces in Central Europe, but they touch principles central to both societies and they serve as a most illuminating indicator of Soviet policies. They demonstrate that changes have occurred within the Soviet Union and in Soviet policies toward the West. However, the political system remains fundamentally untouched, and controls over the population are as systematic and effective as before. We are little closer to or more intimate with the Soviet population than twenty years ago. The Soviet Union has relaxed some restraints in its relations with other states, but slowly and without revising its philosophy, reducing its military strength, or weakening its control of Lenin's "commanding heights." The United States and the Soviet Union remain locked together in a shrinking world, suspicious of each other, unable on the one hand to conquer by force but equally unable to disengage or to find some kind of armed security. In short, the cultural exchange programs reflect the eternal contest between authority and freedom, as well as the age-old pressure that Russia has exerted upon its western borderlands. The present conflict in many ways seems one between Lenin's ideas and the state he established and those of Jefferson and Wilson. It is also a struggle between power and freedom. The concentra-

tion camp and the Berlin Wall, the open library
and the traveling scholar, are its appropriate
symbols.

BIBLIOGRAPHICAL ESSAY

The major source for this volume has been my experience with the Inter-University Committee from 1956 until May 1969. I also benefited greatly from my relationships over those years with the ACLS, the Foreign Area Fellowship Program, the Ford Foundation, and the National Academy of Sciences. I have had many long talks with those Americans who studied in the Soviet Union in the 1930s, with participants in all the varied exchange programs, with officials of our government and of the Soviet government, and with those who have helped administer the responsible British and German organizations. I have discussed academic and cultural exchanges on many campuses in this country and in Western and Eastern Europe, and I have attended countless national and international conferences devoted to Soviet-American relations in general and to this aspect in particular.

Two conferences have proved especially helpful. One, in Suffern, New York, in 1964, brought together those who directed academic exchange programs in all the countries of Western Europe. Another, in Salzburg in November 1973, which Indiana University and the United States Information Agency together organized, provided quantities of information and insight from a number of those responsible for exchange programs in nine Western countries, as well as specialists on exchanges in fields such as medicine, journalism, radio and television, music, film, and religion. The papers and discussions from this second conference have been especially valuable.

Documentary materials were most important sources. I
have reviewed carefully the voluminous records of the Inter-
University Committee, which included applications; reports
of participants; correspondence; Committee reports to the
universities, the Ford Foundation, and the Department of
State; and records of the meetings, large and small, that the
Committee held or in which any of its representatives participated.

I have also studied carefully the published annual reports of IREX, the ACLS, the Ford Foundation, the Rockefeller
Foundation, the Canada Council, the Deutsche Forschungsgemeinschaft, and the National Academy of Sciences. The National Academy's News Reports, the annual reports of its
Foreign Secretary, and the analyses of participants' reports
that its Office of International Relations made available
have provided important information concerning the principal
program for exchanging scientists and scientific information.
The National Academy of Sciences has also served as the base
for the Committee on Scholarly Communications with the
People's Republic of China, which is appointed also by the
ACLS and the SSRC. This Committee's reports, especially the
China Exchange Newsletter, have provided substantial information concerning scholarly visits to China and efforts to
establish an academic exchange program with that country.

The Department of State's publications constituted an
immensely important source. Its Bulletin provided the text
of all agreements and notes exchanged, as well as important
policy statements by leading officials and statistical information concerning the Department's other exchange programs
and activities. The Department's annual reports to the
Congress, published by the Soviet and East European Exchanges
Staff, by the Bureau of Educational and Cultural Affairs, or
by the Bureau of Public Affairs, contain the basic statistical information concerning its exchange programs. The Embassies of West European states in Washington provided copies
of their exchange agreements with the Soviet Union and the
countries of Eastern Europe.

The Department of Health published annual reports of its
own exchanges as well as occasional reports of its delegations.

Two journals, the Bulletin of the Atomic Scientists and
Science, which is published by the American Association for
the Advancement of Science, have been especially valuable,
particularly on Pugwash and on exchanges involving scientists.

The New York Times and the Christian Science Monitor have
devoted more attention to exchanges than other American newspapers, and Newsweek has been the principal weekly journal
source. I have consistently read Pravda through these years
and have used the invaluable Current Digest of the Soviet
Press, published by the American Association for the Advancement of Slavic Studies, for information from other Soviet
journals and newspapers. I have also scoured the principal
professional journals interested in Russian and Eastern
European studies and in international affairs, as well as
important Soviet journals, such as Voprosy istorii.

PRINCIPAL BOOKS AND ARTICLES

I. Soviet-American Relations

     A vast literature in several languages on this subject
includes a large number of immensely useful volumes. I list
here a few of those most valuable for this study: Charles E.
Bohlen, The Transformation of American Foreign Policy (New
York, 1969), 130 pp.; John C. Campbell, American Policy
Toward Communist Eastern Europe: The Choices Ahead (Minne-
apolis, 1965), 136 pp.; Josef Korbel, Detente in Europe:
Real or Imaginary? (Princeton, 1973), 302 pp.; Bennett Kovrig,
The Myth of Liberation. East-Central Europe in U. S. Diplo-
macy and Politics Since 1941 (Baltimore, 1973), 350 pp.;
Anatol Rapoport, The United States and the Soviet Union. Per-
ceptions of Soviet-American Relations Since World War II (New
York, 1970), 256 pp; Marshall Shulman, Beyond the Cold War
(New Haven, 1966), 112 pp.; Anthony C. Sutton's three-volume
Western Technology and Soviet Economic Development, 1917-1965
(Stanford, 1968-73); Adam B. Ulam, Expansion and Coexistence.
The History of Soviet Foreign Policy, 1917-1967 (New York,
1968), 775 pp.; Adam B. Ulam, The Rivals. America and Russia
Since World War I (New York, 1972), 405 pp.; William Zimmer-
man, Soviet Perspectives on International Relations, 1956-
1967 (Princeton, 1969), 336 pp.

II. Negotiating with the Russians

     Charles E. Bohlen, Witness to History, 1929-1969 (New
York, 1973), 562 pp.; Raymond Dennett and Joseph E. Johnson,
eds., Negotiating with the Russians (Boston, 1959), 310 pp.;
Admiral C. Turner Joy, How Communists Negotiate (Santa Monica,
1970), 180 pp.; George F. Kennan, Memoirs: 1925-1950 (Boston,

1967), 582 pp.; George F. Kennan, Memoirs: 1950-1963 (Boston, 1972), 368 pp.

III. Russian and East European Studies Programs

   A. American and Canadian

       Arthur P. Coleman, Report on the Status of Russian and Other Slavic and East European Languages in the Educational Institutions of the United States, Its Territories, Possessions and Mandates (New York, 1948), 109 pp.; Arthur P. Coleman, "Slavonic Studies in the United States, 1918-1938," Slavonic and East European Review, XVIII (1938-39), 372-88; Laing Gray Cowan, A History of the School of International Affairs and Associated Area Institutes, Columbia University (New York, 1954), 106 pp.; Alexander Gerschenkron, "Study of the Soviet Economy in the U.S.A.," in Walter Z. Laqueur and Leopold Labedz, eds., The State of Soviet Studies (Cambridge, Mass., 1965), 44-51; Mortimer Graves, "A Memorandum on Regional Studies," Journal of Higher Education, XIV (November, 1943), 431-34; Mortimer Graves, "Two Experiments in Education," American Scholar, III (1934), 359-60; Ellen McDonald Gumperz, Internationalizing American Higher Education: Innovation and Structural Change (Berkeley, 1970), 250 pp.; Robert B. Hall, Area Studies (New York, 1947), 90 pp.; D. L. B. Hamlin, International Studies in Canadian Universities (Ottawa, 1964), 120 pp.; Alex Inkeles, "Clyde Kluckhohn's Contribution to Studies of Russia and the Soviet Union," in W. W. Taylor, J. L. Fischer, and E. Z. Vogt, eds., Culture and Life (Carbondale, 1973), 58-70; Charles Jelavich, ed., Language and Area Studies: East Central and Southeastern Europe. A Survey (Chicago, 1969), 496 pp.; Robert J. Kerner, "Slavonic Studies in America," Slavonic Review, III (1924-25), 243-58; Richard D. Lambert, Language and Area Studies Review (Philadelphia, 1973), 490 pp.; John M. H. Lindbeck, Understanding China. An Assessment of American Scholarly Resources. A Report to the Ford Foundation (New York, 1971), 159 pp.; Clarence A. Manning, History of Slavic Studies in the United States (Milwaukee, 1957), 117 pp.; Albert Parry, America Learns Russian: A History of the Teaching of the Russian Language in the United States (Syracuse, 1967), 205 pp.; Ernest J. Simmons, "An American Institute for Slavic Studies," New York Herald Tribune (December 30, 1944); Ernest J. Simmons, Intensive Study of Contemporary Russian Civilization, July 5--October 23, 1943 (Ithaca, 1943), 105 pp. (mimeographed); Ernest J. Simmons, "Study of Contemporary Russian

Civilization," Journal of Higher Education, XIV (November, 1943), 439-40; "The Slavonic Conference at Richmond (Va.)," Slavonic Review, III (1924-25), 684-93; Rudolf L. Tőkes, "East European Studies in the United States: The State of the Arts and Future Research Strategies," East European Quarterly, VIII, (1974), 337-52; Gordon Turner, "The Joint Committee on Slavic Studies, 1948-71. A Summary View," ACLS Newsletter, XXIII (Spring, 1972), 6-26; Sergius Yakobson, "The Future of Slavic Studies in American Universities," University of Pennsylvania Library Chronicle, XII (April, 1944), 7-17.

     B. European

       John A. Armstrong, "Slavic Studies in Western Europe. Some Personal Observations," Canadian Slavonic Papers, VIII (1967), 56-67; Elizabeth Beyerly, "The USSR and Eastern Europe: Research and Area Study in Austria," Slavic Review, XXIII (December, 1964), 706-16; Arturo Cronia, La Conoscenza del mondo slavo in Italia. Bilancio storico-bibliografico di un millennio (Padua, 1958), 792 pp.; Arturo Cronia, "Slavonic Studies in Italy," Slavonic and East European Review, XXVI (1947-48), 197-208; Victor Frank, Basile Kerblay, and Jens Hacker, "Soviet Studies in Western Europe," Survey, No. 50 (January, 1964), 90-118; Great Britain. Foreign Office. Report of the Interdepartmental Commission of Enquiry on Oriental, Slavonic, East European, and African Studies, Under the Earl of Scarborough (London, 1947), 192 pp.; Great Britain. University Grants Committee. Report of the Sub-Committee on Oriental, Slavonic, East European, and African Studies, Under Sir William Hayter (London, 1961), 125 pp.; Jens Hacker, Die Entwicklung der Ostforschung seit 1945. Ein Blick auf die bestehenden Institute und ihre Arbeitsweise (Kiel, 1958), 26 pp.; Walter Laqueur and Leopold Labedz, eds., The State of Soviet Studies (Cambridge, Mass., 1965), 177 pp.; Klaus Mehnert, "Survey of Slavic and East European Studies in Germany Since 1945," American Slavonic and East European Review, IX (October, 1950), 191-206; Andrew Rotstein, "Prepodavanie i izuchenie istorii SSSR v britanskikh universitetakh [The Teaching and Study of the History of the USSR in British Universities]," Voprosy istorii, No. 5 (May, 1957), 207-14.

IV.   International Communications and
     Perceptions of Other Societies

      Anna Mary Babey, Americans in Russia, 1776-1917. A Study of the American Travelers in Russia from the American

Revolution to the Russian Revolution (New York, 1938),
170 pp.; Deming Brown, Soviet Attitudes Toward American
Writing (Princeton, 1962), 325 pp.; David Caute, The Fellow-
Travelers. A Postscript to the Enlightenment (New York,
1973), 433 pp.; Norman Daniel, Islam and the West. The Making
of an Image (Edinburgh, 1962), 443 pp.; Raymond Dawson, The
Chinese Chameleon. An Analysis of European Conceptions of
Chinese Civilization (New York, 1967), 235 pp.; Foster Rhea
Dulles, Americans Abroad: Two Centuries of European Travel
(Ann Arbor, 1964), 202 pp.; Durand Echeverria, Mirage in the
West. A History of the French Image of American Society to
1815 (Princeton, 1968), 320 pp.; Peter G. Filene, ed., Ameri-
can Views of Soviet Russia, 1917-1965 (Homewood, Ill., 1968),
404 pp.; Peter G. Filene, Americans and the Soviet Experiment,
1917-1933 (Cambridge, Mass., 1967), 389 pp.; Akira Iriye,
Across the Pacific. An Inner History of American-East Asian
Relations (New York, 1967), 361 pp.; Harold R. Isaacs, Images
of Asia. American Views of China and India (New York, 1962),
416 pp.; Chalmers Johnson, "How China and Japan See Each
Other," Foreign Affairs, L (July, 1972), 711-21; Sylvia R.
Margulies, The Pilgrimage to Russia. The Soviet Union and
the Treatment of Foreigners, 1924-1937 (Madison, 1967),
290 pp.; Philip E. Mosely, "The Soviet Citizen Views the
World," Review of Politics, XXVI (October, 1964), 451-72;
Richard L. Merritt, ed., Communication in International
Politics (Urbana, 1973), 461 pp.; René Rémond, Les États-
Unis devant l'opinion française, 1815-1852 (Paris, 1962),
968 pp.; George R. Stewart, American Ways of Life (New York,
1954), 310 pp.; Cushing Strout, The American Image of the Old
World (New York, 1963), 288 pp.; Gerhard L. Weinberg, "Hit-
ler's Image of the United States," American Historical Review,
LXIX (July, 1964), 1006-21; William Welch, American Images of
Soviet Foreign Policy. An Inquiry into Recent Appraisals from
the Academic Community (New Haven, 1971), 316 pp.; "The Western Image of the Soviet Union, 1917-1962," Survey, No. 41
(April, 1962), 200 pp.; Francesca M. Wilson, Muscovy: Russia
through Foreign Eyes, 1553-1900 (London, 1971), 328 pp.;
William Zimmerman, "Soviet Perceptions of the U.S.," in Alexander Dallin and Thomas B. Larson, eds., Soviet Politics since
Khrushchev (Englewood Cliffs, 1968), 163-79.

V. Western Studies of Exchange Programs

        Frans Alting von Geusau and L. Bartalits, Cultural Ex-
change and East-West Detente. A Preliminary Assessment of
Data Derived from Bilateral Arrangements (Tilberg, The

Netherlands, 1969), 41 pp. (mimeographed); Erik Amburger,
"Deutsch-russische wissenschaftliche Beziehungen im deutschen
und russischen Schrifttum seit 1945," Jahrbücher für Ge-
schichte Osteuropas, X (October, 1962), 395-434; Eric Ashby,
Scientist in Russia (London, 1947), 252 pp.; George Bailey,
"Cultural Exchange as the Soviets Use It," The Reporter
(April 7, 1966), 20-25; Frederick C. Barghoorn and Ellen
Mickiewicz, "American Views of Soviet-American Exchanges of
Persons," in Richard L. Merritt, ed., Communication in Inter-
national Politics (Urbana, 1972), 146-67; Frederick C.
Barghoorn, The Soviet Cultural Offensive. The Role of Cul-
tural Diplomacy in Soviet Foreign Policy (Princeton, 1960),
353 pp.; Frederick C. Barghoorn, Soviet Foreign Propaganda
(Princeton, 1964), 329 pp.; Frederick C. Barghoorn, The
Soviet Image of the United States: A Study in Distortion
(New York, 1950), 297 pp.; Frederick C. Barghoorn, Soviet
Russian Nationalism (New York, 1956), 330 pp.; Robert Blum,
ed., Cultural Affairs and Foreign Relations (Englewood Cliffs,
1963), 177 pp.; Harrison Brown, "Scholarly Exchanges with
the People's Republic of China," Science, LXXXIII (January 11,
1974), 52-54; Robert F. Byrnes, "American Scholars in Russia
Soon Learn About the K.G.B.," New York Times Magazine (November 16, 1969); Anthony C. A. Dake, Impediments to the Free
Flow of Information between East and West (Paris, 1973),
32 pp.; Lewis S. Feuer, "Travellers to the Soviet Union,
1917-1932. The Formation of a Component of New Deal Ideol-
ogy," American Quarterly, XIV (Summer, 1962), 119-49; Charles
Frankel, The Neglected Aspect of Foreign Affairs. American
Educational and Cultural Policy Abroad (Washington, 1965),
156 pp.; Charles Frankel, "The Scribblers and International
Relations," Foreign Affairs, XLIV (October, 1965), 1-14;
Loren R. Graham, "Other Scientific Exchanges with Russia Are
Not So Smooth," New York Times (July 20, 1975); Hans Heymann,
Jr., The U.S.-Soviet Civil Air Agreement from Inception to
Inauguration: A Case Study (Santa Monica, 1972), 54 pp.;
Walter Johnson and Francis J. Colligan, The Fulbright Program:
A History (Chicago, 1965), 380 pp.; Wolfgang Kasack, "Kultur-
politik gegenüber der Sowjetunion," Osteuropa, XXIV (July,
1974), 497-503; Wolfgang Kasack, "Die wissenschaftlichen
Beziehungen zwischen der Bundesrepublik und der Sowjetunion.
Erfahrungen aus den letzten sechs Jahren," Osteuropa, XV
(September, 1965), 587-93; Oliver Korshin, "U.S.-U.S.S.R.
Medicooperation," Exchange, IX (Spring, 1974), 29-32; Dietrich
A. Loeber, Hochschule und Student in der Sowjetunion. Eine
Auswahl von Verwaltungsvorschriften zum sowjetischen Hoch-
schulsystem aus den Jahren 1961-1969 (Bad Godesberg, 1970),
216 pp.; Richard L. Merritt, "Effects of International Student

Exchange," in Richard L. Merritt, ed., Communication in
International Politics (Urbana, 1972), 65-94; Richard L.
Merritt, "Transmission of Values across National Boundaries,"
in Richard L. Merritt, ed., Communication in International
Politics (Urbana, 1972), 3-32; John Miller, No Cloak No
Dagger: Recent Quaker Experiences in East-West Encounters
(London, 1965), 63 pp.; Henri Peyre, "On Professors' Ever-
Recurring Task: Writing Letters of Recommendations,"
ACLS Newsletter, XIII (February, 1962), 5-9; Ithiel de Sola
Pool, Suzanne Keller, and Raymond A. Bauer, "The Influence
of Foreign Travel on Political Attitudes of American Business-
men," Public Opinion Quarterly, XX (Spring, 1956), 161-75;
Joseph R. Quinn, Anatomy of East-West Cooperation. U.S.-
U.S.S.R. Public Health Exchange Program, 1958-1967 (Washing-
ton, 1969), 391 pp.; Alexander Rich, "U.S.-U.S.S.R. Inter-
Academy Exchange Program, 1959-1975," Paper submitted to
U.S. House of Representatives Subcommittee on Domestic and
International Scientific Planning and Analysis (November,
1975), 18 pp.; Joseph Rotblat, Pugwash: The First Ten Years.
History of the Conferences of Science and World Affairs
(London, 1967), 244 pp.; Joseph Rotblat, Scientists in the
Quest for Peace. A History of the Pugwash Conferences (Cam-
bridge, Mass., 1972), 359 pp.; Doris Schenk, "Wissenschaft-
leraustausch mit der Sowjetunion," Deutsche Forschungsgemeinschaft Mitteilungen (April, 1970), 42-47; Doris Schenk, "Die
wissenschaftlichen Beziehungen zwischen der Bundesrepublik
Deutschland und der UdSSR," Das Parlament (August 9, 1973),
28-30; Richard Speaight, Cultural Exchange with East Europe
(Brighton, 1971), 101 pp.; John R. Thomas and William J.
Spahr, The External Information and Cultural Relations Programs
of the Union of Soviet Socialist Republics (Washington,
1973), 153 pp.

VI. Soviet Views

     V. Andreev, Nauchnyi obmen i ideologicheskaia diversiia
[Scientific Exchange and Ideological Diversion] (Leningrad,
1970), 70 pp.; G. A. Arbatov, Ideologicheskaia bor'ba v
sovremennykh mezhdunarodnykh otnosheniiakh. Doktrina, metody,
i organizatsiia vneshpolit propagandy imperializma [Ideologi-
cal Struggle in Contemporary International Relations. Doctrine, Methods, and Organization of the Foreign Propaganda
of Imperialism] (Moscow, 1970), 351 pp.; V. L. Artemov,
Anatomiia lzhi. Kriticheskie ocherki po antisovetskoi im-
perialisticheskoi propagande [The Anatomy of Falsehood.
Critical Views of Anti-Soviet Imperialistic Propaganda]

(Moscow, 1973), 191 pp.; IU. Barsukov, "Vashington. Klevet-
nik bez mundira [Washington: A Slander without a Uniform],"
Izvestiia (July 17, 1970); E. A. Dudzinskaia, "Mezhdunarodnye
sviazi Instituta istorii SSSR AN SSSR v 1969 g. [Internation-
al Relations of the Institute of History of the Soviet Academy of Sciences in 1969]," Istoriia SSSR, No. 6 (November-
December, 1970), 190-94; Victor Furaev, Sovetsko-amerikanskie
kul'turnie sviazi, 1917-1939 [Soviet-American Cultural Relations, 1917-1939] (Leningrad, 1966), 317 pp.; Victor K.
Furaev, "Sovetsko-amerikanskie nauchnye i kul'turnye sviazi,
1924-1933 gg. [Soviet-American Scientific and Cultural Relations, 1924-1933]," Voprosy istorii, No. 3 (March, 1974),
41-57; Victor K. Furaev, Sovetsko-amerikanskie otnosheniia,
1917-1939 [Soviet-American Relations, 1917-1939] (Moscow,
1964), 319 pp.; Sergei M. Goliakov, Voina bez vystrelov [War
without Shooting] (Moscow, 1969), 158 pp.; A. V. Grachev,
"Nauchnyi obmen i ego ispol'zovanie [Scientific Exchange and
Its Use]," in V. M. Vasiliev, ed., Sekrety sekretnykh sluzhb
SShA [Secrets of the Secret Services of the U.S.A.] (Moscow,
1973), 199-218; Nikolai Gribachev, "Kuliki no kochkakh
[Snipes in a Bog]," Izvestiia (September 26, September 27,
1970); Alexander E. Ioffe, "Deiatel'nost' zarubezhnykh ob-
shchestv druzhby s Sovetskom Soiuzom [The Activity of Foreign
Societies for Friendship with the Soviet Union]," Voprosy
istorii, No. 3 (March, 1966), 15-30; Alexander E. Ioffe,
Internatsionalnye nauchnye i kul'turnye sviazi Sovetskogo
Soiuza, 1928-1932 [International Scientific and Cultural
Relations of the Soviet Union, 1928-1932] (Moscow, 1969),
200 pp.; IU. Iudin, "O 'filantropicheskikh' fondakh SShA
[On American Philanthropic Foundations]," Mirovaia ekonomika
i mezhdunarodnye otnosheniia, No. 2 (August, 1957), 123-26;
B. P. Kanevskii, "K kharakteristike amerikanskogo 'soveto-
vedeniia' [Concerning the Character of American 'Soviet
Studies']," Voprosy istorii, No. 5 (May, 1966), 181-86; Ivan
M. Krasnov, "Amerikanskie nauchnye tsentry na sluzhbe anti-
kommunizma [American Scientific Centers in the Service of
Anti-Communism]," Mezhdunarodnaia Zhizn', No. 8 (1963),
50-52; Ivan M. Krasnov, "Izuchenie istorii SSSR v SShA:
Nekotorye tsifry i fakty [The Study of Soviet History in the
U.S.A.: Some Figures and Facts]," Istoriia SSSR, No. 6
(November-December, 1964), 166-83; Asia Efimovna Kunina and
Boris Il'ich Marushkin, Mif o miroliubii SShA [The Myth of
the Peaceloving U.S.A.] (Moscow, 1960), 316 pp.; Boris Il'ich
Marushkin, Istoriia i politika. Amerikanskaia burzhuaznaia
istoriografiia sovetskogo obshchestva [History and Politics.
American Bourgeois Historiography of Soviet Society] (Moscow,
1969), 393 pp.; Zhores A. Medvedev, The Medvedev Papers.

Fruitful Meetings between Scientists of the World. Secrecy
of Correspondence is Guaranteed by Law, translated from the
Russian by Vera Rich (London, 1971), 471 pp.; Zhores A.
Medvedev, Mezhdunarodnoe sotrudnichestvo uchenykh i
natsional'nye granitsy [International Cooperation of Scholars
and National Frontiers] (London, 1970), 270 pp.; Nikolai N.
Mikhailov, Those Americans: A Travelogue (Chicago, 1962),
210 pp.; Lev N. Mitrokhin, Amerikanskie mirazhi [American
Mirages] (Moscow, 1965), 431 pp.; E. Modrzhinskaia, "Anti-
Communism Disguised as Evolutionism," International Affairs
(Moscow), No. 1 (January, 1969), 15-20; Victor Nekrasov, Both
Sides of the Ocean (London, 1964), 192 pp.; A. Nikolaev and
K. Ushakov, "Vysokaia vbitel'nost'--oruzhie protiv proiskov
imperializma [Great Vigilance--Weapon Against the Intrigues
of Imperialism]," Kommunist, No. 11 (July, 1968), 93-102;
V. Ozira, "Kak uchat v shkole biznesa [How Teaching is Done
in a Business School]," Literaturnaia Gazeta, No. 41 (October
9, 1968); A. Panfilov, Radio SShA v psikhologicheskoi voine
[Radio U.S.A. in Psychological Warfare] (Moscow, 1967),
150 pp.; Marat N. Perfil'ev, Kritika burzhuaznykh teorii o
sovetskoi politicheskoi sisteme [A Critique of Bourgeois
Theories on the Soviet Political System] (Leningrad, 1968),
163 pp.; M. I. Radovskii, "Iz istorii Russko-Amerikanskikh
nauchnykh sviazei [On the History of Russian-American Scientific Relations]," Vestnik Akademii Nauk SSSR, XXVI, No. 11
(1956), 93-101; Sergei Romanovskii, Mezhdunarodnye kul'turnye
i nauchnye sviazi SSSR [International Cultural and Scientific
Relations of the USSR] (Moscow, 1966), 239 pp.; V. I. Ruten-
burg, "O nauchnykh sviazakh uchenykh SSSR i Italii [On
Scientific Relations of Scholars of the USSR and of Italy],"
Voprosy istorii, No. 5 (May, 1957), 214-16; Andrei D. Sakharov,
Sakharov Speaks, edited and with a foreword by Harrison E.
Salisbury (New York, 1974), 245 pp.; Vladimir Salov, Sovremen-
naia zapadnogermanskaia burzhuaznaia istoriografiia. Nekotorye
problemy noveishei istorii [Contemporary West German Bourgeois
Historiography. Some Problems of Contemporary History] (Moscow, 1968), 381 pp.; Nikolai N. Smeliakov, Delovaia Amerika.
Zapiski inzhenera [Business America. Notes of an Engineer]
(Moscow, 1967), 301 pp.; Gherman M. Sverdlov, (G. N. Sadovsky,
pseud.), "The Committee of American Friends in the Service
of Society (Quakers)," International Yearbook. Politics and
Economics (Moscow, 1961), 382-86; R. S. Tagirov, "Nekotorye
zamechaniia o sviazi sovetskoi istoricheskoi nauki s mirovoi
istoricheskoi naukoi [Some Remarks Concerning the Relations
of Soviet Historical Science with the Historical Science of
Foreign Countries]," Istoriia SSSR, No. 6 (June, 1961),
128-32; Academician A. V. Topchiev, "Vizit k uchenym SShA

[Visit to the Scientists of the United States]," Vestnik
Akademii Nauk SSSR, XXXI, No. 9 (September, 1961), 81–83;
V. M. Vasil'ev, ed., Sekrety sekretnykh sluzhb SShA [Secrets
of the Secret Service of the U.S.A.] (Moscow, 1973), 303 pp.;
R. V. Viatkin, "Obzory u vostokovedov SShA [Observations on
Asian Studies in the USA]," Voprosy istorii, No. 2 (February,
1971), 178–81; Stepan Volk, Evropeiskie kontrasty. Zametki
sovetskogo turista [European Contrasts. Comments of a Soviet
Tourist] (Leningrad, 1961), 170 pp.; A. Zhukov, "Ten' na
pleten'. Po povodu nelovkikh ob'iasnenki professora R. Byrnesa
pered amerikanskoi obshchestvennost'iu [Shadow on the Wall.
On Some Remarks of Professor R. Byrnes before the American
Public]," Leningradskaia Pravda (May 17, 1970); Georgii
Zhukov, "Cultural Contrasts: Two Approaches," International
Affairs (Moscow), V, No. 11 (November, 1959), 19–27.

VII.   Selected Reports of Participants

A.   Individuals

        Several hundred American and European participants
in the various exchange programs have published books and
articles on their experiences and views, and the Inter-University Committee in addition received hundreds of other
reports. I have also received many other unpublished accounts.
From this great mass of materials, I have selected some of
the most interesting and illuminating published accounts.

        Robert Adamson, "Science Education, Siberian
Style," Scientific Research, III (February 5, 1968), 39–41,
43–44; John A. Armstrong, "The Soviet Intellectuals: Observa-
tions from Two Journeys," Studies on the Soviet Union, I
(1961), 25–37; John A. Armstrong, "A View of the Soviet Uni-
versities," Institute of International Education News Bulletin,
XXXII (1957), 4–9; Jeremy Azrael (Tim Callaghan, pseud.),
"Studying the Students: Between Conformity and Dissent,"
Survey, No. 33 (July–September, 1960), 12–19; Oswald P.
Backus, III, "Recent Experiences with Soviet Libraries and
Archives: Uncommon Resources and Potential for Exchange,"
College and Research Libraries, XX (November, 1959), 469–73,
499; Klaus Berger, "In the Soviet Union," ACLS Newsletter,
XIV, No. 2 (February, 1963), 1–7; James H. Billington, "Soviet
Youth is Getting out of (Party) Line," University, No. 27
(Winter, 1965–66), 9–13; Ralph Blum, "Freeze and Thaw: The
Artist in Russia," New Yorker, XLI (August 28, 1965), 40–217,

passim.; Urie Bronfenbrenner, "The Mirror-Image in Soviet-
American Relations: A Social Psychologist's Report," Journal
of Social Issues, XVII (1961), 45-56; Sylvie Carduner, "Une
classe de français élémentaire a Leningrad," The French Review, XXXVIII (February, 1965), 517-22; Chester S. Chard,
"Archeology in the Soviet Union," Science, CLVIII (February
21, 1969), 774-79; Scott M. Eddie and Arthur W. Wright, "Report on a Summer of Research and Language Study in Central
and Eastern Europe, 1968," The ASTE Bulletin, XI, No. 1
(Spring, 1969), 6-15; George M. Enteen, "The History Faculty
of Moscow State University," Russian Review, XXVIII (1969),
66-76; René Etiemble, "The Sorbonne in Moscow. Adventures
of a Literary Traveler," Survey, No. 30 (October-December,
1959), 14-18; George Feifer, Justice in Moscow (New York,
1964), 353 pp.; Kathryn Feuer, "Russia's Young Intellectuals
or Some of Them Anyway," Encounter, VIII (February, 1957),
10-25; Lewis S. Feuer, "Meeting the Philosophers," Survey, No.
51 (April, 1964), 10-23; John T. Flanagan, "Russian Tour: I
Was a Multilateral Exchange Participant," College English, XXV
(November, 1963), 85-90; David G. Frey, "Limnology in the
Soviet Union," Limnology and Oceanography, X (January, 1965),
i-xxix; George Gibian, "The New and the Old: From an Observer's Notebook," Problems of Communism, XVI, No. 2 (March-
April, 1967), 57-64; John Gooding, The Catkin and the Icicle.
Aspects of Russia (London, 1965), 213 pp.; Richard Harring-
ton, "A Canadian Visits Soviet Central Asia," Canadian Geo-
graphical Journal, LXX, No. 4 (April, 1965), 136-45; Chauncy
D. Harris, "Geographic Research and Teaching Institutions in
the Soviet Union," Archiv für wissenschaftliche Geographie,
XII (1958), 214-21; George R. Havens and Norman L. Torrey,
"The Private Library of Voltaire at Leningrad," PMLA, XLIII
(1928), 990-1009; Calvin Hoover, Memoirs of Capitalism, Com-
munism and Nazism (Durham, 1965), 302 pp.; Edward M. Ifft,
"Science Students at Moscow," Bulletin of the Atomic Scien-
tists, XXIII (April, 1967), 37-40; Richard Judy, "A Report on
Visits to Moscow Computing Centers Institutes," The ASTE Bul-
letin, IX (Spring, 1967), 1-8; Marvin L. Kalb, Eastern Ex-
posure (New York, 1958), 332 pp.; Allan Kassof, "American
Sociology through Soviet Eyes," American Sociological Review,
XXX (February, 1965), 114-21; John Kolasky, Education in
Soviet Ukraine. A Study in Discrimination and Russification
(Toronto, 1968), 238 pp.; Bernard Lovell, Out of the Zenith:
Jodrell Bank, 1957-1970 (New York, 1974), 255 pp.; Ronald
Meek, "The Teaching of Economics in the USSR and Poland,"
Soviet Studies, X (April, 1959), 339-59; Philip E. Mosely,
"1930-1932. Some Vignettes of Soviet Life," Survey, No. 55
(April, 1965), 52-63; Philip E. Mosely, "Russia Revisited:

Moscow Dialogues, 1956," Foreign Affairs, XXXV, No. 1 (October, 1956), 72–83; Talcott Parsons, "An American Impression of Sociology in the Soviet Union," American Sociological Review, XXX, No. 1 (February, 1965), 121–25; Herrmann Pörzgen, "The Influence of Modern Western Literature in the Soviet Union," Modern World (Vienna), V (1965–66), 47–61; Franklin D. Reeve, "Impressions of the Soviet Union," ACLS Newsletter, XIII, No. 4 (April, 1962), 5–12; David Robert (pseud.), "Moscow State University," Survey, No. 51 (April, 1964), 24–31; Avedis K. Sanjian, "Status of Armenian Studies," Bulletin for the Advancement of Armenian Studies, I, No. 1–2 (Autumn-Winter, 1963), 3–31; Francis Sejersted, Moscow Diary (London, 1962), 129 pp.; Stavro Skendi, "Studies on Balkan Slavic Languages, Literatures and History in the Soviet Union during the Last Decade," American Slavic and East European Review, XVI (1957), 524–33; H. Gordon Skilling, "Communism in Eastern Europe: Personal Impressions, 1961–1962," Canadian Slavonic Papers, VI (1963), 18–37; H. Gordon Skilling, "In Search of Political Science in the USSR," Canadian Journal of Economics and Political Science, XXIX (November, 1963), 517–29; William Taubman, The View from Lenin Hills (New York, 1967), 249 pp.; Peter Taylor, "Old and New Horizons," Survey, No. 56 (July, 1965), 3–10; Franco Venturi, Il Populismo russo (Turin, 1972), 3 vols.; David W. Weiss, "The Plight of the Jews in the Soviet Union," Dissent, XIII (July-August, 1966), 1–17; Mitchell Wilson, "Russia's Social Elite," Nation, CXCII (August 26, 1961), 95–99; John Ziman, "Letter to an Imaginary Soviet Scientist," Nature, CCXVII (January 13, 1968), 123–24.

B. Delegations

Philip H. Abelson, "Geophysicists in Moscow: Signs of Easier Relations," Science, CLXXIII (August 27, 1971), 797–800; American Friends Service Committee. Peace Education Division, Reports on the American Peace Delegation's Visit to the Soviet Union and Czechoslovakia, November 6–21, 1968 (Philadelphia, 1969), 43 pp.   (mimeographed); American Friends Service Committee. Peace Education Division, Verbatim Reports of Discussions. Soviet Peace Committee and the American Peace Delegation, November 11, 12, 13, 1968. Pravda Staff Members and the American Peace Delegation, November 15, 1968 (Philadelphia, 1969), 59 pp. (mimeographed); Y. G. Arbatsky, "Recent Advances in Medical Education in the USSR," Journal of Medical Education, XXXVII, No. 9 (September, 1962), 840–61; Earl Callen, "Moscow. Notes on a Scientific Conference," The Atlantic, CCXXXIII (May, 1974), 16–19, 23–26;

Truman Capote, The Muses Are Heard. An Account of the Porgy and Bess Visit to Leningrad (New York, 1956), 182 pp.; Alex Comfort, et al., "British Doctors in Russia. Experiences and Impressions," International Journal of Anesthesia, II (December, 1954), 139-43; Thurston N. Davis and Eugene K. Culhane, "Religion in the Soviet Union," America, CXIV (February 19, 1966), 252-55, 258-59; A. Baird Hastings and Michael B. Shimkin, "Medical Research Mission to the Soviet Union," Science, CIII (May 17, 1946), 605-08; (May 24, 1946), 637-44; Walter R. Hibbard, Jr., "Quantity and Quality in Russian Metallurgical Education," Journal of Metals, X (March, 1958), 174-77; Julian S. Huxley, A Scientist among the Soviets (London, 1932), 142 pp.; Edmund J. King, ed., Communist Education (London, 1963), 309 pp.; Philip B. King, "Colloquium in the Caucasus," Grotimes, X, No. 8 (1966), 20-24; Philip B. King, "A Visit to a Russian Map Factory," Grotimes, X, No. 9 (1966), 19-20; Elinor Langer, "Soviet Genetics: First Russian Visit since 1930's Offers a Glimpse," Science, CLVIII (September 8, 1967), 1153; Colin M. McLeod, M.D., et al., "The United States Medical Mission on Microbiology and Epidemiology to the Soviet Union," Journal of the American Medical Association, CLXII (October 13, 1956), 656-58; W. Renfield, "A Glimpse of Neurophysiology in the Soviet Union," Canadian Medical Association Journal, LXXIII (1955), 891-99; Glenn Seaborg, Atomic Energy in the Soviet Union. Trip Report of the U.S. Atomic Energy Delegation, May, 1963 (Oak Ridge, Tenn., 1963); Eugen Weber, "Innocents Abroad: The XIII International Congress of Historical Sciences," Journal of Contemporary History, VI, No. 2 (1971), 87-99.

INDEX